LITERATURE AND MARGINALITY

LITERATURE AND MARGINALITY

Comparative Perspectives in African, American Australian and Indian Dalit Literature

Parmod Kumar

KALPAZ

ISBN : 978-93-5128-023-1

Price: ₹ 865

First Published 2014

Published by

Kalpaz Publications
C-30, Satyawati Nagar,
Delhi-110052
Ph. : 9212142040
E-mail: kalpaz@hotmail.com

Laser Typesetting: GR Computer, Delhi
Printed at: G. Print Process, Delhi

Cataloging in Publication Data--DK
Courtesy: D.K. Agencies (P) Ltd. <docinfo@dkagencies.com>

Literature and marginality : comparative perspectives in African, American, Australian and Indian dalit literature / Parmod Kumar.

p. cm.
Contributed articles.
Includes bibliographical references.
ISBN 9789351280231

1. Marginality, Social, in literature. 2. Dalits in literature. 3. African literature–Dalit authors–History and criticism. 4. American literature–Dalit authors–History and criticism. 5. Australian literature–Dalit authors–History and criticism. 6. Indic literature–Dalit authors–History and criticism. I. Parmod Kumar.

DDC 809.933552 23

Dedication

This book on Literature and Marginality is dedicated to all those Heroes of Human History who have sacrificed their lives to resist social oppression and deprivation and strived to make this an egalitarian world

Contents

Preface

Preface

This book is really founded on literary trends and practices in the last two decades and more in the twentieth century where an unprecedented scale and the exceptional tendencies is noticed on the part of Indigenous people to speak out against the marginality, racism and oppression that they, and their ancestors, have been subjected to and also raised a rebellious pitch to demand their right in playing a central role in shaping communities, nations and the world. The re-articulation of their history in their own voice and the exploration of alternative modes of living with difference are connected to a global movement. Ngugi, Achebe, Kim Scott, Alexis Wright, Valmiki and Gaikwad and writers of have actually initiated and participated in a complex dialogue that is alive with struggle and possibility. Their writing practices, in all their difference, are fuelled by an ethical imperative to face the implications of living in a contested country, and also to generate anti-colonial ways of being in the world.

'Marginality' is generally employed to interpret and analyse socio-cultural, political and economic spheres, where disadvantaged people struggle to gain access to resources and equal participation in social life. The superstructures of race in Africa, Australia, USA and caste in India inform, deform, and complicate the identities of the marginalized along lines of gender, class and family structure. In the modern day debate, various facets of marginality have been discussed in scholarly circles in almost every disciplinary area including literature, history, sociology, and political science with implications for issues as diverse as justice, gender, equality and inequality. This academic exercise which engage experts from National and International arena has taken into considered and explored the convergences in imagination and expressions of writers like Ngugi, Achebe, Kim Scott, Alexis Wright, Valmiki and Gaikwad.

As a result of these narrative accounts, there is a heightened rwlaisation that there is a no one national memory or one national history. Rather there are a plurality of contradictory memories, imaginaries and histories, generated from different cultural identities and social bodies. The stories that people tell of the past hold the seeds of their hopes, desires and fears for the future. The 'marginalised' writers who have been previously spoken for, written about, categorised and critiqued by 'mainstream' writers have, in the last four decades, begun to be heard by mainstream society. In a diversity of mediums and avenues marginal narratives and stories, in all their multiplicity, enter into the field of mainstream culture and society. In so doing, they enter into a dialogue about the real and their own past, present and future. It has to be said that the inhuman exploitation and deprivation due to caste system, the ceasless racist atrocoties and likewise removal of Indigenous children from their families and communities has taken a central to historical consciousness of all the writers of all these places.

Over the years, the traditional assumptions of disciplines have been challenged and scholars have also explored the role of the "canon" and debated on what the so called "great" (canonical) texts may be in their respective disciplines, and the more profound grounds of their canonicity. There is a great academic need to explore these comparative perspectives in African, American Australian and Indian Dalit Literature. The advent of literary and cultural theories in the literary field has brought major changes in the way of reading, interpreting and understanding literature and culture. This has empowered, in a significant way, marginalised discourses which often remained unnoticed by the hegemonic culture. This has constantly been argued that a comprehensive literary study of marginality and its epistemic role is necessary and would contribute to a better understanding of how humanistic knowledge has been created, structured and transmitted.

A considerable amount of research shows, when seen in the light of a comparative study, that Comparative Literature has expanded our body of cultural knowledge in terms of class, caste, race, language, genre and theory. Over the past decade, however, there have been persistent efforts to trace the comparative dimensions of post colonial studies and these other transnational groupings as fields of inquiry. These efforts have taken the form both of a desire to compare across empires and to conceive of transnational spaces in themselves.

In the first place, and perhaps most importantly, it is important to notice the fact that knowledge has intricate linkages with forces that govern our social life. Invariably, the production and denial of knowledge are akin to the production and denial of power. Consequently, it is not be inappropriate to argue here that, "Social spaces are not blank and open for anybody to occupy, some bodies are deemed as having the right to belong while others are marked out as trespassers, who are...politically, historically and conceptually circumscribes as being out of place." (Nirmal Puwar, Space Invaders: Race, Gender and Bodies Out of Place, p. 8). The point I'm making here is that the political space of global politics is not, therefore, neutral, but underpinned by a powerful hegemonic normative framework that circumscribes who and what we can hear and see. It is not simply a domain in which anybody can turn up and speak out. Instead, it is a space in which certain subjects are produced, while other subjects are rendered unintelligible and denied an authoritative voice. It can be further argued here that the marginalisation of certain voices from global politics is not solely the product of deliberate processes or exclusion, but their exclusion is the result of what Judith Butler says "a normative violence" that denies them the possibility of a culturally intelligible and politically-qualified subject position. Therefore, global politics is a domain permeated by a logic that enables certain actors to speak whilst silencing and marginalising others.

This book aims to contextualise marginality in an Inter-disciplinary framework with reference to past and with its possible effects on life in future and also provide a comparative platform of literary study between Dalit, African, Australian and American discourses. Although the chief concern has been to analyse and review literature on marginality and figure out the points of coming together and departure in terms of marginalised writings. Yet scholarly contributions from every domain are also invited so that the inter-disciplinary or multi-disciplinary approaches can authenticate the main theme. The innovative, exciting, and intellectual discussion by the scholars of all domains will also help in promoting a high order research in this area.

The contributors in the book have so successfully tried to establish marginality as mainstream and whiteness as blankness – "whiteness which was surface only, with no depth, and very little variation". There is an obvious suggestion that to desire a limited and prescriptive notion of nation is to be imaginatively, intellectually and ethically bereft.

These essays have in a big way opened up the possibilities of a counter discourse by exploring that which cannot be contained within the eugenicist and assimilationist logic. In so doing, there is an improvisation on the style in which to give a form to the complexity of experience of marginality. There is an intensive exploration of a style of writing that presents the reader with an experience of sensations and intensities from which meaning and sense emerges. It is as if there is an effort to speak of the past historical events to envision a future in which the 'real' people might be able to flourish. It is a future of which the readers and writers, the creators, have not yet been constituted. *If one has* to summarise the chief tone and tenor of the book, I would say that this book seeks to both question the adequacy of the novel, and the English language, to represent Indigeneity, and to propose a style of writing that generates new speaking positions for Indigenous people. And also, to shift the narrative of the 'stolen generation' or black or deprived generation from hidden and marginal Indigenous history onto the stage of mainstream world history.

Parmod Kumar

List of Contributors

Rajesh Kumar, MLN College, University of Delhi.

Komal Agarwal, Research Scholar, Jawaharlal Nehru University.

M.B. Gaijan, Head, Deptt. of English, Samaldas Arts College, Bhavnagar University, Bhavnagar – 364002.

Pooja Chaudhary, Research Scholar University of Delhi.

Isha Anand, Research Scholar University of Delhi.

Putul Sathe, Department of English, SNDT College of Arts, SNDT Women's University, Mumbai.

Mritunjay Kumar Yadavendu, Department of Sociology, Delhi School of Economics, University of Delhi, Delhi-110007.

Deepthy R. Chandran, Research Scholar, Department of English University of Delhi, Delhi-110007

Tapan Basu, Assistant Professor, Department of English, University of Delhi, Delhi-110007.

Sharan Kumar Limbale's, The Outcaste and Richard Wright's Black Boy.

Moola Ram, Assistant Professor of English, Ramanujam College University of Delhi.

Bishnu Mohan Dash, Assistant Professor, Department of Social Work, Bhim Rao Ambedkar College, (University of Delhi), Main Wazirabad Road, Yamuna Vihar, Delhi-110094, India.

A.K. Chaturvedi, Associate Professor of English, S.L.P. Govt. P.G. College Gwalior, 269 CP Colony Morar, Gwalior (MP)-474006.

Pradeep Trikha, Professor, Dept. of English, MLS University.

Renu Singh, Research Scholar University of Delhi.

Dinesh Misra, President Emeritus, Indian Society of Authors.

Mridusmita Baruah, Senior Research and Teaching Assistant (SRTA), School of Interdisciplinary and Tran disciplinary Studies, IGNOU, New Delhi.

Manoj Srivastava, Research Scholar, Indian Institute of Technology, Delhi.

Prachi Patil, Jawaharlal Nehru University.

Pawan Kumar, Department of English, Jawaharlal Nehru University.

Pragya Bajpai, Research Scholar University of Delhi.

Anuradha Deepak, Associate Professor in English, KLP College, Rewari (Haryana).

Asha Sharma, Associate Professor (Eng. Lit.), M.D.U. Rohtak, Haryana.

1

COMPARING LITERATURES OF MARGIN : DALIT AND AUSTRALIAN ABORIGINAL AUTOBIOGRAPHIES

Rajesh Kumar

A considerable amount of research shows, when seen in the light of a comparative study, that Comparative Literature has expanded our body of cultural knowledge in terms of class, caste, race, language, genre and theory. Over the past decade, however, there have been persistent efforts to trace the comparative dimensions of post colonial studies and these other transnational groupings as fields of inquiry. These efforts have taken the form both of a desire to compare across empires and to conceive of transnational spaces in themselves.

In the first place, and perhaps most importantly, it is important to notice the fact that knowledge has intricate linkages with forces that govern our social life. Invariably, the production and denial of knowledge are akin to the production and denial of power. Consequently, it's not be inappropriate to argue here that, "Social spaces are not blank and open for anybody to occupy. Some bodies are deemed as having the right to belong while others are marked out as trespassers, who are...politically, historically and conceptually circumscribes as being out of place." (Nirmal Puwar, Space Invaders: Race, Gender and Bodies Out of Place, p. 8). The point I'm making here is that the political space of global politics is not, therefore, neutral, but underpinned by a powerful hegemonic normative framework that circumscribes who and what we can hear and see. It is not simply a domain in which anybody can turn up and speak out. Instead, it is a space in which certain subjects are produced, while other subjects are rendered unintelligible and denied an authoritative voice. It can be further argued here that the marginalisation of certain voices from global politics is not solely the product of deliberate processes or exclusion, but their exclusion is the result of what Judith Butler says "a normative violence" that denies them the possibility of a culturally intelligible and politically-qualified subject position. Therefore, global politics is a domain permeated by a logic that enables certain actors to speak while silencing and marginalising others.

Judith Butler deploys the concept of 'Cultural Intelligibility' to refer to the production of a normative framework that conditions that can be recognised as a legitimate subject. She argues that subjects are per formatively constituted through the repetition of specific norms within a tightly controlled regulatory framework. It is this normative framework that provides the conditions of recognition through which subjects emerge as legitimate and culturally intelligible beings. However, these norms are constituted through the exclusion of that which cannot be accommodated within its framework. Butler further argues that 'exclusionary matrix by which subjects are formed thus requires the simultaneous production of a domain of abject beings, those who are not yet "subjects", but who form the constitutive outside to the domain of the subject.' The hegemonic normative framework has a powerful role in the production of politically-qualified and culturally intelligible subject position.

She also draws on it in her later texts (*Undoing Gender and Precarious Life*), to demonstrate how the human being is normatively produced within particular racial and cultural frames. She ties the idea of Cultural Intelligibility to the possibility of a liveable life (that is, a life that is recognised as having value and legitimacy). Butler (*Gender Trouble:viii*), argues that before any individual can live a "liveable" life, they have first to be recognised as a viable subject. If they cannot be recognised in this way then their lives will be impossible, illegal, unreal and illegitimate. Any regime of cultural intelligibility thus depends on what she calls in 1999 preface 'normative violence' (*Gender Trouble:xx).*

The Dialectics of Marginality

The term "Marginality" is a historically specific social construct marked by contingency mainly because it is a discursive formation. It refers to the overt actions or tendencies of human societies whereby those perceived as being without desirability or function are removed or excluded from the normative framework thereby limiting their opportunities and means for survival. It may manifest itself in multifarious forms varying from genocide/ethnic-cleansing and xenophobic acts/activities at one end of the spectrum, to more basic economic and social hardships at the unitary (individual/family) level.

The dialectics of Marginality creates discursive openings for marginalised voices by questioning and displacing the locations of power within discursive spaces and opens up avenues for exploring alternative forms of communication that exist outside the realm of the dominant discursive space. Thus, with its potential to interrupt the modernist epistemic structures, literature of Margin becomes an entry point to explore the emancipator potential of dialogue. How are the conditions of marginality created and sustained within social systems? And what communicative possibilities might be theorized in engaging in dialogue with the positions at the margins. This paper seeks to explore the role of dialogue in the realm of marginalisation, and suggest theoretical entry points for engaging with those voices that have traditionally been silenced in the dominant discursive spaces.

One very important point of marginality is that, 'Discourse of Marginality' is an area of inquiry concerned with the condition of being erased from the discursive space. As a field of study, it has traditionally focused on writing history from below. It has introduced questions of voice and access in contesting the dominant constructions of knowledge. Situating the mainstream knowledge as subject of inquiry, it demonstrated how such knowledge continues to serve positions of power and maintain social structures that sustain the conditions of marginality. In this context, literature of margin interrogates those epistemic structures that participate in the silencing of the subaltern subject. It raises key issues for consideration for dialogue theorists that have traditionally been overlooked in the broader literature on dialogue.

It can be argued that marginality is the condition constructed by the posited relation to a privileged centre, an 'Othering' directed by the imperial authority. But the abrogation of that centre does not involve the construction of an alternative focus of subjectivity, a new 'centre'. Rather the act of appropriation in the post-colonial text issues in the embracing of that marginality as the fabric of social experience. The 'marginal' and the 'variant' characterise post-colonial views of language and society as a consequence of the process of abrogation. Discourses of marginality such as race, gender, caste, psychological 'normalcy', geographical, social distance and political exclusion, all intersect in a view of reality which supersedes the distinction of centre and margin and replaces it with a sense of the complex, interweaving and syncretise accretion of experience.

The dialectics of marginality presents two constructs operating side by side, the one that is inclusive, underscoring elements of belonging, juxtaposed with the second that stresses what it is not. In other words, it has yielded two opposing models for identity formation: the first establishes identity in *inclusionary* terms as the result of constitutive formations structured around existing racist, castes, demographic, social, historical and cultural moralities and the second functions through recourse to *exclusionary* constructs in which identity is simply expressed in negative and dissociative registers.

It is important to note that the central point at issue for the discourse of marginality is the question of power in the realm of dialogue. The subaltern studies project suggests that the possibilities of dialogue are intertwined with the positions of power and privilege of dominant social actors, and the economic systems served by mainstream discursive spaces. It raises questions regarding the representation of the subaltern subject in the dialogical act, and fundamentally interrogates the role of the academic/researcher/intellectual engaged in the process of dialogue. Through these different questions raised by the subaltern studies project, we suggest that dialogue theory can make important strides in the realm of understanding communication processes in marginalised settings and exploring the emancipator potential of dialogue.

Deetz and Simpson are of the following view and note that power is pervasive across social structures that "routinely preclude otherness and block conversation...systems of domination usually preclude genuine conversation" (p. 147). The authors caution that structural inequities are deeply embedded in human experiences rendering them natural and invisible. Marginality provides an entry point to interrogate these privileges and explore the conditions of silences that are historically produced through the communicative exercises of omission. As a field of inquiry, marginal system of knowledge is concerned with the omissions and absences in the dominant constructions of knowledge, thus paying attention to the erasures in the discursive space. In its concern with recovering the voices of marginal subjects, the field of marginality offers a foundation for engaging in dialogue with those sectors of the social system that have traditionally been erased by the modernist agendas of the dominant epistemic structures.

It is important to notice that discourse of marginality is essentially concerned with writing literature from below. The very essence of writing literature from below is to challenge the dominant constructions of knowledge, with specific focus on that which is left out of such dominant constructions. The objective of marginal studies is to document the historiography of the people by documenting their agency and politics, which had always been left out.

The position of subalternity, I believe, is marked by its absence from the dominant systems of dialogue and representation. This absence is fundamentally tied to questions of access to power and the ways in which such access shapes the content and form of dialogue. Subaltern studies scholars point out that power lies at the core of the dialogues that take place in mainstream social systems, and the limits that are imposed upon these dialogical spaces with respect to the stakeholders that are able or unable to participate in them. Furthermore, the nature and forms of dialogue that become possible within social systems are dependent on the presence of communication infrastructure and human capacity to engage in those participatory processes of modern civil societies that are accorded legitimacy.

The significant question that concerns the subaltern studies scholar is the question of representation of the subaltern within the dialogical space: Who speaks for the subaltern? Whose voice gets heard? One might well ask, therefore: How does the subaltern identity get articulated within the discursive space? It has been suggested that the dialogue is built upon the existence of "the other" with whom one engages incommunicative exchange. In the realm of subaltern studies, this other is marked by her absence from the spaces of dialogue that are recognised by the mainstream actors of modern social systems as legitimate spaces for engaging in dialogue. In other words, the subaltern is "subaltern" precisely because she/he has been erased from the discursive space. Her presence is dialectically connected with dialogue, existing outside the dominant spaces of social systems that constitute dialogue. In other words, the possibility of dialogue is connected with its impossibility. In the realm of dialogue, the subaltern remains as an erasure. He or she remains in the subject position of the subaltern as a marker to be talked about, talked for and talked to. He or she remains as a site to be acted upon through top-down modes of communication within modern social systems. Situating the condition of subalternity within the realm of power equips us with an understanding of the situations and contexts in the flow of power that create and sustain the silencing of subaltern voices. It also offers us opportunities for engaging with the subaltern voices by resisting the flow of power within social systems and exploring alternative possibilities, both materially and discursively. In doing so, subaltern studies turns dialogue into a political act, inherently connected with the ideology of the involved actors and with the possibility of social change. The dialogue is limited to certain actors within social systems, and who engages in dialogue is determined by the distribution of power within social systems.

The possibilities and limits on dialogue are predicated upon the access that social actors have to the discursive spaces of dialogue. This in turn, is shaped by the ways in which power is distributed within social systems. Subaltern interpretations of dialogue suggest that the logic of dialogue within modern social systems is inherently tied to the interests of the capital and the ways in which this capital operates to create and sustain conditions of marginality. In other words, the interests of the dominant social actors are played out through the mainstream platforms of social systems as the subaltern sectors continue to exist at the margins of such systems.

Testimonio/Life Stories/Autobiographies

There is no denying the fact that the marginalised groups participate in alternative communicative spaces and avenues that are typically shunned by the mainstream. Moreover, these forms of communication have the power to fundamentally rupture the dominant notions of what constitutes communication, and reconstitute our standardised notions of what counts as communication. Resistance is enacted through the very choice of communicative strategies, forms and channels, the inclusion of which fundamentally disrupt the ways in which we come to understand communication and dialogue. One such mode of a communicative text that enacts the voice of the marginalised is the American Spanish *testimonio* (testimonial narrative in English/ Hindi) and others being *autobiographies* and *life stories.* The *testimonio* serves as a site of social change by presenting the marginalised voice in its accounting of events and the narrative construction of these events. As a representation of those subjects who have traditionally been excluded from authorized representation, the *testimonio, autobiography* and *life stories* operate as resistive strategies. As a new narrative genre that developed in the 1960s in close association with the national liberation movements and the generalised cultural radicalism of the decade, *testimonio* is representative of the resistance literature. Furthermore, the introduction of the *testimonio* into the dominant discursive space ruptures the very notion of "what is valued and understood as [culture] by dominant groups" (Beverly, 2004, p. 19). It is the *testimonio, autobiographies, and life stories* once again as subaltern/marginalised texts that challenge the privilege associated with the dominant constructions of knowledge. The texts challenge academic knowledge by opening up alternative possibilities. The introduction of the subaltern voice offers alternative explanations and interpretations of phenomena. The constitution of knowledge through subaltern participation offers different insights into phenomena that challenge the very interpretations offered by the mainstream academic. The introduction of *testimonio, life stories and autobiographies* into our understanding of what constitutes communication allows us to open up to the ways in which we as academics participate in serving the dominant power structures. By situating academic knowledge as a form of knowledge among many other possibilities, literatures of margin open up the discursive spaces to listening to the voices of marginalised/subaltern participants.

It seems to me that in Dalit as well as Australian Aboriginal autobiographies, it is through detailed analysis that their aesthetic strategies for exploring the complex somatic and emotional nuances of pin can be perceived, that the transformative powers of autobiographies, and arguably literary testimony, become apparent. Moreover, this aestheticisation of pain is both emotional and sensuous. The autobiographies under consideration contain detailed physical and emotional descriptions of pain. It is in its juxtaposition with small and ordinary pleasurable sensations that pain is at its most poignant. These autobiographies are shaped by questions about the universality of pain, cultural specificity of national narratives, and literary theory's relevance to suffering in the real world.

Many literary theorists working on representations of pain, suffering in literatures bring issues of cultural specificity into their works and do so in order to examine the real world implications of their interventions, arguing that literature is a unique space in which to reveal the social structures that create conditions of suffering and propose alternative realities. These approaches have proved extremely fertile and have produced influential works of manifested comparative literary criticism. Pain/suffering, as it is represented in literature, has so far been studied as exemplary, as providing evidence to help understand how a range of pains are experienced. This involves a search for defining features of pain narratives, for the points of similarity across literary texts, points which gain their 'validity' by being applicable to a range of other pains. One of the joys of aesthetic narratives is that they place different forms of pain in relation to each other through a process of tangential linking.

It is to be born in mind that all the autobiographies seem to be giving the message that pain and suffering have become a pre-requisite for authenticity and authority amongst minority groups. Individuals who have personally experienced great pain are awarded the right to speak for the group. Their words and leadership are valorised through narratives of suffering. The potential danger here is that pain becomes fetish zed and hyper-valorised as a means of gaining power. The body as privileged symbolic space is here read in light of the politics of pain as both an exclusive defining identity and experience that is culturally co modified into potentially problematic social currency. This is a phenomenon which Sara Ahmad refers to as 'the fetishisation of the wound in subaltern politics' and relates to the contemporary 'culture of compensation' and 'transformation of injury into an entitlement that secures forms of privilege' (Ahmad, 2004: 32).

I'm reminded of Lionnet's (1997) groundbreaking essay "Geographies of pain: captive bodies and violent acts in the fictions of Gayl Jones, Bessie Head and Myriam Warner-Vieyra". She argues in this essay that female novelists create literature both to reveal enduring gendered injustice and to depict potential alternate realities. Dalit and Australian Aboriginal autobiographies too reveal detailed descriptions of pain and suffering to which they were subjected due to their different dimensions of marginality and depict potential alternative realities. These auto biographers are discussing the ways in which the wider social, political and cultural systems affect the lives of individuals. Literature is seen as both reflecting and potentially changing such systems of knowledge. All these writers pay detailed attention to the nuances of pain explored through the literature. They dwell on the messiness of sensation, on the physical experience of violence or the visceral aching of being alone and excluded from the society.

All the autobiographies under consideration seek to describe what happens when a person is pushed to the extremes of pain and suffering. Their arguments are based upon the premise that at such a point cultural and linguistic differences fade into the background because the physicality of pain is so world-destroying that the sufferer is reduced to his own state of affairs. This is an assertion which seems to be true for all human beings. They describe the route along this pain journey identifying other features of pain that seem to be universal in scope, that physical pain are later on politically converted into the assertion of political power and self assertion. Writers of both domains of writing, with their very gesture of asserting particularity, juxtapose one pain with another, draw attention to the fact that pain does reside within a meaningful conceptual category.

A Comparative Perspective

The semiotic system by which the indigenous peoples of Australia and India (categorizing Aborigines of Australia and Dalit of India as being off springs of 'indigene' group) have been represented looks -- as Terry Goldie writes in an article entitled "The Representation of the Indigene" – something like a chessboard in which the semiotic pawn signifying the indigenous person and can only be moved in very circumscribed ways. Terry Goldie is of the view that the shape of the signifying process as it applies to indigenous peoples is formed by a certain semiotic field, a field that provides the boundaries within which the images of the indigene function. The existence of such semiotic field constitutes an important aspect of the 'subjugated knowledge's' to which Foucault refers in *Power/Knowledge*. The indigene is a semiotic pawn on a chess board under the control of the White sign maker (in the case of Aboriginals in Australia) and the caste Hindus sign maker (in the case of Dalit in India). And yet the individual sign maker, the individual player, the individual writer, can move these pawns only within certain prescribed areas. The sign-making is all happening within two fields of discourse: one is that of British imperialism and the other is that of caste oppression by the caste Hindus.

As well as extending the chessboard analogy, it would not be over-simplistic to maintain that the play between white and indigene (in the case of Australia) and Dalit and the caste Hindus (in the case of India) is a replica of the black and white squares, with clearly limited oppositional moves. The basic dualism, however, to be noted here, is not that of good and evil but that of oppressor and the oppressed, racialism and caste oppression.

The Indian state has been an important reference point for the Dalit in their quest for social justice. Ambedkar is said to have observed, 'You have now a way of bringing about change, an improvement in your life conditions. That way is through political action, through appropriate laws... you can make [the] government provide for you what you are now denied–food, clothing, shelter, education...' (Gore 1993: 213 and Shah 2001: 223). Adopting the policy of protective discrimination, the state has, indeed, granted a number of special privileges to the Dalit: reservations in the legislature and bureaucracy, socio-cultural safeguards, and programs for economic upliftment. The practices of untouchability and bonded labour have also been legally abolished.

However, the Dalit relationship with the state has evolved in the past few decades. Especially since the 1980s, the Dalit have felt that the state machinery, despite the constitutional provisions, has failed to protect them against exploitation, guarantee their rights, and improve their socio-economic position. Leaders of the Bahujan Samaj Party (BSP)-led Dalit movement in Uttar Pradesh have argued that in such circumstances, capturing power is essential. The former BSP President and Dalit ideologue, Kanshi Ram, is said to have observed, 'Political power is the key by which any lock (obstacle) can be opened' (S. Pai 2002). Ram and others in the BSP have taken Ambedkar's dictum on state power a step further. Ambedkar had stressed upon effective participation by the Dalit in the decision-making process. He had never equated power with post or office. But those in the BSP do. The rise and success of the Mayawati-led BSP in Uttar Pradesh has created a new identity and awareness among the Dalit. Mayawati has emerged as a symbol of their dignity and aspirations. Dalit women seem to strongly identify with her.

In comparing the two literatures, it has been necessary to compare the Australian Aboriginal and Dalit societies as well. Given the effective fact that the two societies are different in terms of place and time, country, region, conditions and languages, it is understandable that there should be certain similarities and on the other hand certain limitations and differences too. Dalit and Aboriginal literatures are mirror images of the lives, sorrows, problems, pains and revolts of Dalit and Aboriginals.

There are numerous expressions of red-hot experience and fighting instinct in these literatures. More than anything else, the 'right' or 'ability' of the marginalised group to write literature comes under immediate contestation. Both literatures speak about struggles for human rights and against exploitation. Despite differences of country and conditions etc., the similarity in the life experience of the two communities derives from the fact that both were targets of excess injustice and exploitation — their experience of pain is of a world-scale. There are similarities in the feelings of ownership, entitlement and superiority demonstrated by the white and savarna societies, on the one hand, and of revolt against caste/racial discrimination by Dalit and Aboriginals on the other. Moreover, Dalit and Aboriginal literary commentators have rejected the patronizing, sympathetic representations of white and *savarna* writers, as well as the unrealistic and pitying portrayals of Dalit and Aboriginals. Dalit and Aboriginals speak and write about people who suffer from injustice in their own societies as well as in other societies. That is why the human being has become the counterpoint of both these literatures. Phrases such as "only he or she who has suffered this anguish knows its sting" clearly delineate narrative authority for the Dalit writer. It can be seen how the entire life – narrative in both literatures is based on the idea of the communal identity. Subjectivity in these autobiographies is complicated by the deep connection between the individual self and the communal self. The autobiographical narrative is perceived as the actual site of the power struggle, where the voice of the marginalised individual contests the institutionalized narrative of the dominant group.

Convergences

Dalit writings and Aboriginal writings bear considerable resemblance because first, the predicament of the Dalit in India and Aboriginals in Australia go together in the context of oppression; second, thematically human suffering because of social discrimination is similar in both writings; and thirdly and most importantly, the emotional worlds they inhabit - constituting their pain, rebellion, hopes and desires - are similar though there is a lot of difference in the geographical background. An important similarity between Dalit autobiographies and the autobiographies of Aboriginal community is the difficult struggle these writings face to gain the right to speak. More than anything else, the 'right' or 'ability' of the marginalised group to write literature comes under immediate contestation, and Dalit writers as well as Aboriginal writers have likewise been forced to fight for the right to speak as well as to redefine the boundaries of what can be said. Dalit writers and Aboriginal writers have attempted to negotiate the challenge of securing narrative authority by emphasising one, the 'experience of discrimination' and two, necessary criteria for writing autobiographies. These autobiographies are not simply the narration of a life-story, but they are also used as a means of political assertion. They are a process of 'self-emancipation' in the creation of a 'dissident space' within the public sphere. At the same time they are also a process of 'self-creation' through the narration of a public persona. Thus, these autobiographies also serve as means for Dalit as well as Aboriginal writers to reclaim narrative authority over the construction of the 'Dalit self' or 'Aboriginal self'. While dominant Indian society has identified Dalit as 'inferior', 'polluted' etc., and White British society has identified Aboriginals as 'inferior'. These auto biographers rewrite selfhood, so to speak, in their description of their life and the life of their communities. Dalit society and Aboriginal society are not inferior as is claimed by the dominant communities, but are 'different' or 'oppressed' or 'inventive in the face of extreme exploitation'. Thus, rather than describe their life only as one of 'victimhood', pain becomes transformed into a uniting, 'enlightening' experience in which an assertive identity is realized and incites the individual to action and political struggle. Watching their community continually oppressed by the upper-castes (in the case of India) and the white people (in the case of Australia), the protagonist of the particular autobiography does not experience his/her pain 'lying down', but rather pain incites him/her to unite with his/her community in a fight against caste/racial discrimination. Similarly, the process of 'reliving' this pain, while writing the autobiography is not viewed as a process of healing or forgetting in order to move on with one's life. It is a way of solidifying individual connection with the larger imagined community and at the same time contributing to the political assertion by presenting 'facts' of one's life to contest castes (in India) and racism (in Australia).

The white settlers of Australia have used Aboriginal people as slaves, indentured labourers and teenager girls have been used as maidservants. In order to teach the captured black people a lesson, the white people and station-masters subjected them to painful torture. They were beaten to death, particularly in prisons; women were brazenly raped by station owners and masters; pregnant women suffered abortions from being assigned extremely difficult tasks; children were separated from mothers, wives from husbands, and their families were destroyed. There are hair-raising accounts of these tortures and excesses found in *Bringing Them Home* published by Human Rights and Equal Opportunity Commission (HREOC). Dalit too have been tortured for a very long time. Dalit have remained outcast and the Hindu Varna system imposed slavery on them, such was the condition of the outcast communities that they had neither a village nor a home. The Adivasis have been pushed into forests and caves. Needless to say that God did not ordain the slavery of Dalit and Australian Aboriginals. Human beings created it themselves. Having imposed slavery on Aboriginals and Dalit, White and *savarna* societies forcibly extracted labour from them. Whites assigned separate educational institutions, separate eating places, separate spaces in trains and buses, and separate residential areas to Australian Aboriginals. Untouchables, too, were kept outside the village. Arrangements were made for them to have separate settlements, separate river banks, and separate cremation grounds. Since *sudras* were denied any right to education by the Hindu caste system, the question of separate educational institutions did not arise. Later, during the British days, when they did begin to receive education, as Omprakash Valmiki states they had to sit in a separate corner or outside the threshold of the class room. Actual descriptions of this arrangement can be found in Valmiki's *Joothan* and Sharan Kumar Limbale's *Akkarmashi.*

Though Dalit Movements and Aboriginal movements have proceeded along different paths and taken different turnings, both movements are struggles for human rights and against exploitation. Aboriginal people in Australia and Dalit in India have both experienced inhuman degradation; their struggle is against it. Despite differences of country, region, conditions, society and language, the similarity in the life experience of the two communities derives from the fact that both were targets of excess injustice and slavery — their experience of pain is of a world-scale. There are similarities in the feelings of ownership, entitlement and superiority demonstrated by white and savarna societies, on the one hand, and of revolt against racism by Aboriginals and caste discrimination by Dalit on the other hand. Because of these similarities Dalit writers and Aboriginal writers see the pain of each other as their own, which they have communicated and expressed through their literatures.

Divergences

As far as divergences or dissimilarities between Dalit writings and Aboriginal writings are concerned, to begin with, if Aboriginal autobiographies can be viewed as a dialogue between Aboriginal and non-Aboriginal people (i.e. White people) about the history of injustices that Aboriginal people have experienced fighting against racial discrimination on the one hand, Dalit autobiographies on the other hand, contest one, the basis of caste discrimination and two, the institutional claim that caste no longer functions as a social force in modern India. There are differences of country, region, conditions, society and language found in both writings. If the Dalit are the protagonists of India's boycotted society, the Aboriginals are the protagonists of Australian society. The Aboriginals have been degraded by white society and their differences are mainly based on colour and blood, and the Dalit have been degraded by *savarna* society whose differences are based on 'caste'. White children could feed at a Black woman's breast, but even the touch and shadow of the Dalit were considered untouchable by the touchables. While the Blacks and whites belong to different racial groups, the Dalit and *savarnas* do not. The main cause of the Aboriginal's slavery was economic where as the main cause of the Dalit's untouchability is social. Aboriginal people perform labour but their labour is not considered undignified. Dalit do the lowest types of work and their work is considered undignified. While Aboriginal people cannot hide their colour of skin, untouchables can hide their caste. In Australia, Aboriginal people were given subhuman treatment because of their colour. In the case of Dalit it is because of their 'caste', based on birth. It was because Dalit are 'untouchable' that they are subjected to discrimination and humiliation by *savarnas.* That means Dalit's predicament is much worse than that of the Aboriginal people.

Australian Aboriginal literature protests against the two centuries of colonial rule, loss of indigenous rights, culture, languages and identity. It tries to reconstruct the identity and history of the Aborigines from an Aboriginal perspective and deconstruct the same that have been created by the whites. The stolen generation, which was one of the atrocious consequences of colonialism, is the crucial theme of Aboriginal literature given the fact that most aboriginal writing is autobiographical and most aboriginal writers were stolen children. They were stolen from their people and culture in the name of education and etiquette and trained to become good domestic servants in white households. Most of the autobiographies under consideration depict how the Aboriginal women writers give testimony to being removed from their mothers, parents or homes through 'compulsion' or 'duress' by the station-owners for whom they worked. The argument put forth by the station owners or managers was that the children would be taken to get education, but to the dismay of the girls they found they were being used as 'slave' labour. Many examples of this could be found in *My Place* and *Wandering Girl.* Another major issue is the issue of half-castes, who were born out of the relationship between white men and Aboriginal women, sometimes vice versa, but considered illegitimate for most of them were born outside the wed-lock. They were neither accepted by the whites nor admitted by the blacks and were removed by the government saying that since they have white blood, aboriginal mothers are not eligible to look after them and that they could be trained to become civilized beings. Sally Morgan, Glenyse Ward, Ruby Langford and even Elsie explain how the Aboriginal Affairs representatives had come to "look for the half-caste kids". Their mothers would tell them to 'stay in the bunkhouse all day'. The children would never be caught during those official visits. Glenyse Ward, Daisy Corunna and others too, all bear witness to the experience of girls who were sent to work as domestic servants. All recount the hard physical work, the racist insults and the wages that they never received.

Thus, we may conclude, then, that both writings evince a form of 'resistance literature'. They exemplify a form of 'testimony' to the kind of injustices that occur to them and also to the struggles to survive because of the human rights denied to them. Therefore, it is the 'truths' of Aboriginal and Dalit writers' experiences that engage the readers of these autobiographies. It is not the 'truths', or the legitimated speaking positions as recorded in the history books, or the newspaper reports that the readers of these autobiographies search for. It is the 'truths' revealed in the speaking positions of those who have been treated as invisible, or who have been silenced by the dominant voices. In the writings by Dalit and Aboriginal men/women, it is the 'petite narratives' of the life story that are a 'witnessing' of other experiences rather than the legitimated histories.

It seems to me that all the autobiographies under consideration seek to describe what happens when a person is pushed to the extremes of pain and suffering and their arguments are based upon the premise that at such a point cultural and linguistic differences fade into the background because the physicality of pain is so world-destroying that the sufferer is reduced to his own state of affairs. This is an assertion which seems to be true for all human beings. They describe the route along this pain journey identifying other features of pain that seem to be universal in scope: that physical pain are later on politically converted into the assertion of political power and self assertion. Writers of both domains of writing, with their very gesture of asserting particularity, juxtapose one pain with another, draw attention to the fact that pain does reside within a meaningful conceptual category. All the auto biographers seem to be giving the message that pain and suffering have become a pre-requisite for authenticity and authority amongst minority groups. Individuals who have personally experienced great pain are awarded the right to speak for the group; their words and leadership are valorised through narratives of suffering. The potential danger here is that pain becomes fetish zed and hyper-valorised as a means of gaining power.

REFERENCES AND FURTHER READING

Ahmad, Sara. (2004). *The Cultural Politics of Emotion*. London: Routledge.

Bama. (2000). *Karukku.* Translation from the Tamil by Lakshmi Holmstrom, Chennai: MacMillan India Limited.

Beverly, J. (2004). *Testimonio: On the politics of truth.* Minneapolis: University of Minnesota CA: Sage Publications.

Deetz, S. and Simpson, J. (2004). Critical organizational dialogue. Open formation and the demand of "otherness". In R. Anderson, L. A. Baxter and K.N. Cissna (Eds.).

Dialogue. Theorizing difference in communication studies (pp.141-158). Thousand Oaks, Ginibi, Ruby Langford. (1988). *Don't Take Your Love to Town*. Australia: Penguin Books.

Gore, M.S. (1993). *The Social Context of an Ideology*, New Delhi: Sage Publications.

Guha, R. (1982). Preface. In R. Guha (Ed.), *Subaltern Studies I* (pp. vii-viii). Oxford University Press: Delhi.

Guha, R. (1997). Introduction. In R. Guha (Ed.), *A Subaltern Studies reader 1986-1995,* (pp. ix-xxii). University of Minnesota Press: Minneapolis.

Jadav, Narendra. (2003). *Outcase*. Translation from the Marathi, New Delhi: Penguin.

Limbale, Sharan Kumar. (2003). *Akkarmashi:The Outcaste*. Translation from the Marathi by Santos Bhoomkar. New Delhi: OUP.

Lionnet, Francoise. (1997). Geographies of pain: captive bodies and violence acts in the fictions of Gayl Jones, Bessie Head and Myriam Warner-Vieyra. In O. Nnaemeka, ed., *The Politics of (M)othering: Womanhood, Identity, Resistance in African Literature*, pp. 205-27. London: Routledge.

Moon, Vasant. (2001). *Growing up Untouchable in India: A Dalit Autobiogrpahy.* Translation from the Marathi by Gail Omvedt and Introduction by Eleanor Zelliot, New Delhi: Vistaar Publications.

Morgan Sally. (1987). *My Place*. Fremantale: FACP.

Pai, S. (2002). *Dalit Assertion and the Unfinished Democratic Revolution: The Bahujan Samaj Party in Uttar Pradesh*, New Delhi: Sage Publications.

Prakash, G. (1992). Postcolonial criticism and Indian historiography. *Social Text, 31/32,*8-19. Press.

Roughsey, Elsie. (1983). *An Aboriginal Mother Talks of the Old and the New.* McPhee Gribble Publication.

Shah, G. (2001). 'Dalit politics: has it reached an impasse?', in N.G. Jayal and S. Pai (eds.) *Democratic Governance in India: Challenges of Poverty, Development and Identity*, pp. 221-31, New Delhi: Sage Publications.

Spivak, C.G. (1988). Subaltern Studies: deconstructing historiography. In R. Guha and G.C. Spivak (Eds.), *Selected Subaltern Studies* (pp. 3-36). Oxford University Press: New Valmiki, Omprakash. (2003). *Joothan: A Dalit's Life.* Translation from the Hindi by Arun Prabha Mukherjee. Kolkata: Samy Publication.

Ward, Glenyse. (1987). *Wandering Girl.* Broome: Magabala Books.

2

AESTHETICISING PROTEST : A COMPARATIVE STUDY OF THE INDIAN DALIT AESTHETIC MOVEMENT AND THE BLACK ARTS MOVEMENT WITH REFERENCE TO SELECT POETRY OF NAMDEO DHASAL AND SONIA SANCHEZ

Komal Agarwal

Abstract

Aesthetics is a term that is generally associated with 'serious', 'mainstream' literature. But, on deeper reflection, one will realise how we cannot really lock the term into watertight compartments. Aesthetic pleasure, or *rasa*, can be experienced in any form of art or literature which has a 'serious' import and has all the elements that lead to the fruition of a work of literature/art into aesthetic pleasure. Hence, the theory of aesthetics can be considered to be a very democratic theory. It is with this approach that this paper attempts a comparative study of Indian Dalit literature and African-American Literature, thereby seeking to dismantle the very category of 'marginality' that we associate with them. According to the ancient Indian theoretician of drama, *Bharata, rasa* is the combination of *vibhava*, *anubhava*, and *vyabhicaribhava.* Hence, one can contend that *rasa* can be tasted by the audience/readers in any literature/art across the world, irrespective of caste, class, race, gender, nationality etc. This exploration becomes all the more interesting when we take for study the Dalit Aesthetic Movement and the Black Aesthetic Movement, movements which were engaged in politics through the medium of literature and art. This paper explores the aesthetics of Dalit and African-American writings, specifically in the poetry of

Namdeo Dhasal and Sonia Sanchez, literary figures prominently associated with the Dalit Panther Movement and the Black Arts/Aesthetic Movement respectively. The paper studies the employment of poetic language not only for aesthetic pleasure but also for furthering the community voice of protest of the Dalit and the African-Americans against discrimination on the basis of caste and race respectively. Thereby, drawing a parallel between the two politico-cultural movements, different spatially and temporally, but converging on the subject of caste and racial othering, and the demand for recognition through aesthetic means.

Key Words: Aesthetics of Protest, Politicizing Poetic Language, Questioning Marginality

> Are they the only ones who've came forth from a human mother's womb?
>
> Are the rest of us the progeny of cats and dogs?
>
> What sort of an illusion is it in which they live?
>
> . . . .
>
> Now they must stop this.
>
> Now they must change.
>
> They must mend their own ways
>
> Before trying to correct others.
>
> . . . .
>
> They think human beings are completely blind;
>
> They think human beings are inferior;
>
> They think human beings are a helpless lot;
>
> They are afraid of the shadow of man;
>
> . . . .
>
> They suffocate; they're galled; they spit venom.
>
> Never hereafter must one write anything shrouded in obscurity
>
> One must plough it all up with a donkey pulling the yoke—and start from the scratch. "Ode to Dr Ambedkar: 1978 EQUALITY FOR ALL OR DEATH TO INDIA"
>
> by Namdeo Dhasal[1]

Who's gonna make all that beautiful mean something.
like I mean who's gonna take blk / is / beautiful
and make more of it than blk / capitalism. . . . .
like. this. is an SOS me. calling. . calling. .
some / one please reply soon.

—"blk/rhetoric" by Sonia Sanchez[2]

The extracts of the two poems quoted above have one thing in common. Both look at poems as weapons to be raised against oppression and both have a sense of urgency, when it comes to motivating people born in their lot to use the very same weapons fearlessly without mincing words. Likewise, this paper is an exploration of the common meeting grounds of two seemingly disparate aesthetic traditions, namely, the Indian Dalit Aesthetics and the Black Aesthetics, locating them in two specific movements, namely the Dalit Panther Movement and the Black Arts Movement. This study takes, as illustrations, select poems of Namdeo Dhasal and Sonia Sanchez, poets who were prominent cultural and political representatives, (along with other poets, writers and artists) of the Dalit Panther Movement and the Black Arts Movement respectively. The study will also examine the dynamics of performance and language and its relationship with the processing and the manifestation of aesthetic experience; the epistemology of the audience/ reader, and, the role of the performer/poet in bringing about the aesthetic experience and in exploring the potential of performance/art to bring about social changes.

Although the two movements might not have any comparison along the spatial and temporal registers, and their aesthetics might also seem diverse and quite mismatched. Yet, on deeper reflection, one might notice the points of convergence regarding the voices that they try to raise against caste-based or racial oppression, and the theories of literature, art, and performance that the two traditions evolve, especially in their conception of art as being the aesthetic chronicle of a society/ race. Now, since caste, race, and society are all political constructs, hence, in defining the purpose of literature, art and performance as the intertwining of the aesthetic and the communitarian, the two movements forward the conception of poetry, art, literature, and performance as endowed with political vigour.

Owing to the complex and manifold relationship between language, literature, performance and literary art, one easily mistakes that the only use of words is cognitive, thereby undermining the literary experience as a whole. Since literature is fashioned from language rather than the written word, and it is speech which gives a kind of vitality to language, one can presume that literary arts are essentially per formative, spoken arts, a fact which is illustrated not only by poetic language and dramatic arts, but also by novelistic narratives, all of which either offer word images or evoke entire, lived worlds.

Literary language is therefore, not abstract, but graphic, and a literary experience involves perception of images and sounds, in addition to providing avenues for analysis or interpretation of the same, and the subsequent application of the same to one's immediate circumstances and the society at large. When a literary vision is grasped, the word and the speaker's awareness become one. Thus, a union of the body and the mind constitutes true speech and writing, which is both alive and creative. A literary object acquires life-force when the visual or verbal presence evokes a world of images in which man is reconciled to his empirical experience.

This paper is a reflection on the political nature of art and aesthetics, or the hand in glove nature of the political and the aesthetic. Thus, the motive of the present endeavour is to bring to light the fact that irrespective of the nature and form of art, or the political designs or lack of the same in an artistic/creative enterprise, there is a unity of the aesthetic and the political consciousness in an experience of art/performance. This, as the study will show, becomes all the more pronounced when the people from the margins, like the Dalit or the African-Americans engage with politics through the medium of literature. Thus dismantling the very fringes to which they belong, and becoming mainstream literatures and artists in terms of artistic production and aesthetic fruition, as their literature or art is not just meant for 'their' people, but also for, and targeted at the 'dominant sections' of their respective societies. Hence, one can conclude that the arena of literature or art is a democratic one. It recognises no margins, knows no boundaries, does not practice discrimination, and includes everyone in its ambit.[3] Additionally, the study will investigate how art/performance/poetry can be, and often is, committing its aim being to delight as well as to instruct,[4] and how consequently, it leads to a liberating vision and when required becomes a tool of resistance and change.

Existing scholarship on a comparative study of the two movements has not really dealt with the aesthetic dimensions of the two movements, and that is the missing link that this paper seeks to explore. K.S. Singh elaborates on the similarities between Indian Untouchables or Dalit and the American Blacks[5], discussing how both have suffered from "cumulative deprivations and inequalities in their respective societies" (163). He discusses in his essay how both the Dalit and the African-Americans have been engaged in protest movements of several types to "ameliorate their socio-economic condition, as well as their cultural, religious, and other deprivations. . . Their protest ideology involves resistance, opposition, confrontation and conflict with the dominant groups (oppressors) . . . to achieve their desired goals of social equality, social dignity and de-stigmatized social identity" (166). He notes further a new ideological phase started in the history of social protest movements with the formation of the Black Panther Party in the US and the Dalit Panther Movement in India. While the immediate cause of the formation of the Black Panthers was the increasing brutality by the white police, the increasing atrocities perpetrated by the caste-Hindus on the Dalit were responsible for the formation of the Dalit Panthers. (172)

J.M. Waghmare, by way of comparing Dalit and African-American writers, observes: Both Dalit and Blacks (non-Whites) are in search of their cultural identity. Their experiences are based on social and cultural inequalities. Both write to strike a social balance, for equality. The language of both these groups of people is that of literary and cultural revolt. The literature of both is firmly held by creative possibilities. (Kumar 49, translation mine)

Basing his classification of the Dalit movement on the lines of Gail Omvedt, Nagaraj identifies three specific epochs in the Dalit movement in the twentieth century: proto-Dalit activism (1900-1930); the emergence and consolidation of Ambedkarite paradigms (1930-1972), and the birth of the Dalit movement which begins with the birth of the Dalit Panther movement of Maharashtra in 1972 and spread to other parts of the country in the same decade (95).

The Dalit Panther movement started with Marathi literary magazines propagating anti-establishment and Left trends in Marathi literature (S.D. 1398). Born in Bombay in 1972, was a militant organization of Dalit youth, its leadership mostly drawn from a new generation of young poets and writers during a period when the atrocities against Dalit in the villages, often of brutal and horrifying forms, seemed to be increasing by leaps and bounds (Omvedt 73). The Dalit Panther Movement was formed under the leadership of Raja Dhale as president, Namdeo Dasal as defence minister and J.V. Pavar as its general secretary (K.S. Singh 173). Although the Dalit Panthers drew inspiration from Jotiba Phule and Dr. B.R. Ambedkar, they drew the organizational structure and strategies from the Black Panther Party and were also greatly influenced by black literature (K.S. Singh 173). They proved to be the spark that set off a wave of organizing efforts throughout the country (Omvedt 73). It was for the first time in the history of India that creative writers headed an organization which was engaged in political proceedings (Kumar 50-51, translation mine). Writing about the body of Dalit literature and poetry, K Satchidanandan makes the following observation,

"Dalit literature has indeed created its own alternative aesthetic by redrawing the map of literature, by discovering and creating a whole new continent of experience that had so far been left to darkness and silence . . . by disturbing the sterile complacency of the dominant social groups, and by challenging their set mores and fixed modes of looking at reality, their stale habits of ordering knowledge, beauty and power and their established literary canons, bringing to focus neglected, suppressed or marginalised aspects of experience, vision, language and reality and forcing the community to refashion its tools and observe itself critically from fresh and different angles. . . Dalit poetry . . . challenges the assumptions and injunctions of classical poetics by breaking its rules of "propriety", "balance", "restraint" and "understatement". Dalit literature also questions the middle-class notions of linguistic "decency" by using words that classical aesthetics would consider "uncouth" (*chyutasamskara*), "rustic" (*gramya*) or "obscene" (*asleela*)." (78)

Although the above observation is about Dalit literature and poetry in general, yet, if brilliantly outlines the features that differentiate Dalit literature from other genres or types of literature, and hints at what Dalit aesthetics can ideally comprise. According to Nagaraj, the most important strategy of the Dalit movement is a coupling of the cultural theory of despair with the politics of hope (105). In the words of Arjun Dangle, "Dalit literature is a creative rebellion, which is based on revolt, unacceptance and scientific viewpoint. Dalit writers do not only write for entertainment, but for a social purpose" (Kumar 47, translation mine). In fact, the inextricability of Dalit aesthetics with the political condition of the Dalit can be gauged in Hovell's observation, "Dalit poems have a purpose, the poets speak about and for a community. Some of these poets say that if their political and social goals were met tomorrow, they could stop shouting and writing." (65)

Taking the same argument further and applying it to his study of Dhasal, Shaleen Kumar Singh observes that Dhasal is both poet and Panther. His poetry and that of the larger Dalit movement cannot be separated from its historical, political and social context. He adds that the poetry of this movement has a purpose, the poets speak about and for a community. It is noteworthy here that Dhasal also launched *Vidroha* (Revolt), a little magazine of protest writing (Chitre 158). In his poem, "Ode to Dr Ambedkar: 1978 EQUALITY FOR ALL OR DEATH TO INDIA," Dhasal proclaims:

Never hereafter
Must one write anything,
Shrouded in obscurity.
No longer must one indulge,
In oblique poetry.
No longer must one erratically swoop,
One should catch it by its very roots. (81)

Chitre is of the opinion that, "Namdeo cannot separate his activism from his poetry, and his poetry is only the literary form of his activism" (15). In the poem, "Mandakini Patil: A Young Prostitute, My Intended Collage," Dhasal uses plain language, but pointed words to appeal to his fellow Dalit and human beings, "People who are merely involved in living are actually dead and gone cold" (Chitre 60). In fact, about this intermingling of the social and the political in his poetry, Dhasal notes, "I had to prepare ideological ground for my political commitment to Dalit Panther. We would have nothing to do with the so-called progressive and left parties as long as the problem of untouchability was not their topmost political priority. Around 1968-69, I gradually came to believe that untouchability would we our prime target" (qtd. in S.K. Singh) Chitre is right when he says," Namdeo's universe is untouchable too. It is loathsome and nauseating universe, a journey into it is a journey from the sacred into the profane. Or, if we were to see it in purely secular and material terms, it is a journey from the clean to the dirty, from the sanitized to the unsanitary, from the healthy to the diseased." (qtd. in S.K. Singh)

Dhasal admits further, "I do not differentiate between political poetry and non-political poetry. . . My so-called political poems belong to that rich period of my life when Dalit Panther was on the right track. That is where the force in those poems comes from . . . I have a mission in life and that is to oppose all forms of exploitation— economic, social, cultural. My poetry is a product of my spontaneous commitment to my mission. . . Call it political poetry, call it social poetry if you like, but as long as there remains contradictions and conflicts between individual and collective life that affect my feelings, my poetry will be about them. . . What is poetry but autobiography, anyway? Even political poetry is autobiographical." (Chitre 170-73)

Now, it is generally accepted that poetry, as a genre, is a sort of a conversation between the readers/audience and the poets/speakers. Talking about the sense of urgency inherent in poetry, and the thrust of Namdeo's poetry, Chitre writes,"With its affinity for the spoken word, poetry (other than theatre) is the one literary genre that conveys subtle tones of intimacy and powerful thrusts of urgency even in its textual incarnation. . . In its elemental form, poetry is located in the human voice. Even when it is appropriated and re-voiced as a performed text, it does not cease to have a live addressor and a live addressee. . . Namdeo Dhasal restored this quintessential quality of live performance to his . . . poetry from the outset. . . [so much so that when] Vijay Tendulkar wrote a foreword to this first edition of *Golpitha* . . . [he] was struck by its rootedness in space and time, and by the language that defied penetration beyond a point." (9-10)

The latter half of the paper will elaborate on how poetry was the most prolific form of writing even in the Black Aesthetics Movement, and the performative style of Sanchez is what makes her poetry stand apart from other contemporary writings. However, coming back to Dhasal, Chitre points out how Dhasal sometimes uses "words that do not exist in the vocabulary of the other or have different connotations for aliens" (24). Chitre, describing the craft of Dhasal's poetry writes, "His poems are driven by the voice of the poet initiating a rhythmic movement, creating sweeps, swirls and loops through syntactical inversions and convolutions, forceful stokes contrasting with fine-lined details. The reader is drawn into its music and dazzled by occasional phrases and images, innovative turns of phrase and striking metaphor. His poems defy linear denouncement and literal translation because at the heart of his creative process are Namdeo's technique of free association and the spontaneous contextual leaps he makes." (27)

In fact, Dhasal's collection *Golpitha* (named of a red-light district in Mumbai),depicts the tough life of a Dalit and is marked with 'raw energy exuded by each of its words entirely unfamiliar to the established literary circle of its time, writes S.K. Singh. He also quotes Rakshi Sonawane, who has made the following observation about this collection, "The book scandalized the Marathi literary world, which had always been dominated by upper-caste writers. *Golpitha* was initially attacked for not being a literary work worth the name. Taking artistic liberty with free verse, Dhasal lashed out against the system, using words that had never been printed." (italics mine)

According to Anand Teltumade, the creation of the Dalit Panthers led to the recognition of the Dalit as the defeated class turning into a group of revolutionary warriors and hence the identification of their struggle with the struggle of all the oppressed people of the world (translation mine, 16-17). However, he also furthers the opinion that their fighting spirit was mostly limited to their writings or their speeches (translation mine, 19), thus meaning that it was not an armed struggle.

Dhasal is not only concerned with the upliftment of the Dalit, but envisions an egalitarian society in general. His poetry integrates—rather than divides—humanity. In his "Allahu Akbar," he talks of communal harmony between the two sects of Islam, "Let's filter out the Shia and the Sunni *dargahs* inside ourselves / Let's weep upon every grave / Allahu Akbar" (Chitre 53). He is also worried about issues that plague humanity in general, like poverty and hunger. In his poem "Hunger," he writes, "Hunger, just tell us, to what race does this ape belong. / If you can't answer that, we'll fuck seventeen generations of you. / We'll fuck your mother hunger, hunger. . ." (Chitre 80).

At this juncture, referring back to the theories of *rasa* aesthetics, we can easily see how scatological words and repulsive vocabulary act as the *vibha*s (determinants) for the tasting of *Bibhatsa Rasa* (the sentiment of the grotesque, the odious), and sometimes also *Bhayanak Rasa* (the sentiment of anger) in the readers/audience. In fact, rummaging through Dhasal's poetry, one can easily find many such references, "the public urinal" and "[t]he shining liver of a seven-year-old gathers rust" in "Ode to Dr Ambedkar", "ferocious python is moving through the intestines" in "Songs of the Dogs and the Republics", and "Man's lost his speech / His god's shitting skeleton" in "Kamatipura" (Chitre 37; 63; 74).

Moving to the other Movement that the paper is dealing with, it was the disenchantment with the goals and strategies of the Civil Rights Movement that led to the Black Power Movement and the subsequent widespread revival of nationalist feelings among blacks. Malcolm X's passionate and open resistance to what he perceived as attempts by American whites to eradicate African Americans became a model for the Black Power movement (Gates and McKay 1794). The concept of Black Aesthetics surfaced in the 1960s in America at the time of the Black Power Movement and the Black Arts Movement.

The most controversial representation of Black Power during the 1960s was the Black Panther Party for Self-Defence, founded in Oakland, California, in 1966 by Huey Newton and Bobby Seale. The Black Panthers declared themselves revolutionaries and announced their intention to bring Black Power to black people by any means necessary. The Panthers openly displayed their dedication to a gospel of the gun (Gates and McKay 1794-95). They were a group of radical and militant Blacks who emphasised revolutionary nationalism rather than cultural nationalism (K.S. Singh 173).

The sixties and the early seventies marked a growing interest in black consciousness, writing, and art, thanks to the roaring popularity of the Black Arts Movement. Both inherently and overtly political in content, the Black Arts movement was the only American literary movement to advance "social engagement" as a sine qua non of its aesthetic.

The Black Arts Movement in America was a time during which various definitions of a black aesthetic were being approximated in America by the African-Americans. The Black Aesthetic is more a 'concept in definition' than a 'concept.' In the *The Black Aesthetic*, which is a collection of essays by various authors like Larry Neal and Amiri Baraka, Addison Gayle Jr. sets forth his own manifesto for the Black Arts and his understanding of the black aesthetic. Larry Neal, in his essay, *The Black Arts Movement*, writes, "The Black Arts Movement is radically opposed to any concept of the artist that alienates him from his community. Black Art is the aesthetic and spiritual sister of the Black

Power concept. . . The Black Arts and the Black Power concept both relate broadly to the Afro-American's desire for self-determination and nationhood. Both concepts are nationalistic" (Gates and McKay 1797).

In accordance with their definition of themselves as participants in a movement, African American writers and artists turned to the African American masses for their inspiration and defined their goals in broadly collective social and political terms. The objective of these writers was to create works that would be, in the words of Maulana Karenga, "functional, collective, and committing or committed." Hence the Black Arts of the 1960s proposed to create politically engaged expression as a corollary to the new black spirit of the decade (Gates and McKay 1796-97).

African American writers and artists, as a vital sector of the movement, sought to transform the manner in which black Americans were represented or portrayed in literature and the arts (Gates and McKay 1796). James A. Emanuel, whose essay features in Gayle's *The Black Aesthetic*, highlights the change that is palpable in the literary works of the times, "The nature of literature itself. . . appears to be changing for black authors and their followers. It seems to be more social, more programmatic, more therapeutic." (192-223). Hoyt W. Fuller wrote, "The black revolt is as palpable in letters as it is in the streets" (qtd. in Gayle 3-12).

The Black Arts movement believed that occasional, per formative, musical, authentic, and affective sounds of a black voice committed to struggle could serve as persuasive and effective weapons in the campaign to liberate a black nation. Hence, Black Arts practitioners sought to combine the African American vernacular resonances of sermons, popular music, and black mass "speech" into a rousing new form of poetry (Gates and McKay 1797).

Poetry was the creative genre that saw the most accomplished experimental and distinguished work by the black artists of the sixties. Because poetry normally requires far less time to compose than prose genres such as the novel or short story, it was ideally suited to the felt immediacy of struggle characteristic of Black Arts and Black Power advocated and adherents (Gates and McKay 1797). Amiri Baraka, a principal architect of the Black Arts, stated in one of his early works:

We have awaited the coming of a natural
phenomenon. Mystics and romantics
knowledgeable
workers
of the land.
But none has come.
(Repeat)
but none has come.

will the machine gunners please step forward? (qtd. in Gates and McKay 1799)

The fact that poetry and revolution were interconnected is evident in a lot of poetry from the times. For example, Nikki Giovanni writes in "For Saundra": "i wanted to write / a poem / that rhymes / but revolution doesn't lend / itself to be-bopping. / . . . / and it occurred to me / maybe I shouldn't write / at all / but clean my gun / and check my kerosene supply / perhaps these are not poetic / times / at all" (qtd. in Gates and McKay 1983-84).

Maulana Karenga holds a similar opinion, "The real function of art is to make revolution, using its own medium" (qtd. in Gates and McKay 1974). Amiri Baraka's poem *SOS* can be the most classic example of the same:

Calling black people
Calling all black people, man woman child
Wherever you are, calling you, urgent, come in
Black People, come in, wherever you are, urgent, calling
you, calling all black people
calling all black people, come in, black people, come
on in. (qtd. in Gates and McKay 1883)

Even Julian Mayfield, whose essay has been complied in Gayle's *The Black* Aesthetic, writes, "The Black Aesthetic, for those trying to create today, is necessarily the business of making revolution, for we have tried everything else. . . Let another generation deal with the niceties of beauty and art. This generation has its work cut out for it" (qtd. in Gayle 24-31).

Amiri Baraka makes this agenda very clear in his poem *Black Art*:

. . . We want "poems that kill."
Assassin poems. Poems that shoot
guns. Poems that wrestle cops into alleys
and take their weapons leaving them dead
with tongues pulled out and sent to Ireland. Knockoff
poems for dope selling wops or slick halfwhite
politicians Airplane poems, rrrrrrrrrrrrrrr
rrrrrrrrrrrrrr . . . tuhtuhtuhtuhtuhtuhtuhtuhtuh
. . . rrrrrrrrrrrrrrr . . . Setting fire and death to
whities ass. . . . . . .
We want a black poem. And a Black World.
Let the world be a Black Poem
And Let All Black People Speak This Poem
Silently or LOUD. (Baraka 1883-84)

Sonia Sanchez, after hearing a powerful speech by Malcolm X during the early 1960s, became a vernacular poet for the African-American masses (Gates and McKay 1902). It is because of the effect he had on Sanchez that her first book of poetry, *Homecoming* (1969) reflects her social activism and black militancy (Sarana and Cucinella 319). She was deeply committed to the belief that the black people must understand their black cultural identity (Sarana and Cucinella 319). In the late sixties, she helped to forward the movement for black studies at San Francisco State College (Gates and McKay 1902). She writes to, about, and for black people (Sarana and Cucinella 322). Sanchez writes in the poem "we a bad people (for gwedolyn brooks / a fo real bad one)". . . our high must come from

thinking working
planning fighting loving
our blk / selves
into nationhood (Weaks and Perry 320)

According to Sarana and Cucinella, Sanchez deals consistently and unwaveringly in her work and in her activism with being female and black in a society structured by racism, sexism, and classism (319). In the poem "homecoming," Sanchez writes:. . . .

this is for real.
black
nigger my beauty.
baby.
i have learned it
ain't like they say
in the newspapers. (Gates and McKay 1903)

According to Gates and McKay, Sanchez's most remarkable quality is "her dazzling performative style. . . She invokes the vocal intonations of Africa and African America in her performance, moving audiences to call/response" (1902). Ultimately, her works recognise the reaffirming aspects of valuing a black heritage and of claiming subjectivity as a black man or woman (Sarana and Cucinella 322). In her poem "poem at thirty," Sanchez refers to the metaphor of travelling that is can be connected with the displacement of slaves from Africa, ". . . I am here waiting/ remembering that/ once as a child/ i walked two/ miles in my sleep./ did i know/ then where i/ was going?/ travelling. I'm/ always travelling./ . . ./ i a not afraid/ of the night" (Gates and McKay 1903-04).

Because *Homecoming* and *We a Bad People* emerge out of the Black Arts Movement, they respond to the political and social unrest of the 1960s (Sarana and Cucinella 320). In the poem "A Blues Book for Blue Black Magical Women", Sanchez elucidates on what it is like to be a black woman, history, and the power that such a woman can feel very much inside herself:

there is no place
for a soft/black/woman.
there is no smile green enough or
summertime words warm enough . . .
. . . . .
i see my history
standing like a shy child
. . and my singing
becomes the only sound of a
blue/ black/ magical/ woman.
walking.womb ripe. walking. loud with mornings. walking
making pilgrimage to herself. walking. (Gates and McKay 1906)

Sanchez was intensely aware of the politics of language, which marks *Homecoming*, as the poems in this volume begin the legitimatizations of Black English by taking "Black speech and put[ting] it in the context of world literature" (qtd. in Sarana and Cucinella 320). Sanchez uses this urban black speech to underscore the homecoming to which the title refers, "The act of returning home as a rejection of fantasy and an acceptance of involvement" (qtd. in Sarana and Cucinella 320). This involvement demands a return to "things" black speech, music, rhythm and the rejection of the values of white America (Sarana and Cucinella 320). In this sense, Sanchez's poetry might serve as an example of what Henderson observes about Black Poetry, "Structurally speaking," writes Henderson, "Whenever Black poetry is most distinctly and effectively Black, it derives its form from two basic sources, Black speech and Black music" (141- 52). In fact, that is precisely one of the reasons why reviewers of Sanchez's poetry find it "complex, disturbing, challenging," often negotiating between "awakening political consciousness and. . . imagination to order or shape words and create sounds that represent the highest degree of poetic art" (qtd. in Sarana and Cucinella 322).

In her *We a Bad People* (1970), Sanchez continued experimenting with form, particularly with radical spelling, emphatic use of capitalization and slashes, and a singing or chanting voice (Weaks and Perry 318). The poems "We a Bad People" and "Blk/Rhetoric" from this collection, while attacking the racial problems of her country, also celebrate the black community (Weaks and Perry 318). Sanchez has no qualms in celebrating the fact that she is a black, and this is what is written into the poem "We a Bad People":

We a BAD people and every day
We be getting
BADDER (Weaks and Perry 321).

Hence, one can grasp how during the Dalit Panther Movement as well as the Black Arts Movement, particularly through the specimens of the poetry of Dhasal and Sanchez, the use of slang, pointed or abusive language, stylistic experimentation with written and spoken language, and the infusion of performative elements are all directed towards the eradication of the discriminative mindset of certain caste or racial groups, with a vision for a just society, a society for all. Poetry is reconnected to its oral, folk, and musical sources, because poetry as a genre has always combined music and speech, and has inscribed and performed a living tradition. Dhasal's and Sanchez's improvisational and idiosyncratic forms provide a way to 'hear' their works through their vocabulary, intonations, and visual signs, thus altering our concept of poetry itself as a written form of expression, taking us back to the days of Kalidas and Sophocles, when poetry was performed and not really read in isolation.

Aesthetic cognition is brought about by the poetic/signifyin(g) language and rhetoric, through a shared tradition of orality (speech, folklore and music), and is realised by means of enactment/ performance/reading. Art, performance, and poetry, to use Sanchez's phrase, becomes a kind of a *subconscious conversation* between the performer/poet and the audience/reader, one in which the audience/ reader and the performer/poet become a single knowing subject during the aesthetic experience, one in which a collective/community consciousness comes about because of the transformative power of performance and language. While this is the underlying assumption and explanation of the process of aesthetic experience in the context of the Indian aesthetics, precisely, this very process is the impulse behind and the desired end of the Black Arts Movement and the answer to its quest for defining a Black Aesthetic, one component of it being, as Don L. Lee proclaims, "The language of the street, charged so as to heighten the sensitivity level of the reader," and thus act as a catalyst in the generation of a heightened consciousness in the reader/audience regarding the political agenda of black cultural nationalism (qtd. in Gayle 239). It is not difficult to grasp that the same holds true of Dalit aesthetics as well, and hence the ties between the two aesthetic movements which can be read back and forth.

The different modes of expression and enactment of both Dalit and Afro-American poetry are verbal, emotional, as well as physical. This sort of employment of language does not only shape consciousness, but can, and also does change consciousness. It would not be wrong to end with what K.S. Singh writes about the Dalit and the African-Americans as the conclusion of his article, that "due to the emergence of Dalit consciousness and black consciousness, the Dalit have become dignified and the blacks have become beautiful for their respective communities" (176). Thus, poets and artists during the two movements under discussion become public voices of community consciousness, especially through the sense of urgency, experimentation, and performativity imbued in their works. Thus, in both Dalit Aesthetics and Black Aesthetics, ethics, politics, and aesthetics became one. In fact, aesthetics is politicised, and politics becomes aestheticised. This unification of aesthetics and politics can create, or facilitate the creation of a new, egalitarian world, free of caste-based and racial biases and lead towards a liberating vision of the society.

NOTES

1. Trans. Dilip Chitre 81-86.
2. Weaks and Perry 321-22.
3. However, there is no denying the fact that the nature of aesthetic experience might be different for different individuals or groups of people.
4. There has been a debate on the nature and purpose of poetry/drama/literature/art since ancient times in the greatest of cultures and literary traditions. While in the Greek culture, Plato regarded poetry as useless since it had no lessons to teach but was meant only for entertainment, his disciple Aristotle theorized on the twin purpose of art, that of offering instruction as well as delight. In the Indian aesthetic tradition, Bharatmuni wrote *Natyashastra* in the 3rd century B.C., where he outlined the primary function of poetry/drama as that of offering delight to the readers, but he did not rule out the possibility of instructions and teachings that were inherently present in art.
5. Singh uses such dated terms as "Indian Untouchables" and "Black Americans" which might sound detrogatory today. This paper will, however, refer to them as Dalits and African-Americans, since they sound the least prejudiced and free of caste or delimiting racial connotations as far as my understanding goes.

   3http://navsarjan.org/navsarjan/dalits/

   4http://wikiepedia.in 5 *[Manu VIII.270]*

REFERENCES

Baraka, Amiri, "Black Art," Gates and McKay, 1877- 1902.

Chitre, Dilip (selected, trans. and intro.) (2007), *Namdeo Dhasal: Poet of the Underworld: Poems 1972-2006*, Chennai, Navayana Publishing.

Emanuel, James A, "Blackness Can: A Quest for Aesthetics," Gayle 192-223.

Fuller, Hoyt. W, "Towards a Black Aesthetic" Gayle 3-12.

Gates, Henry Louis, Jr. and Nellie Y. McKay (eds.) (1997), "The Black Arts Movement: 1960. 1970," *The Norton Anthology of African American Literature*, New York, W. W. Norton Company.

Gayle, Addison, Jr. (1971), *The Black Aesthetic*, New York, Doubleday and Company, Inc.

Henderson, Stephen E, "From "The Forms of Things Unknown", In *Understanding the New Black Poetry: Black Speech and Black Music as Poetic References* (1973), *African American Literary Criticism, 1773 to 2000*. Ed. Hazel Arnett Ervin, New York: Twayne, 1999, 141- 52.

Hovell, Laurie (1989), "Namdeo Dhasal: Poet and Panther," *Journal of South Asian Literature*, 24.2, *Miscellany*, 65-82, Michigan State University, Asian Studies Center, http://www.jstor.org/stable/40873091, 19 Feb. 2013.

Kumar, Ajay (2006). *Dalit Panther Aandolan* [*Dalit Panther Movement*], Ed. S.S. Gautam, New Delhi, Gautam Book Centre.

Mayfield, Julian, "You Touch My Black Aesthetic and I'll Touch Yours," Gayle 24-31.

Michael, S.M. (ed.) (2007), *Dalit in Modern India: Vision and Values*, 2nd ed., New Delhi, Sage Publications.

Michael, S.M. Introduction, Michael 13-41.

Nagaraj, D.R. (2012), *The Flaming Feet and Other Essays: The Dalit Movement in India*, Ed. P.D.C. Shobhi, Delhi, Permanent Black.

Omvedt, Gail (2012), *Dalit Visions: The Anti-Caste Movement and the Construction of an Indian Identity*, rev. ed., Tracts for the Times, New Delhi, Oriental BlackSwan.

S.D. (1973), "Children of God Become Panthers", Spec. issue of *Economic and Political Weekly*, 8.31-33, Special Number, 1395+97-98, http://www.jstor.org/stable/4362913, 19 Feb. 2013.

Sarana, Sister Shiree and Catherine Cucinella (2002), "Sonia Sanchez (1934-)", *Contemporary American Women Poets: An A-Z Guide*, Ed. Cucinella, Connecticut: Greenwood Press.

Satchidanandan, K. (25 Jan. 2013), "Mainstreaming the Subaltern", *Frontline*, 77.

Singh, K.P. "Liberation Movements in Comparative Perspective: Dalit Indians and Black Americans", Michael 162-78.

Singh, S.K. "Namdeo Dhasal: A Radical Voice of Dalit Protest," http://drshaleenkumarsingh.blogspot.in/2009/02/namdeo-dhasal-radical-voice-of-Dalit.html, 25 Jan. 2013.

Weaks, Mary Louice and Carolyn Perry (1995)), "Sonia Sanchez (1934-)", Southern Women's Writing: Colonial to Contemporary, Florida, University Press of Florida.

Bio-Note: I am currently enrolled in the ph.D Programme at the Center for English Studies, Jawaharlal Nehru University. I have recently submitted my dissertation for the award of the degree of Master of Philosophy in English at the same centre. My M.Phil work is titled Popularising and Identi(ty)fying the Folk: A Study of Rajasthani Folk Songs and Popular Culture and the Resultant Formations of Identities.

3

GUJARATI DALIT WRITINGS : A LITERATURE OF MARGINALISED

M.B. Gaijan

Gujarati Dalit have sound and profound spiritual voice. But, due to untouchability, for centuries, that remained only heard in the untouchable's ghettoes, at the outskirts of villages. Still the tradition is maintained by the rural Dalit, still under the open sky at night, they sing the spiritual songs *Bhajans* with Ektara, the traditional typical musical instrument.

As literacy started and increased in the 20th century among the Gujarati Dalit, they started to write their saga sufferings and untold pain. Their secular voice becomes audible since before the independence. Dr. Ambedkar and Gandhiji both remained the great force for Dalit/ Harijan writings in Gujarat. In Gujarat Dr. Ambedkar had served in Vadodara state for a short time that had remained great force for Gujarati Dalit writers to write from Ambedkarite perspectives. Under Dr. Ambedkar's influence before the independence, Gujarati Dalit had started to cry against injustice and cruelty committed on them. Earlier it was in simple poetic form. Essays and stories were also composed in a simple language so the Dalit brothers could understand the message. But that remained marginalised.

But after Gandhiji's active efforts to emancipate untouchables from centuries old oppression and cruelty, the mainstream Gujarati writers highlighted the issue in their creativity. He renamed untouchables as *Harijan* and under *'Harijan Sevak Sangh'* he had started the mission to emancipate the unaccepted Hindu Humanity of the nation. Under Gandhiji's mega influence a novel literary trend started in Gujarat where *Harijan* was first time brought at the centre by the Non-Dalit Gujarati writers. The literature produced during 1935 to 1960 was mainly this sort of sympathizers writing which presented helpless, pitiable condition of untouchables so called "*Harijans*" the children of God.

But after independence as the literacy increased among Gujarati Dalit, the marginalised literary trend whose icon was Dr. Ambedkar became alive again. Dr. Ambedkar's philosophy, struggle, efforts were seriously studied and evaluated by the Dalit of Gujarat. As a result from the mid 70s the first generation of Gujarati Dalit has started writing, quite different from the mainstream Gujarati writings.

Gujarati Dalit writer's first prefer poem to express their emotions. The remarkable aspect of this writing is that it is created by Dalit and it is the furious cry against injustice, inhumanity and cruelty. Non-Dalit later on talk for Dalit in Dalit' tongue. At the earlier stage it was not noticed by the mainstream society.

Cruelty and killing of Dalit were/ are not new things. There is law and orders but still injustice is committed on Dalit. At many places Dalit become victims of cruelty. Poet Chandu Maheriya in his poem writes ,,How long they have to bear the chains of cruelty?

> "How long you will bear these?
> These cruel traditions of killing!
> Started from the era of Rama Rajya,
> That chain of brutality ....
> Does not stop now....
> Even at the end of the 20th century......."[1]

Secular democratic Republic Indian is yet to be born where all are equal, no discrimination on the base of caste, class, race or gender. Still India is a community of castes, one is high, another is low, it is a society of caste-based capitalism, upper caste-based capitalist class is at the top and lower-caste-based mass is at the last. In this condition powered-upper caste-based class obviously create injustice and cruelty on Dalit. It is a crude reality of Indian society. The orthodox class by using the fruits of science and technology in 21st century still they cherish centuries' old orthodoxy and hated towards Dalit. So cruelty, injustice and boycott of are going on. Gujarat is not the exception of that. Injustice and cruelty on Dalit are still going on.

Dalit should do cleaning job for the society (upper caste), this was the inhuman, spiteful religiously supported statement. Still the orthodox believe that Dalit must do their job – cleaning. But Kantilal Makwans' poem presents anger and protest;

"In one direction I am standing and in another you are
If I refuse cleaning what will happen to you?!
Countless emerged the shit globules in the gutter
which cannot be removed by spade,
Their shapes are like *Tripunda, Trishulas*
and some like lady's finger of month September,
if I ask the charge at each globule it would be painful to you,
If I refuse cleaning what will happen to you?!

Since Valmiki who sink down while cleaning the gutter
How can Moraribapu know the saga!!
Who made us from poet to gutter cleaner?
Find out those stories curved on the stone monuments,
The crowds of cockroaches climb on the body
And body shivers with the cold,
If I refuse cleaning what will happen to you?!"[2]

The poem is highly realistic. Gutter cleaning profession is mainly done by Dalit in Gujarat. There are many reasons behind accepting this cleaning work. Still a class of Dalit who does not have good education, no other work for their survival, they have to accept this filthy work. Gutter cleaning is a disgusting and dangerous work. While cleaning the gutters, many times cleaners die. When it comes in the news paper it becomes source for a Dalit poet. The poet has mentioned Moraribapu a leading Ramayana *Kathakar*. The poet writes in the poem the death of Dalit by suffocating while cleaning is not a new thing. It is started since long. For survival Dalit have to helplessly accept cleaning job but after understanding ideology they also started challenge and protest against unjust process.

Cruelty and injustice to women in general is still taking place in our society. Many times they are inhumanly treated. Their basic human rights are violated. They become victims of harassment, rapes and death. Dalit women suffer a lot, inhumanly, unbelievably. When she suffers nobody comes to help her except in some cases. Pravin Gadhavi's poem presents the pathetic truth in his poem "*Barter*";

"She was denuded and was paraded
In the public place of the village

Under the scorching mid day sun.
Neither she was a married woman nor a divorcee,
Neither she was a damsel nor a woman at her forty,
She was not a sex worker nor she was a woman
Her name was not in the electoral list.
She was not from any village,
She had no religion.
Nor she had tongue,
She had neither dignity nor honour,
Her sin was that by birth untouchable she was."[3]

The poet tries to picture the crude reality and helpless suffering of Dalit woman. These sorts of cruelty on Dalit women are reported many times. It is a fact of Indian society women suffer at two levels sometimes at home and many times at away from the home.

At the end of the poem, the poet is writing she suffers because of two factors, first she is a woman and second is she is a Dalit woman, so the poet writes take back the Constitutional Rights, "Reservation" and give her human dignity, honour back to the Dalit woman.

Dalit woman is nothing but the untold saga of suffering, her one tragedy ends another begins. In this sort of life struggle they also try to cope with changing world of 21st century. They also express their feelings, thoughts through their creativity. Gujarati Dalit women writers' creation is note worthy. Daxa Damodara's poem *Anaconda* is highly realistic and novelty in literary world;

"In the dark and deep jungle of anarchy,
Behind the dark and dirty mask of caste-ism,
On the branches of big and small trees,
With forked tongue,
Smells the blood of helpless being,
Enormous and unable to move,
Terrible and terrifying,
With a little chance rushes to attack,
Gallops...
Moving twisting....
Moving twisting....

......................Helpless.
Centuries after centuries have gone
Why, still neither its hunger is satisfied nor it dies
The Anaconda of untouchability?"[4]

The poem is a reality of our time. Caste plays very significant role in Indian society, at every stage of life, public and private, Gujarat is not an exception of that. Secular India is yet to be created. The poem suggests due to caste-ism untouchability becomes like a big boa-constrictor. Untouchablity takes different shapes in Indian society but totally it does not disappear.

Story is the second choice of Gujarati Dalit writers. Many Guajarati writers have written stories. A few of them are highly realistic and appealing. The stories written by Gujarati Dalit represent reality of rural as well as urban Gujarat. At both the places Dalit suffer differently because of being a Dalit.

Hasmukh Vaghela's story *Zol* (The Flame)[5] represents reality of rural Gujarat. In rural Gujarat still Dalit ghettoes are at the outskirt of the villages. Still the upper castes egoist orthodoxy is prevailing in the society. Dalit have to face the fact. Injustice and cruelty is taking place. The story opens with all members of the Dalit colony are extremely frightened because they are threatened by the *Darabara*, the upper castes to set fire on their houses. Kalubha, the son of *Sarapanch*, upper caste, he comes in the centre of Dalit colony and shouts demands Daliya, Daliya is a Dalit youth; "Son of pigs, if you love to live and love your wives-children, present Daliya here, otherwise whole colony will set on fire and will die alive." (Zol:311) Understanding the terror of the event, the old Fuladosa begs to pardon Daliya for no reason. The old man told; "Bapa, Daliya is a child, pardon him....if you say, on behalf of him I take shoe in my mouth and beg you to forgive, *Bapa* please don't do anything wrong". (*Zol* :311-12) But Kalubha rudely abuses all.

The story presents picture of *Holi* festival of a village. At the evening on the *Holi* festival, at the outskirt of the village with the help of wood and cow/buffalo-dung cakes *Holi* was arranged. It was believed to set fire to *Holi* was/is the degraded work according to the mythical story of Prahalada and Holika. So in rural areas *Harijans* had/ have to set fire to *Holi*. For that job they were/are given a little reward. In this story the *Sarapanch* orders Daliya to set fire to *Holi*, simultaneously he also orders to keep distance. Thus untouchability is practiced. Daliya obeys the order. Sets fire to the *Holi*.

The story further presents, on that evening *Darabars*, the upper castes come with iron-covered *lathis* and they form first circle around the *Holi*, then other castes and *Harijans* are at far away from the *Holi*. Coconuts are offered to the burning flames of *Holi* and who gets coconut from the flames of the *Holi* are known as the hero of the village. Kalubha, young man of the *Darabara* community is strong and sturdy, six feet in height. As a son of *Sarapanch* nobody dares to challenge him. He has also a strong body so he could get coconuts from the flames. So he is considered as a village-hero, a leader of his community.

In this story Daliya is a thin, weak Dalit youth. On that evening of *Holi* festival who gets coconuts is declared the hero of the village. Dalit cannot enter in this competition for village-hero. But here Daliya unexpectedly jumps and gets a baked coconut then runs away. That has raised fury among the *Darabara* community. They connect coconut catching issue with their honour. And to protect their honour they decided to destroy Dalit crops, set fire to Dalit' colony. It is the reason so Kalubha lost his temper and comes in the colony. He finds Kanku there. Kanku is Daliya's wife. She begs for Daliya's life. But blind by lust and fury Kalubha has denuded her, raped her. She cries for help but none helped her. She is left alone to cry. Her house was set on fire. At late night Daliya returns to his colony. His house is burning and wife is crying. He could judge what has happened. Painfully helplessly he tells to Kanku; "Get up Kanku, we do not want to live on this land of cowards, stand up, let us go to the land where even coward air may not touch to our coming children". Telling this, holding hands of his wife the couple jumps in the fire of his house. To save their lives Dalit run away leaving their ghetto. The story is pathetic but based on reality.

Pathik Paramar's *Tejo Vadha*[6] is a very appealing story. The story presents crude, unbelievable reality. It is story of Tejo, a revolutionary Dalit youth who is appointed in as a teacher in very remote village of Gujarat. He is also a columnist. He has written two three columns on the contemporary education condition and a few stories on political corruption. As a result of that he is posted in remote village. While on other hand the political-flatters were appointed in schools nearby the city. In the village he is an unwanted teacher. Because of untouchability, discrimination is taking place. He thinks;

> "Is it a village or cattle comp? Why a son of Harijan cannot teach the children of village? Only the upper caste can teach? Am I not a qualified teacher? If I teach them, will they be polluted? Why my drinking water pot is kept separated?"(*Tejo Vadha*: 15)

All these questions disturb him a lot. He feels continuously insulted. Villagers do not accept him as a teacher. He thinks;

> "I want to tell something but I can't. I cannot write. After throwing me in deep ditch of mud you become happy, aren't you? But I am like lotus flower in mud. My pan can't be controlled by any."(*TejoVadha*: 15)

The story presents predicament of Tejo. He thinks thus when he is walking at evening without anybody's company. In urban area it is tough for a Dalit to get a "good" house on rental base. In rural areas it is impossible. So Tejo gets a house in Dalit colony. At that particular evening, he gets very unpleasant experiences. There is ban on wine in Gujarat but reality is different. Takhubha, the upper caste, insults him and show a bag of wine. He walks on the rocky path where villagers rarely go.

When he reaches at the pit nearby the village where Dalit women are used to empty their bowls he sees Champa, his house owner's daughter. She is entrapped by Mangalsinh. Looking at Tejo Mangalsinh becomes furious and rushes with knife at Tejo. He threatens him to kill.

Next day in the morning when he gets up late, he knew that a few Dalit women have secretly gone to fetch water from the well of upper castes. The upper castes *Darabars* knew the matter and they attacked on Dalit colony with weapons. As a result, "Three Harijans were killed on the spot, many injured. Deadly silence controlled the village."(*TejoVadha*:17) The story presents there is no enough water facility for Dalit so the Dalit women secretly fetch water from the upper caste well. But the upper castes, as usual believe the well is polluted. Thus cruelty committed on Dalit. Tejo thinks about the crude reality of the rural areas;

> "Theft, loots, killing, threatening, wine, quarrels, rapes, corruptions, caste-ism, sectarianism, classism, nepotism!....injustice and cruelty on Dalit women. Village is nothing but the place of sufferings. City is better than this." (*TejoVadha*:17)

He also thinks that it is the hell. He decides to leave the village but under the wrong FIR filed by the upper caste he is arrested by the police. The story presents crude reality. Still in rural areas untouchability based cruelty taking place.

To portray the saga of suffering, the Dalit writers prefer novel form. A few Gujarati Dalit writers have given highly appealing, realistic novels. Joseph Macwan's *Stepchild* is one of them. It is translated into English. But still there are more Dalit novels written in English. Harish Mangalam's *Aganzal*[7] (The Flames of Fire) is an autobiographical novel. It is a story of protagonist, Veeru. His family members, Dalit' condition in villages everything is minutely and realistically presented. The novel presents practice of untouchability in rural areas. The novel presents the picture post independent era but still untouchability is existing in many forms. When Veeru was in standard 7th at that time, about the school novelist writes,

> "So called upper castes teachers were not teaching to Dalit' children. The ghost of untouchability was dancing everywhere. ....Farmers were thinking; 'after getting education if Dalit will get job then who will do labour in our farms".........Dalit' condition was worse than animals.....upper castes were calling them by names. They were standing even away from the shadows of Dalit. Because of the fear of being polluted the upper caste teachers were throwing sticks at them." (*Aganzal* :16)

In this sort of adverse condition Veeru struggles. Right from the childhood he prefers rational and revolutionary path. He establishes a library and finds only learning is the best means for Dalit' emancipation. The novel presents the journey, how a rural Dalit youth emerges from nothing to something.

Daxa Damodara is a mature young Dalit woman writer. Her novel *Savitri*[7] is an excellent work of art. The novel presents life story of Jotiba Phuley and Savitribai Phuley. The writer has re-interpreted Indian history and re-created the struggle of Savitribai and Jotiba. First girls' school for untouchable was started by this couple. They had established "*The Satya Shodhak Samaj*", *Bala Hatya Pratibandhaka Gruha* (A home for the pregnant mothers, they were allowed give birth of babies, if they wished they could get their babies or left in the home) and library. It is story of Savitribai. She struggles right from her childhood. As a faithful and committed companion she always remains with Jotiba in his life mission. After his death she tries to fulfill his uncompleted dream. While serving the plague victims, especially Dalit, she becomes victim of bubonic plague and dies. The novel has sound bases so it can be evaluated from different angles.

Recently published novel *Vajra Prahar*[8] by Kantilal Parmar presents reality rural life. Practice of untouchability and cruelty on Dalit are presented in the novel. Because of cruelty Dalit migration is also highlighted in this novel.

After evaluating Gujarati Dalit writings, a few remarkable aspects clearly emerge before the readers;

- There is anger, protest, and struggle for identity – in their creativity they justify why there is anger, protest, and struggle.
- Cultural assertion.
- Demand for justice, equality and human acceptance.
- Contribute in nation building-environment, education, corruption, social service, etc.
- Contemporary cruel realities, injustice, boycott, killing of Dalit are highlighted in their works.
- Dalit have their own media to present their voice. Still unaccepted by the mainstream. Thus it is the voice of marginalised even in the early 21st century.

REFERENCES

1. Maheriya Chandu, *Asmita*: Khet Vikas Parishad, Khet Bhavan, Ahmedabad, 1984. p. 51.
2. Makwana Kantilal, *Nai Upadu Mathe Melu* (*I'll not Carry Dirt on My Head*), Hayati, ISSN 2231-0282, Gujarat Dalit Sahitya Akademi, Dec. 2012, p. 5.
3. Gadhavi Pravin, *Barter*, in *Dalit Vani*, ed. by Harish Mangalam, Gujarat Dalit Sahitya Akademi, Ahmedabad, 2006, p. 23.
4. Damodara Daxa, *Anaconda*, in *Bharatiya Dalit Naree Lekhan* ed. by Faruk Shah, Hayati, ISSN 2231-0282, Gujarat Dalit Sahitya Akademi, March. 2012, p. 43.
5. Vaghela Hasmukh, *Zol* (The Flame), in *Varta Lok*, ed. by Harish Mangalam, Pathik Parmar, Madhukant Kalpit, Arvind Vegada, Gujarat Dalit Sahitya Akademi, Ahmedabad, 2008, pp. 311-318.
6. Mangalam Harish, *Aganzal* (The Flames of Fire), Gujarat Dalit Sahitya Akademi, Ahmedabad, 2007, p.16.
7. Damodara Daxa, *Savitri*, Gujarat Dalit Sahitya Akademi, Ahmedabad, 2008.
8. Parmar Kantilal, Vajra Prahar, Gujarat Dalit Sahitya Akademi, Ahmedabad, 2012.

4

WOMEN, RACE AND NATION (REPRESENTATION OF MARGINALISED DALIT WOMEN IN PRESENT, PAST AND FUTURE INDIA)

Pooja Chaudhary
Isha Anand

Abstract

With the barging of the concept of 'marginality', Dalit in India and Blacks in America and slaves in Africa are most prominently and frequently discussed in English Literature. It is no more an astonishing fact that Dalit in India and Blacks in America have been the most exploited, subjugated and oppressed classes among the marginalised population. Marginality means exploitation done morally, sexually, socially and economically. Dalit literature is based on Dalit consciousness and it represents the harsh lived experiences of marginalised Dalit women. More so, women of these classes suffer thrice removedeness; isolation oppressed by the so-called high caste people (which equally affects both male and female Dalit), oppressed by the design of the Hindu patriarchal system and oppressed by Dalit males. The literatures across the globe are full of the images who have undergone pangs of sufferings due to their caste/race and gender. This paper examines and explores the past, present and future of Dalit women. By juxtaposing these phases, the paper seeks to highlight the prevalence of certain maladies and strengthened the future of Dalit women in India, despite all sorts of sufferings.

Key Words

Barging, Marginality, Subjugated, Opressed, Consciousness, Patriarchal, Juxtaposing

Introduction

The word Dalit—literally referring to "oppressed" or "broken"—is generally used to introduce a section of people who were once known as "untouchables", those belonging to castes outside the fourfold Hindu Varna system. Dalit is a designation for a group of people traditionally regarded as 'untouchables'. Dalit are a mixed population, consisting of numerous social groups from all over South Asia. They speak a variety of languages and practice a multitude of religions. There are many different names proposed for defining this group of people, including Panchamas (fifth varna), and Asprushya (untouchables). Dalit and similar marginalised people are found in India, Nepal and Bangladesh. In countries, like Africa and America, these are designated as[1] slaves or blacks, Burakumin in Japan, Cagots and Roma in Europe, Al – Akhdam in Yeman[2].

In India, caste system assigns individuals a certain hierarchical status according to Hindu beliefs. Traditionally, there are four principal castes (divided into many sub-categories) and one category of people who fall outside the caste system—'The Dalit'.

The caste system finds its origin in functional groupings, called *varnas*, which have their origins in the Aryan society of ancient Northern India. In their creative myth, four varnas are said to have emanated from the Primeval Being. The Creator's mouth became the Brahman priests, his two arms formed the Rajanya warriors and kings, his two thighs formed, the Vaishya landowners and merchants, and from his feets were born the Shudra, artisans and servants. Later, there developed a so-called "fifth" varna, the Untouchables.

This caste system became fixed and hereditary with the emergence of Hinduism and its beliefs of 'pollution 'and 'rebirth'. The Laws of Manu (*Manusmitri*), which date roughly to the 3rd century A.D. preached the sanctity of the varnas and uphold the principles of gradation and rank. They refer to the impurity and servility of the outcastes, while affirming the dominance and total impunity of Brahmins. Those from the "lowest" castes are told that their place in the caste hierarchy is due to their sins in a past life. Vivid punishments of torture and death are assigned for crimes such as gaining literacy or insulting a member of a dominant caste. Among the writings of Hindu religious texts, like 'the *Manusmitri*' is undoubtedly the most authoritative one, legitimising social exclusion and introducing absolute inequality as the guiding principle of social relations.

> *"A once-born man (Sudra) who insults a twice-born man (Aryan) with gross invective, shall have his tongue cut out; for he is of low origin."*[3] — *[Manu VIII.270]*

This very phrased by Manu clearly speaks aloud about the heights of discrimination and degraded point of view about Dalit. The condition of Dalit woman was worsened as compared to Dalit male.

Our traditional caste monopoly is tough and hierarchical. This assumption is based on piousness and [garbage], pollution announced by birth and large high castes Hindus. In olden times, since Ramanayana, Dalit used to live in utter isolation. The word Dalit comes from Marathi language and means ground, suppressed, crushed, broken into pieces. Dalit in India, are marginalised and blacks in Americans always found a chunk of population called "marginalised population". Several book shelves of the world depicts the same pathetic plight of Dalit. This Dalit Literature written by various thinkers,scholars and Litterateurs speaks aloud about the acts of discrimination and exploitation made against these people. Among Dalit, the sad condition of Dalit Women is highly pitiable and thus requires great attention of the society. The plea of Dalit women is of utmost significance in the contemporary Indian situation, particularly in the context of new social ambience silenced today by narrowing their democratic space.[5]

The Marginalised and under-privileged rediscover their articulation and self identity through autobiographies. Dalit Women are subjected to extreme forms of social, physical and mental trauma and backwardness according to the official figures. Dalit Women are raped every day. Bagul's Murali, *Devdasi's*, portrays that abuse and endurance of Marginalised Women, is about prostitutes and women who fall prey to sexual exploitation.

Past Dalit women were indulged in inner conflicts rather than outer conflicts, that is to identify herself in this Patriarchal society *Devdasi's* by B.B. Borkar or *'Seva Sadan*, House of Service of Munshi, they occasionally compromised with the situations. They strived for food, clothing and shelter. Thus, turned to Devdasis, became victims by male cruel hands and they brought their cruel malignant fate. They have no grievances against life, no reactions, no efforts to come out of such kind of life, hunger, poverty, servility, and submission to the circumstances. The ultimate end of life of the Dalit, was toiling, laboring women in this slum. They all represents a middle class life.

Baburao Bagul's, Janaki comes into the world, as the child of a beautiful Dalit, Murali (Devdasi). She becomes a victim of her mother's helplessness, misery and the perverted social order, disgusted with bodily function, bodily enjoyments. Sometimes feels that her women body should be replaced by a male body. She nurtures in her mind feelings of revenge. The reason behind that is, she had been taken as 'a tool of pleasure' and shaped accordingly.

Dalit Women were victims of caste-based atrocities, they were raped when working in the factories and fields. They were casually stripped and molested and even invited death, if they dared to quench their thirst from a common well. Their life was quite similar to their upper caste counterparts but the fact is that, Dalit Women have been victims of Patriarchal society for ages and still have very little right over Human Rights. By the term 'Dalit Women', we are creating imagined category. This imaging is necessary, because we hope that Dalit Women is the new future, will give new critical dimension to Indian feminist movement as well as to Dalit Movement. Dalit Women suffered three faced oppression at the cruel hands of gender, caste and class. There were many pressing issues being faced by Dalit Women in pre-independence period and some of them are seen in continuous even today, this is due to their marital old binding with males at home as their life partners. This paper depicts nothing but about the whole little world of Indian Dalit Women representing her helplessness, exploitation, mental, physical, economical and social torture. Women were not allowed to worship temples before Independence, fetching water from common wells etc. By turning back the pages of History, the picture of Dalit Women is seen as an individual who is dependent on the male counterpart for everything, whose birth on this earth was to bear burden of her lower caste and lower social status, meant to be exploited and assaulted by people of urban society, whether she is an Indian, American, or Australian.

Their attempt to assert their rights are often met with strong resistance from the higher castes, resulting inhuman torture, filth, rapes, massacres and other atrocities. The images of savage reality that emerge through Dalit stories, the level of violence against Dalit Women is quite similar to the ordeal of Black Women in the United States.

> This is hell
> This is a Swirling Vortex
> This is an ugly agony
> This is pain wearing dancer's anklets.
> [Namdeo Dhasal:Kamatipura]

A significant proportion of Indian Dalit Women faced verbal abuse, sexual harassment, domestic torture and rape of inner as well as her outer self. The piece of misery continued with Dalit Women working as forced and bonded labourers. Young Dalit girls suffered systematic sexual abuse in Temples, worked as prostitutes for men from dominated upper castes. All these severe atrocities were faced by Dalit Women in India before the arrival of the Britishers.

[4]But only a minor improvement was seen with the coming of the Britishers, who named them as Women as Scheduled of Castes and Tribes. Even Britishers failed to change the mind set of Orthodox Hindus who considered them as Untouchables, thus isolated them from their society. It was conscious endeavour of Bhim Rao Ambedkar. When these Marginalised women stepped out of their homes as took part in freedom struggle, the real self came out all of a sudden as a "TIGRESS'. But the condition did not improve even after Independence. Women born in Dalit castes have to produce their own critical interpretation of the issued patronized by other feminist in India like security control over body, sexual and fertility. Various writers like Meena Kandasamy who herself is a Dalit in her autobiography, has very well delineated of the 'Women Untouchable'. Women being the weaker gender though physically, are maltreated even by those, who themselves demand dignity and respect from others. Ruth Manorama, a social activist and the Head of a newly constituted 'Federation for DALIT Women' has rightly[5] called Women Dalit among Dalit.

Present Dalit is extremely forceful, conscious of her status as a female in a Patriarchal Society. She is no more a creature of sympathy. She comes rather as harbinger of struggle. Women in[6] Annabhau's novels, forsake tradition and emerge with strength to fight against adverse incidents. Whether she is Radha of *'Fakira'* or *'Vaijayanta'* who loves art more than life or Durga of *'Makadicha Mal'* [Monkey Hill], the familiar social and mental conflict of all these women has been responsible for the birth of revolt. Some sell honour because of helplessness and poverty. Thus they try to escape from this poverty.

They write autobiography, read the "almanac" of their actions to themselves and questions. All these women contemplate on the god. Whether it is Girija in "*Hathaa bhatt*" [Home Brewery] or Sona in "*Chitra*", they discard their ugliness and struggle to lead a happy life. Now a days, these ladies are enjoying an equal status to man in a society. *Aghori* [Monstress], Janaki of *'Sood'* [Revenge] Nandini of *'Aghori'* [Monstress], will be one step ahead of man.

Sometimes seems that her women should be replaced by a male body, she nurtures in her mind feelings or revenge. The reason behind that is she had been taken as a tool of pleasure and shaped accordingly. Dalit Woman is rebellious, change – oriented and thoughtful she is the one who herself sets her own goal, discovers her own path.

Dalit woman are urban, employed, educated. Dalit woman caught in the vortex of old-new ideas, the handful of women participating in meetings, conferences processions, demonstrations, etc., so, in this context, the attitude of society towards them have changed a lot. Her social, familial conflict, problems of educated Dalit women, the agony of *'Devdasis,' 'andhashraddha'* (BLIND FAITH), the revival of old customs and morals, ignorance, Tribal woman, *Banjara* women, rural women and in urban area toiling in sundry work, female village level workers, teachers and nurses, the life of all these has become insecure and problem – ridden. There was a dire need of to give justice to these exploited, grieved souls. In the present study the attitude of men in viewing them has not changed even today, e.g., raped, killed by husbands, exploited every now and then. As a man considers woman as enticing, in the same way woman looks at her as a character of hate-jealously, and sympathy. There are women who live under the illusion that an earning woman is an independent woman and lives like a queen of her home.

The Sea of Change

Direct political participation of Dalit women in local governance (Panchayati Raj) is a central human right in itself and enables the realisation of a host of other human rights. Political voice and decision-making power concerning basic services, economic development and social justice are critical factors in challenging and transforming structural caste-class-gender discrimination, and enabling Dalit women to realise their fundamental rights. Political participation also demands accountability from state and non-state actors to guarantee and respect these women's equal political voice and development. This requires a transformation of power relationships[7] both within institutions of governance and in the women's social environment. Through there are some autobiographical writings, and some literary texts, Dalit women's writings has not become a force as yet. Malika Dhasal s autobiography *Mala Uddhvasta*[8].

Mayawati,the Chief Minister of Uttar Pradesh, India's most populous state. After three short tenures between 1995 and 2003, she served four term in her office. Her supporters referred to her as Behen Ji, which means a sister. At age of 39, she became the youngest politician to be elected as the Chief Minister of UTTAR PRADESH, a person of dignity and political inspiration for millions of India's Dalit, who were oppressed by the Hindu upper castes for centuries. There are allegations that she has used her status to amass alarge amount of personal wealth.

According to an article in The Indian Subcontinent Times, Uttar Pradesh Chief Minister and Dalit leader Kumari Mayawati has found a place among the Forbes 100 Most Powerful Women (born 15 January 1956), is an Indian politician. She is the current in the political world giving jitters to Indian National Congress President Sonia Gandhi. According to the Forbes list released on 28th Aug. 2008, Mayawati is ranked 59th just behind Queen Elizabeth of UK.

In the present, aspires to be Prime Minister, from her perch as chief minister of Uttar Pradesh, India's most populous state. In 1995, at 39, she was the youngest politician elected to the post and was also the first Dalit (India's lowest, untouchable caste) to head a state government. Commands a large following and goes simply by Mayawati.

Future of Dalit Women

As over viewing, the past and present, the picture of future becomes quite clear. It is seen,that the Dalit Women is no more a statue of tears but can wipe-off others tears, for she is independent now, also in future, Indian Dalit Women would be more powerful to earn equal status in male-Patriarchal society. In the frame of development (Education, Health, Economy etc.) she proved as equal in the eyes of constitution. She is no more a victim at home and outside home. Various steps have been taken by our Indian Government for the upliftment of Dalit Women,they are reaching to higher levels for example in politics, Mayawati worked as a Minister, as a Dalit writer, Urmila Pawar, wrote on her mother's pangs of sufferings in her famous book, The Weave of My Life, so future Dalit would be more aware for their equal rights and partnerships at every level. *Gulabi gang*, which is a group of Indian Women vigilantes and activists originally from Bundelkl.and, U.P. are active members across North India. So these Dalit have reached up to Television screens for example, Sampat Pal Devi, at Big Boss, who is without any personal interest has been fighting for better future of Dalit Women since 2006. Various reservation policies are being included like Reservation bills etc. Also future Dalit Women are taking 50,000 cash amount for their daughter's marriage, and for *Pakka* Houses Project, these Dalit Women are attaining other cash amounts, for water facilities. They are enjoying equal rights among Dalit males too. Other Dalit Women aim at achieving is 33 per cent of the 543 LOK SABHA SEATS, including 40 per cent of scheduled caste or scheduled tribes of Adivasis. Since 82 seats are reserved for Dalit and *Adivasis*, it will leave only 280 seats in the unreserved category, although, women may contest these as well.

The future Dalit Women would be more solid in thought and action as compared to past and present, not only in India but in other countries too. They are also working in Panchayats and Zilla Parishads. Dalit Women's participation in MNREGA activities as a worker, in Panchayats for planning work and as supervisor of work-mate has greatly increased. In 2009, in work it was in strength, 2.811 in all eight districts of the DWLAI Programme. Dalit Women are now 'unionised' and have a collective voice to get their demands met.

This is very true about them:

"They have two eyes like us,

Two hands like us and

Same red colored blood in veins like us."

So we all are same like brethrens and sisters.

NOTES

1. http://navsarjan.org/navsarjan/dalits/
2. http://wikiepedia.in
3. Dalit Women in India: Issues and Perspective (By Prahlad Gangaram Jogdand).
4. http;/english/org./india.1503/02/13./india.htm.Dabra
5. https;//en.wikipedia.org/wiki/Annabhau_sathe
6. http://adniel.tripod.com/org.in.htm
7. http://hrw.org /english/ docs/2007/02/13india1503.htm..Dabra
8. htpp//www.pintersociety.com

REFERENCES

http://Wikipedia.in

manu viii-270.

http:/adniel.tripod.com/org.in.htm

Dalit Women in India :issues and perspectives.

Luital Samira: Occasional papers; The Position of Dalit http://navsarjan.org/navsarjan/Dalit Women.

http://www.pintersociety.com

http://hrw.org/english/2007/02/13.india1503htm.Dabra

5

READING RESISTANCE IN DALIT WOMEN'S AUTOBIOGRAPHIES

Putul Sathe

The arrival of Dalit literary criticism and Dalit literature located within the Ambedkarite movement was accompanied by a new founded Dalit political identity and social consciousness. In this context G.N. Devy has identified Dalit writings as one of the forces, which have challenged the bourgeois nationalist perspective in Indian literary historiography. Within Dalit literature, autobiography is a literary and cultural expression of internal caste based discrimination. As cultural and literary expression Dalit autobiographies have created a praxis, which has challenged existing literary structures through their articulation of cultural and caste based discrimination.

The literary historiography of Dalit literature [is derived] from this principle of racial inequality of Indian society. It focuses on the question of otherness, difference, marginality, canon and the categories of aesthetics. In order to voice the protest of the marginalised, Dalit literature often follows the subversive historiography path of personalising history. It is therefore, . . ., that autobiography is the most potent and often exercised form of fiction produced in Dalit literature. (Devy 2009 : 129)

Dalit autobiographies governed by "subversive historiography path of personalising history" becomes a political gesture in the context of Indian literary historiography to focus upon a sort of "epistemic mutations" (Mohanty 1998:120) not only in "cultural criticism but in social and historiography as well" (120). The agenda of personalising history point to the central political claim of the autobiographical narratives that certain subaltern sensitivities have been repressed or left unarticulated. As cultural narratives, the autobiographies emerge as site of articulation of resistance creating the possibility for representation of the self and the community. The present paper will focus on Urmila Pawar's *The Weave of My Life* (2008) and Baby Kamble's *The Prisons We Broke* (2008) as narratives of resistance, which project voices of previously silenced subaltern women to create emancipator spaces. As narratives of resistance they are small voices located on the margin of social and cultural imagination traversing the realm of Dalit literature and women's autobiographical writings.

Sharankumar Limbale in his book Towards an Aesthetics of Dalit Literature: History, Controversies and Considerations (2004) had drawn to the rise of alternative literary paradigms by Dalit writers through their resistance to caste based discrimination in their writings. Hence Dalit literary and cultural representations have moved beyond the 'discourse of pity', which was the case in the works of upper caste writers. The articulation of resistance was wedded to identity politics and Arjun Dangle has advocated the 'differentness' to understand this different literary–ideological-cultural paradigm.

Within the field of autobiographical writing, women's autobiographies emerge as site of difference, since they provided an alternative to 'maleness' of autobiographies written by men and simultaneously within the category 'woman'. As a polyphonic sign in a double voiced discourse, autobiographies by women are performances which have negotiated with a seamless, decentred self. Autobiographical writings have been "one of the most important sites of feminist debate precisely because it demonstrates that there are many different ways of writing the subject" (Anderson 2007 : 87). In the context of women's writing in India, women could write about only a few things in the absence of a sustained, high level of formal education. Beginning in the 19th century, it was high caste Hindu women, who started writing autobiographies which were located in the new emerging material and social condition resulting from reforms and legislative innovation in public sphere. Hence the autobiographies revolved around sati, widow remarriage, child marriage, divorce and the age of consent (Sarkar 1999). Women's autobiographies then became site, where tension were articulated resulting from colonial modernity. The dominant ideology of nineteenth century cultural nationalism celebrated India's spirituality superiority over material West and remained silent about caste/gender based humiliation and was not concerned about racial humiliation. The autobiographies of upper caste women have to be located within this framework. The question of caste was invisible in their writings. Sharmile Rege in her study of autobiographies in Marathi written by upper caste women has drawn attention to this erasure.

The majority of modern Brahmin women's autobiographies have been narratives of upper caste women, their struggles with tradition and their desire to be modern. It is this self that claims to be universal, modern unmarked by caste through its journeys of companionate marriage, modern institutions and marital discord. Caste is the 'other' of the modern as if it belongs only to Dalit women. This claim of the upper caste women's autobiography to represent modern Marathi/Indian women serves, on the other hand, to render invisible their complicity in privileges of brahminical patriarchy, and on the other, it classifies the narratives of women whose self-definition is located explicitly in caste as a relational identity, as if it were the 'other' of modern and feminist. (Rege 2006 : 50).

Within this paradigm Dalit women's autobiographies through their articulation of caste based inequalities traced the "hidden histories of hurt and humiliation"(Rao 2003 : 3) and as gendered texts was an initiative to engage with Dalit and social patriarchy. Writing of resistance brought to forefront gendered subaltern alternative historical voices of politicized activist Dalit women and underscored the epistemological disadvantages of unmarked feminism (S Anand 2009). Dalit women's autobiographies through their struggles and literary representations have questioned the genealogy of Indian feminism where the position of caste has not been articulated and drew attention to the complex relationship between feminism and caste's complex history. Anupama Rao as probed the specificity of this position.

Dalit feminism poses anew the position of how we might understand caste's complex history as a form of identification and as a structure of disenfranchisement and exploitation, how we revisit the forgotten and repressed histories that illuminate the criticism of feminism by its most vulnerable and exploited constituency. (Rao 3).

Baby Kamble's text can be located within the existing oeuvre of protest writing in Marathi. According to Maya Pandit the translator of Baby Kamble's autobiography, this autobiography is probably the first autobiography by a Dalit women in Marathi. Most of the Dalit autobiographies written by men were for a mixed readership of Dalit and non-Dalit readers. This narrative on the other hand is not only a text representative of the Dalit community but is an engagement with the "history of Dalit oppression" (Kamble 2008:IX) and is "located in the tradition of direct self-assertion" (IX). The text confronts Brahminical hegemony and patriarchal structures within Dalit society. Located on the margins of 'social imaginary', the representation of marginality writes resistance and the text is cultural site with "tremendous transformative potential for oppressed people"(XI). This performance is not an individual act but is collective in nature.

I wrote about what my community experienced. The suffering of my people became my own suffering. Their experiences became mine. So I really find it very difficult to think of myself outside of my community (136).

Articulation of collective experience is a political act of resistance and in the process the autobiography becomes a socio-biography and creates a subject position, which is at once individual and collective. The auto biographer is "simultaneously the author of an individuated act of truth-telling and the subject of a shared historical memory" (Udayakumar 2008: 421). The articulation of subjectivity violates the concept violated the concept of singular individual self and the narrative voice that "narrates the humiliation has questioned the hegemonic power of the dominant Brahminic authority"(Ramakrishnan 2011: 69). Articulation of humiliation becomes a mode of understanding the social system of 'graded inequality' embedded in the caste system from the point of view of a gendered untouchable identity. The experience of untouchability was both a "layered experience and . . . an evil that is stunning in its banality"(Geeta 2009: 92). Addressing the hegemonic nature of caste structure the text registrars resistance and the narrative point to "moral corruption of the society which legitimises caste oppression". (Ramakrishnan 67).

Such was the condition of our people. We were just like animals, but without tails. We could be called human because we had two legs instead of four. Otherwise there was no difference between us and the animals. But how had we been reduced to this bestial state? Who was responsible? Who else, but people of the high caste! They destroyed our reasoning, our ability. (Kamble 49).

Articulation of resistance is articulation of marginality and is located within the 'discourse of participation', which is "framed in terms of sympathetic immediacy, per formative speech acts and ritual action"(Pandhian 2008:40). In keeping with this choice, the autobiography is not about centralising a single person and the text is distanced from the "formal and establish the ordinary as [the] chosen domain"(35). The text describes the childhood of Baby Kamble as part of community life, the struggles of Dalit society, celebration of festivals, rituals performed at Dalit weddings, the impact of Ambedkarite movement, the plight of Dalit women and the world of Dalit labouring body. The act of narrativising the "ordinary" raise moral issues that cannot be addressed in purely artistic or socio-political terms (Ramakrishnan 2011) and the text creates a cultural space that brings out how "experience, affect and politics are inseparable" (Pandhian 40).

The recounting of humiliation along the multiple axis of gender, class and caste is not a victim narrative, rather is a mode of resistance to the hegemony of caste system. Caste structure used structural violence to maintain caste hierarchy and this was "integral to the molecular structure of caste" (Rao 2011:114). The labouring body of the *Mahar* women was the marker of caste and women's subordination was the gateway to caste system. Humiliation as Gopal Guru has pointed out is an individual, collective, social and political phenomenon. Dalit women's experience of caste based humiliation results in the visibility of caste, which scripts a polemical attack on gender and caste structures of brahminical patriarchy. Within this paradigm the Dalit women is also located within Dalit patriarchy and experiences the worst form of exploitation when Dalit men do not hesitate in chopping off the nose of those Dalit women who fail to conform to Dalit patriarchal norms (Kamble 98). The body of the violated Dalit women provide a critique of Dalit patriarchy and destroys the myth of Dalit patriarchy as democratic. Dalit women negotiate not with multiple patriarchies, but with what Uma Chakravarti has termed as 'graded patriarchies' operating within the grid of brahminical patriarchy.

Moving beyond literary paradigms, as part of protest literature the text has to be located and read within the larger counter discourse of Amdekarite movement, which questioned the liberal, unified humanist vision of a nation controlled by elites, who tried to "control and regulate the unchartered spaces of living communities" (Ramakrishnan 71). As a site of this articulation the text spells out the tenants of Ambedkarite project, which was not an abstract one but brought to the centre stage of Indian political modernity the stigmatized Dalit community as a political community. The autobiography maps the journey of Dalit, who were "history's losers" (Rao 2011:208) to create a "crucial space of alterity"(208) not through "ameliorative logic of a reformed Hinduism"(209) but by existing from brahminical fold through conversion to Buddhism.

Urmila Pawar's autobiography titled 'The Weave of My Life' (2008) has been categorized as a "A Dalit Woman's Memoirs" and the metaphor of woven things runs throughout the narrative. Woven together the text is made up of several texts and inscribes a complex notion of the margin. The trajectory of Urmila Pawar is very different in terms of modern education, salaried employment and involvement in women's movement which takes her away from the world of physical labour and struggle for livelihood. Dalit autobiography as a literary and cultural genre as pointed out after 'The Prisons We Broke' were life narratives, which brought out struggles of *shudra* (low caste) and *atishudra* (Dalit) men and women but one perceives the emergence of individual identity, which was in contrast to one's community and represented success stories resulting from affirmative action of the state and the onset of neo-liberal programmes during the 1980s to 1990s. Narendra Jadhav's autobiography is representative of a life story of a de-caste Dalit. But at the same time atrocities against Dalit still continue. Pawar's autobiography traverses a range of positions, representing 'graded margininalities' and can be read as a "complex narrative of a gendered individual who looks at the world initially from her location within the caste but who also goes on to transcend the caste identity from a feminist perspective"(Pawar 2008: XVII). Pawar's autobiography is both a continuation of the tradition of Baby Kamble of portraying the inhuman condition of the community, but it moves forward where caste identities morphed into a larger human identity influenced by Buddhist philosophy. The dialectics between self and community finds a larger articulation with Pawar re-defining the category 'Dalit' to include a radical humanist category.

'Dalit'! How are we Dalit now? They asked angrily. We had to make an elaborate explanation. Dalit does not mean socially oppressed people. It also signals rational, secular people who have discarded the oppressive system and concepts like God, fate and caste system.

Pawar's re-definition of Dalit as a radical liberating agency while promoting "grater historical sensitivity"(Pawar 325) marks the arrival of a gendered self as "situated, local and partial"(329) along the multiple axis of class, caste and gender. Intersectionality as a particular perspective draws upon marginalised subjects inscribing the belief the "....those who have experienced discrimination speak with a special voice to which we should listen"(Matsuda quoted in Nash 2008 : 3).

The memoirs present a detailed account of the community along with Pawar's journey to emerge as a feminist, thereby the issue of 'difference' to the centre stage. The narrative opens with a detailed description of the labouring Dalit women travelling from nearby villages to the market at Ratnagiri to sell various things through a hilly and dangerous terrain.

Women were compelled to make the journey to the market for they had to sell their wares for survival. (Pawar 2).

The articulation of resistance occurs through mapping of hurt and humiliation across various structures and practices. The culture of backbreaking physical labour has been documented in great detail, when Pawar recalls the hardship of women, who went to collect oysters and crabs in the middle of the creek, bending down in knee deep water and returned with their hands bruised and bleeding. Some of them were drowned while bending in deep water and did not notice the water level rising. Enacting the violence embedded in caste identity draws attention to the lived reality of Dalit women, which the text throughout will vividly portray.

At another level the writing of resistance is the moment, when the narrator wakes up to the implication of being a member of low caste (Ramakrishnan 721). There are several such episodes in the text. One such episode is when Pawar goes to deliver the baskets to her mother customers and she would be made to stand outside their houses at the threshold. Pawar would then put the baskets down and the customers would "sprinkle water on them to wash away the pollution, and only then would touch them"(Pawar 65) and would "drop coins in my hands from above, avoiding contact as if their hands would have burnt had they touched me"(65).

The act of writing of resistance is a performance in the public domain with certain ideological underpinnings, which call for a revision of the dichotomy between the self and the society, the private and the public and the question the legitimacy of narratives that inform the history of the nation. Dalit life narratives are 'testimonies', which forge the right to speak both for and beyond the individual and contest explicitly or implicitly the official forgetting of histories of caste operation, struggles and resistance (Rege 13) and hence the narrative demands "new modes of narration and signification"(Ramakrishnan 66).

Central to both the texts is the articulation of a Dalit feminist standpoint which results in the creation of cultural and literary space, which is concerned with the recovery of Dalit gendered discourse. This discourse has provided a critique of the failure of dominant groups to critically and systematically interrogate their advantaged situation in terms of knowledge production and leaves them crippled, scientifically and epistemologically (Rege 328).

Within this literary space reading resistance calls for an engagement with marginalised gendered voices and involves understanding the "complex relationships of social location, experience and history"(Rege 72) and results in building Dalit feminist pedagogies. This site includes a range of possible meanings and knowledge systems both from dominant and radical discourses. Re-visiting the margin and centre results in reading and understanding resistance that moves beyond "epistemic charity" (Rege 73). And finally the category literature in this context included literature, history and politics and calls for a need to produce new and liberating revisions of history.

6

SPECTRE OF CASTES HAUNTING LAKSHMIPETA, SRIKAKULAM : SOCIOLOGICAL EXPLANATIONS

Mritunjay Kumar Yadavendu

Abstract

The ghastly massacre of 5 Dalit on 12th June, 2012 in Lakshmipeta village in the Srikakulam district of Andhra Pradesh left the democratic sections aghast. More than 50 men, women and children of the Mala, Dalit community suffered serious injuries, out of which 19 are still struggling with their lives in two private hospitals in Vishakhapatnam, Andhra Pradesh in this dastardly attack by the land-owning Kapu community. This is a continuation of outrageous carnages in Andhra Pradesh since Karama, Chedu, and Tsunduru massacres. This exposes the republican, democratic charade of the India, which constitution provides right to life and dignity to every citizen. The incidents of Lakshmipeta show that the hapless Dalit are disowned by the Indian State. Where brethren are, insulted, tortured, raped, maimed and killed in each passing day.

The paper maps out the gruesome massacre of Dalit in Lakshmipeta that makes the mockery of India being the largest democracy whose politicians trumpet the slogans of social justice and dignity. The paper also analyses how this heinous attack on Dalit in Lakshmipeta is a stark indicator of the exploitative, insidious nexus of upper caste politicians, police and other functionaries of the state machinery. The paper explores that this gruesome killing has its roots in the land dispute/conflict between Kapus and the Malas. It also explains the strong bond between state power and caste hatred of this kind.

Key Words

Lakshmipeta, Dalit, caste atrocities, land, development, justice, democracy.

On the 26th of January 1950, we are going to enter into a life of contradictions. In politics we will have equality and in social and economic life we will have inequality. In politics we will be recognising the principle of one man one vote and one vote one value. In our social and economic life, we shall, by reason of our social and economic structure, continue to deny the principle of one man one value.

How long shall we continue to live this life of contradictions?

How long shall we continue to deny equality in our social and economic life?

If we continue to deny it for long, we will do so only by putting our political democracy in peril. We must remove this contradiction at the earliest possible moment or else those who suffer from inequality will blow up the structure of political democracy which this Assembly has so laboriously built up.[1]

Alongside of modern evils, a whole series of inherited evils oppress us, arising from the passive survival of antiquated modes of production, with their inevitable train of social and political anachronisms. We suffer not only from the living, but from the dead![2]

Caste is one of the main crutches of class rule in the Indian society. As an inhuman social institution, which evolved out of the archaic division of labour from the very beginning, the caste system is integrally linked up with women's oppression on the one hand, and landlessness of the broad masses on the other. In other words, as a legitimizing power of the exploiters and being intertwined with patriarchy and land question, caste was and is one of the most effective tools in the hands of both colonial and the present semi-feudal and semi-colonial Indian State acting as the supervisor and custodian of ruling class interests. Thus smashing the material basis of the caste system is the goal that had/has been an inseparable task of the revolutionary forces in their fight for the casteless and classless society.

After 1947[3], there has been hardly any substantial change in the plight of the Dalit in India. While a section of the 'middle castes' benefited from the Nehruvian policies and succeeded in improving their position in the economic hierarchy, the 'lower castes' composed of the

Dalit and tribals continued to be the worst sufferers of the harmful consequences of the imperialist policies since the 1960s. Even the anti-zamindari legislations and Tenancy Regulation Acts that came into force in the 1950s and 1960s in various Indian 'states' utterly failed to address the question of land-to-the-tiller such that Dalit' deprivation of land continued unabated.[4] At the same time, the Dalit were at the receiving end of the economic displacement, social disruption, ecological distortion and cultural dislocations. At an economic level, while it transformed the erstwhile feudal landlords into an agricultural bourgeois class, the strangle hold of the upper castes coupled with the newly emerging elite from the middle castes over the rural population remained more or less intact. In the 'largest democracy' that India is, Dalit are denied vital resources like water, agricultural implements, and are subjected to worst forms of untouchability, social boycotts, violence, rapes and killings.

Colonial policy of imperialism prompted by the pressures of capital accumulation in general led to a disruption of the socio-economic formation in colonies including a distortion of the traditional village communities, changes in land relations including the introduction of private property in land, enforced monetization and exchange relations, imposition of forced labour, destruction of handicrafts and domestic industries, imposition of metropolitan cultures and so on. However, as far as the caste question is concerned, the Britishers pursued a cautious and calculated approach in India. Even while adopting measures against '*sati*' and child marriage aimed at reforming the upper segment of Hindu religion with a view to integrating it with imperialist market, except the state-sponsored conversion of 'low caste' people into Christianity and isolated missionary intervention with regard to certain heinous caste practices, no significant step was initiated by the colonial administration to alter the caste foundations of Indian society.[5] On the other hand, the colonial policy was one of manipulating the anti-caste movements of lower caste people that arose in the country as part of the renaissance movement and the anti-colonial struggle to divide the anti-imperialist unity of the people. At the same time, British imperialism ruthlessly suppressed several tribal and peasant struggles mostly led by tribals and Dalit that challenged the colonial-caste-feudal order.[6]

At present under imperialist policies of the comprador Indian state that served imperialist, capital have strengthened the caste oppression in new forms. Just as in the case of the communal divide of the people, the Indian State and the ruling system through their political representatives have succeeded in propping up caste based parties ultimately serving comprador bourgeois-bureaucratic-landlord classes through caste based vote banks thereby dividing the fighting unity of Dalit and toiling people. Identity politics or caste based politics are the new catchwords obscuring the realities of iniquitous class structures within and around the identities or communities and the mud of the time invariably carried out by them. They are so theorised as to persuade the exploited to accept and stay happy with their 'difference' in place of equality and liberation they should strive for.[7] Though a small section among the Dalit has managed to better its position through reservation, the neoliberal policy of demolishing general education and closing down of public sector, public distribution and overall downsising of the state itself has made even that option a mirage. Along with this, all kinds of decadent caste practices ranging from caste-genocides, untouchability to "honour killings" etc. are propped up with ulterior ruling class motives.

The incidents of atrocities evidently show the stubborn persistence of caste in 'modern India'. For those who are oppressed by the caste system, its existence is evident, albeit in fragmented or distorted forms. 'Caste riots', caste atrocities and the reservation debates make it difficult for us to accept views that mask the continuous existence of this system of domination by regarding them at the most as atrocities of the past. And what happened in Lakshmipeta, Srikakulam district of Andhra Pradesh is a glaring example of it. Though there have been caste rivalries and caste tensions in India since centuries, there is a distinct unprecedented increase in the tempo following the transfer of the power in 1947. According to National Campaign on Dalit Human Rights statistics, every 18 minutes a crime is being committed on a Dalit, everyday 27 atrocities takes place against Dalit; 3 Dalit women are raped and 11 Dalit beaten. Every week 13 Dalit murdered; 5 Dalit' homes or possessions burnt; 6 Dalit kidnapped or abducted[8]. And here it is noteworthy that only very few incidents get reported.

> India is a peculiar country and her nationalists and patriots are a peculiar people. A patriot and a nationalist in India is one who sees with open eyes his fellow men treated as being less than man. But his humanity does not rise in protest. He knows that men

> and women for no cause are denied their rights. But it does not prick his civil sense of helpful action. He finds a whole class of people shut out from public employment. But it does not rouse his sense of justice and fair play. Hundreds of evil practices that injure man and society are perceived by him. But they do not sicken him with disgust. The patriot's one cry is power for him and his class. I am glad I do not belong to that class of patriots. I belong to that class which takes its stand on democracy and which seeks to destroy monopoly in every form. Our aim is to realize in practice our ideal of one man one value in all walks of life - political, economical and social.[9]

The oppression of the Dalit continues unabated in the Andhra Pradesh. Whichever dominant castes are in power, people belonging to those castes continue to conduct violent attacks on the Dalit. When Nandamuri Taraka Rama Rao (NTR) was in power, six Dalit were brutally killed in Karamchedu (17th July, 1985). When Nedurumalli Janardhan Reddy was in power, they chopped off the heads of eight Dalit in Chunduru of Guntur district (6th August, 1991), and dumped them in the Tungabhadra. Now when Botsa Satyanarayana, who calls himself a BC (Backward Class), is the Pradesh Congress President, Botsa Vasudeva Naidu and his horde of Toorpu Kapus, armed with swords and axes, have tortured and killed the Dalit of Lakshimpeta in Srikakulam district.

I went to Lakshmipet on 18th June and was there till 25th of the month. In this dastardly attack by the land owning Kapu community 5 Dalit were brutally killed whereas more than 50 Dalit men, women and children suffered serious injuries, out of which 19 are still struggling with their life in two private hospitals in Vishakhapatnam. A visit in Vishakhapatnam private Seven Hills Hospital in Vishakhapatnam where 11 seriously injured men and women at the Dalit Mala community are struggling for their lives shows the chilling brutalities of the upper caste monsters, who have been perpetrating these monstrosities on the Dalit and other marginal people since centuries. This was a continuum of outrageous carnages in Andhra Pradesh since Karamchedu, and Chunduru. This exposes the republican, democratic charade of the Indian state, whose constitution provides right to life and dignity to every citizen.

The incidents of Lakshmipeta shows that the hapless Dalit are disowned by the Indian State, which brethren are, insulted, tortured, raped, maimed and killed in each passing day in this country. The gruesome massacre of Dalit in Lakshmipeta makes the mockery of India being the largest democracy whose politician shamelessly trumpets the slogans of social justice and dignity from every public platform. The heinous attack on Dalit in Lakshmipeta is a stark indicator of the exploitative, insidious nexus of upper caste politicians, police and other functionaries of the state machinery. Since the formation of the state land owning castes in various regions be it Kammas or Reddies or Kapus or Kalingas or Velamas have been unable to bear the sight of Dalit tilling land on their own and developed grudges against them claiming that the Dalit have no rights to land, conducted violent attacks on them or expelled them from villages. There is a strong bond between state power and caste hatred of this kind. In this brutal, inhuman incident, which ashamed every democrat in this country is one more black chapter in the post independent history of India.

Lakshmipeta is the biggest massacre by the upper caste after Karmchedu and Chunduru. These upper caste monsters surrendered the Dalit, chased and hunted them for two and half hours with spears, lathis and axes. The upper caste kapus of neighboring villages, following the bonds of kinship and caste, also participated in the attack by the Kapus of Lakshmipeta. 26 years old Chittiri Sridevi, Borada Kasalu, Nivirti Ramudamma, Nitirti Venkatmma were widowed by this gruesome upper caste attack. A month ago the mother-in-law of the Dalit Panchayat president was brutally attacked by Kapu men, after that police picket was put up in the village, but strangely just a day before the massacre on 12th June it was withdrawn in the name of Assembly by-election.

This gruesome blood bath has its roots in the land dispute/conflict between Kapus and the Dalit Malas. Land is not merely an important economic asset; its ownership is also socially valued, sought and denied. In rural societies, ownership of land was and to a large extent is still coterminous with social status. Hence, its unequal distribution reflects both prevailing social stratification and also helps maintain the hierarchical structure of the society. In contrast, fair distribution of land strikes directly at the roots of an unequal social order and skewed power relations, and frees the Marginalised from the clutches of perpetual bondage, for want of a sustainable livelihood. The landless, whose only remaining asset is their labour, are effectively separated from the other means of production, namely land, and remain dependent on large land holders for their survival. Powerful landlords have always opposed land reforms, fearing not only loss of control of assets, but also their dominant position in society, which straddles the economic and the political realms. The denial of access to land, thereby, functions both as a means of exclusion as also a mechanism of bondage.

The pattern of land distribution in India, therefore, reflects the existing socioeconomic hierarchy. While large landowners invariably belong to the upper castes, the cultivators belong to the middle castes, and the agricultural workers are largely Dalit and tribals. The data of absolute landless families proves that the feudal society is firmly anchored in large parts of India, notwithstanding claims to the contrary. Most Dalit victims of abuse in India are landless agricultural labourers who form the backbone of the nation's agrarian economy. Despite decades of land reform legislation, over 86 percent of Dalit households today are landless or near landless. Those who own land often own very little. Land is the prime asset in rural areas that determines an individual's standard of living and social status. As with many other low-caste populations, lack of access to land makes Dalit economically vulnerable. Their dependency is exploited by upper-and middle-caste landlords and allows for many abuses to go unpunished.

Land was acquired by the government for Madduvalasa reservoir built on two tributaries of Nagavali river, Suvarnamukhi and Vegavathi which, while displacing thousands of people irrigated 15000 acres of land. In Lakshimpeta village, after the construction of the reservoir, 240 acres of land intermittently comes out of the submergence when water dries up. As the land turns fertile, rich crops were being raised on it with profitable cultivation in the past five years. The government paid a compensation of two lakh rupees per acre to Kapu land owners and settled 190 Kapu families and 60 Dalit families about seven kilometres away from the reservoir. The Dalit families were not paid any compensation or given employment though they were also displaced and resettled except for four families, who had assigned lands—only 40 thousand rupees per acre were paid to each of these four Dalit families. Meanwhile one each from 40 families of the Kapu caste was provided with employment in the reservoir office departments in addition to compensation amount for land. All 250 families were settled in *pacca* houses built by the government. Having been deprived of land for centuries, the Dalit of Lakshimpeta, as in most other cases, aspired to take over the unaffected land under the project and they have been asserting their rights over the land which now falls under the control of the government.

As the 240 acres of land—that once belonged to Kapu community became government land after compensation was being paid—came out of submergence every now and then, 180 acres of land has been cultivated by the Kapu families while only 60 acres by 60 Dalit families in the last five years. Kapu community in the village claimed that the entire land belongs to them as it once belonged to them. Dalit argued with the local revenue administration that they should be allowed to cultivate this land as it was now government land.

The local administration maintained silence as the Kapu caste people were supported by powerful lobbies within the ruling party from the state to the bloc levels within the same caste. Both sides of the dispute approached the court for justice. The court as usual stayed the cultivation from both sides till its judgment. This triggered fury among the Kapu community and they blamed squarely the Dalit community for the court order, though both communities had approached the court. The former local block president of Congress Party, Botsa Vasudevanaidu instigated the Kapus against the Dalit with the active encouragement from PCC (Pradesh Congress Committee) chief, Botsa Satyanarayana. Congress leaders like Botsa Satyanarayana, Dharmana Prasada Rao (Minister for Roads and Buildings in Andhra Pradesh Government) from North Andhra region have become the powerful agents of land grab in the region for thermal power plants, industrial corridor projects and mining. They are maintaining land mafia's and have acquired thousands of acres of land for their own families. They are responsible for the police firings and state-sponsored killings of the people, who are protesting against land grab in the region. They are the powerful political leaders of the region who are in real sense representatives of globalisation and displacement of hundreds of thousands of people in the region.

As the tension in the village grew, the government put up a police picket in the village. Instead of solving the issue, the bloc has been placed under the atrocity-prone area. This shows such an attack, as the one on Dalit on 12 June, has been expected to happen. In these circumstances, the government itself is directly responsible for the massacre of Dalit. On June 12, majority of police personnel at the picket were sent away on by-election duty. The police forces returned to the village only after giving enough time to the caste chauvinists to carry out the massacre unhindered. History testifies to this set pattern of conduct of the state forces as every time they remained mute witnesses to the upper caste brahmanical fascist attacks on Dalit. In fact the India State forces like police, paramilitary and army always either sided with upper caste big landing owning communities or stayed as onlookers over the atrocities as they represented the interests of the brahmanical upper caste Indian State.

As the Dalit people were not prepared to face the brutal attack from the brahmanical casteist forces, they either prayed their attackers to leave them or couldn't move away to safety. The motivated and calculated nature of the attackers was evident from their preparedness to strike on the Dalit fatally. All the victims targeted were the main bread-winners of their respective families. All of them were mainly landless peasants.

The infuriated Dalit of Lakshimpeta refused to bury the dead for the next three days as the government did not arrest the culprits and their abettors, the kingpins in the massacre and the ruling parties' leaders. The Dalit people protested the government's inaction placing the dead bodies of their kith and kin in front of the village. The administration did not use SC and ST Atrocities Act against the culprits and their abettors till all Dalit and democratic forces raised their voices in protest. A week after when the law was evoked, it was used against small insignificant elements among the culprits, leaving out safely the main abettors and political leaders like Botsa Vasudeva Naidu, Botsa Satyanarayana and others.

Conclusion

The people were demanding a CBI (Central Bureau of Investigation) enquiry into this incident and the time bound trial of the upper caste murderers in a fast court. The demand of special court for speedy trial has been conceded. It has to be set up at Lakshmipeta village, instead of Srikakulam this year, months after the incident took place, under the pressure of the agitations by several Dalit and other progressive organizations. Allotment of agricultural land to each Mala family in Lakshmipeta is also one of the demands which have to be won. With this situation where Dalit are always suppressed, what would a real democracy entail? It would involve a genuine assertion of people's power from the grass roots? People themselves will determine their future? Probably, YES. The determination of the people of Lakshimipeta to fight against casteism and to build a casteless society is better reflected in the following words of revolutionary poet Faiz Ahmad Faiz:

> The cage may be in your power, but you do not control
> The season of the flowering of the bright rose.
> And so what if we do not see it?
> For the ones following us will witness
> The brightness of the garden, the singing of the nightingale.

NOTES

1. Ambedkar, B.R. 1949. *Writings and Speeches*- Ambedkar's Speech in the Constituent Assembly on 25th November, 1949.
2. Marx, Karl. 1867. *Economic Manuscripts: Capital Vol. I, Preface*, Moscow, Progress Publication.
3. The political parties which believe that the Indian society has semi-feudal and semi-colonial mode of production are of the opinion that India did not get independence in 1947, but this was mere power transfer. They argue that the though the British left India in 1947, India continued to dance to the tune of its colonial masters.
4. Ghosh S.K. 2009. *Naxalbari: Before and After*, Kolkata: NAPL Publisher.
5. *Ibid*.
6. Kaviraj, Narhari. 2001. *Santal village community and the Santal Rebellion of 1855,* Kolkata, Subarnarekha.
7. Singh, Randhir. 2008. *Marxism, Socialism, Indian Politics: A View from the Left,* New Delhi, Aakar Books.
8. National Campaign on Dalit Human Rights, 2007. Cast Out Caste, *A Newsletter on Dalit Human Rights*, September Issue.
9. *Ambedkar, B.R. 19th January 1931 at the Round Table Conference in London.*

REFERENCES

Primary source

Feild Trip

Secondary source

Ambedkar, B.R. 1949. *Writings and Speeches*-Ambedkar's Speech in the Constituent Assembly on 25th November, 1949.

————————. *1931. 19th January 1931 at the Round Table Conference in London.*

Ghosh S.K. 2009. *Naxalbari: Before and After*, Kolkata, NAPL Publisher.

Kaviraj, Narhari. 2001. *Santal village community and the Santal Rebellion of 1855,* Kolkata, Subarnarekha.

Marx, Karl, 1867. *Economic Manuscripts: Capital Vol. I, Preface*, Moscow, Progress Publication.

National Campaign on Dalit Human Rights, 2007. *Cast Out Caste*, A Newsletter on Dalit Human Rights, September Issue.

Singh, Randhir. 2008. *Marxism, Socialism, Indian Politics: A View from the Left,* New Delhi, Aakar Books.

7

DALIT WOMEN-INSIDE AND OUTSIDE CASTE-A STUDY OF DALIT WOMEN IN TAMIL NADU WITH REFERENCE TO KARUKKU

Deepthy R. Chandran

Tapan Basu

Abstract

Marginality is a term applicable universally to the people of the world who are living in conditions of abject poverty and are isolated from the general luxuries of life. These depressed groups are meant to suffer several deformities because of their caste, class, race or sex. In India, Dalit people or the so-called untouchables are the most neglected groups. Within these depressed sections of the society, women are the worst sufferers. They are said to face double or triple marginalisation because of their gender apart from their discrimination out of caste, class or race. Dalit women need special attention than their male counter parts, as they are the victims of Dalit men's patriarchy also. This paper is an attempt to trace the patriarchal deformities faced by the Dalit women, outside their community and within it. Bama's *Karukku* is analysed to have an outlook of Dalit women in Tamil Nadu.

Key Words

Patriarchy, Dalit women in Tamil Nadu, Dalit movement in Tamil Nadu, Dalit Panthers in Tamil Nadu, Dalit literature in Tamil Nadu, Bama, *Karukku*.

Introduction

"One can speak of the social problems of men without involving the family, but one cannot speak on women without dealing with their family functions" (Mies :15). Patriarchy has wrecked the lives of women in India and it affects the social, political and economic scenario badly. For centuries, woman is considered low to men in every spheres of society. The general notion of the society is that, woman's sphere of action is essentially limited by the horizons of the small family world. The preliminary duty of woman is supposed to be towards her family. Men can go out and have fun but women are not allowed to do that. They are always under the strict rules of men who rule the family. "The roles of wife, mother and house-wife are by all means regarded as the central ones for the woman. That means her life is regarded as being basically determined by her biological functions" (Mies : 5). In all other spheres of the society, she is considered odd, no matter how much she is talented and capable, she is 'merely a woman'. Our society is structured in such a way that women folk are the ones who is meant to suffer and are Marginalised in every way. The mindset of society is moulded in this way from centuries ago and is the so-called patriarchal society.

"Patriarchy in its wider definition means the manifestation and institutionalization of male dominance over women in society in general. It implies that men hold power in all the important institutions of society and that women are deprived of access to such power" (Singh (1990) : 3). The politics of patriarchy "lies in the fact that the family, caste, religion and the dominant value system are surcharged with the spirit of male superiority. Women are suppressed and exploited by men" (Singh (1990) : 13). Patriarchal society binds women's each movement by perceptions and prohibitions. She is considered to be the unpaid labourers (maids) of a family. Women do not enjoy equality with men in social, economic, political or cultural sectors. Women seem to have no individuality and freedom. Women activists and feminists for years have been racing their voices against this unequal patriarchal system that prevails, but it has never been resolved which itself appears to be rigidly patriarchal. Educated women are also tied down by the same feudal and patriarchal norms.

Women are not given honour or respect in any religion or caste. In politics also, she couldn't attain much seats or even reservation bill is yet to be passed. Law also is not favourable to her. As De Beauvior says, "Almost no where is her status the same as man's and frequently it is much to her disadvantage. Even when her rights are legally recognized in the abstract, long-standing custom prevents their full expression in more's" (Singh (1990): 14). Religion, politics, and law are all manipulated and manoeuvred by the 'normative structure', which is highly patriarchal. Feminist movements in India have posed challenges to established patriarchal institutions such as the family, and to dominant social values and structures, most significantly in the arena of legal interventions in the areas of violence against women" (Geetanjali: 1). Against this established system of patriarchy, various women's organisations and feminist movements have fought, but still it remains as it was.

Women's organisations and movements always emerged as a branch of the main movements like nationalist or caste movements. In the nineteenth century, there were very few women's movements, which were organised for women, by women; usually they were organised by men for women. Therefore these women's organisations were strictly patriarchal and were controlled by men. A women's organisation meant to be an organisation set up for the welfare of children and women, which is not necessarily by women's themselves. Women activists protested and raised their voices among the men folk and their voices went unheard. It was only in the 1970's that feminist groups as such emerged in India. They began to recognise their rights which are subdued by men. The emergence of women's movements resulted in an increase of educational and employment opportunities for women and in politics also. It was the period in which there were many 'people's movements' like, "the Naxalite movement in West Bengal, Bihar and Andhra Pradesh, the anti-price movements in Maharashtra and students movements in different parts of the country" (Geetanjali: 15). The male activists or nationalist leaders criticized the women's movement arguing that "the most burning problems of the majority of women in the world are food, shelter, health, work and not the patriarchal attitudes of husbands" (Mies: 8). The main organisations and nationalist groups have accused feminists of prioritising gender over nation or class. This was a great challenge to the women's movements. Moreover feminist movements depicted their lives and ignored minority and Dalit women's strives. Hence the women's organisations also got split up based on caste and religion and class which resulted in dissimilation of power.

Women in every strata of the society are the preys of this patriarchal anarchism. But the most struggling sections among these are the women who face double marginalisation because of their caste and of their gender. Caste system is one of the widely discussed topics today and everyone knows the dangers of caste system in our society. The person who belongs to a lower caste or Dalit is exploited in the society because of his/her caste. And the plight of a Dalit woman is unimaginable to the upper caste women and to the educated Dalit women living in urban areas.

Though the system of patriarchy is structured by ancient Hindu texts especially Vedas, Dalit who stand out of the so-called 'Vedic structure' also facilitates the patriarchal norms in their society. It is an irony that the lower caste people or Dalit who are fighting against the Hindu norms practice such inequalities upon their women folks. Hence Dalit women's assertion for their rights and identity goes without any results. Dalit women's movements for their rights fail to shed light upon their identity as a Dalit or as a woman.

Plight of Dalit Women

Having been a victim of two exploitations is a hard thing. A Dalit girl is chained from her childhood onwards under this double threat of caste and gender. From her childhood onwards, she has been made socialised into 'accepting the male hegemony as well as the caste hierarchy'. Even among women she is perceived as the 'other'. "She is at the perceiving end of a long, socially-engineered pecking order, which asserts the relative 'superiority' of one category of human being over another" (http://www.countercurrents.org/stephen161109.htm). The men of the higher castes and the majority groups rape Dalit women. Rape becomes a political tool to keep the economically poorer sections in their destined place. "This is one of the effective ways to crush and silence the brewing dissent of the underdogs, because women happen to be the custodians of honour of their men folk. In urban areas a woman dare not move in the night in fear of the lurking patriarchal lecher. It does not mean that day time is safe" (Singh (1990): 13). Dalit women are deprived physically due to malnourishment, educationally, culturally and politically. They have been denied systematically of their human rights to education, properly equal wages and for employment. Dalit women suffer the lowest status in society and are brutally marginalised in social hierarchy.The caste system declares Dalit women as 'impure' and are considered in the same way, by Dalit men also. Dalit men fight against Brahmins when they are outside the family, and when they are inside the family they impose the same 'Brahmanical system' to their women. This is referred as 'Sanskritization' by M.N. Srinivas.

"Sanskritization is the process by which a 'low' Hindu caste, or tribal or other group, changes its customs, ritual, ideology and the way of life in the direction of a high and frequently 'twice-born' caste. The Sanskritization of a group has usually the effect of improving its position in the caste hierarchy" (Srinivas: 77).

"The laws of the *Manusmriti* have a devastating effect on the level of education reached by Dalit women" (Kumar: 230). The caste and patriarchal norms legitimize the poor economic conditions of Dalit women. Due to Sanskritization, the Dalit began to emulate the customs and rituals of the Hindus which resulted in strict patriarchal norms of Dalit families. The system of dowry also is a result of this.

While tracing the history of patriarchy in India, one feels shocked to learn that "In the Vedic period, female *brahmavadinis* (students) went through the same rigorous discipline as their male counterparts, the *brahmacharis*" (Kumar: 289). Some famous women were *Ghose, Lopmudra, Maitreyi* and *Gargi* who were highly respected and honoured during that time. The women's position in society however lost its charm and were stigmatised as impure. Subsequently, they were deprived all rights and are considered as mere sex objects. The seizing of power and rights from the hands of women crowned men in higher positions. Women, who even contributed hymns to *Rig Veda*, were denied of studying or even having them. Later, *Vedas* and *Smritis* were misinterpreted by men according to their wish and gradually chained women. The system of patriarchy remains because, women are unable to assert their rights and identities.

Dalit Women in Tamil Nadu

The plight of Dalit women in Tamil Nadu is not different from the above description. In Tamil Nadu, the rights of Dalit liberation and assertion started with the non-Brahman movements as in Maharashtra.

Iyothee Thass, Erattaimalai Srinivasan, M.C. Rajah, Iravath Nair, L.C. Guruswamy, Dr. P. Varadarajuly Naidu, N. Sivaraj, L. Elayaperumal Vai, T.B. Pandian, Periyar E.V. Ramaswamy and Balasundaram are some of the leaders associated with Tamil Dalit movement at various stages.

The early phase of non-Brahmin movement took the form of an organisation formed by the people who are not Brahmins, against the Brahmanical supremacy. The non-Brahmin movement never voiced the sufferings of the depressed classes of the society. They revolted against the Brahmins and the movement powered in the hands of *Nadars* and other upper caste leaders. Within the non-Brahmin movement, there existed an inequality between the non-Brahmin upper castes and the lower-castes, which finally resulted in the Dalit movements and organisations.

In Tamil Nadu, the non-Brahmin movement took place only after the 1900's. But long before it, people started their revolt against the Brahmins. "In 1897, 'The Visvakulatharana Association of Madras' voiced its grievances against the supremacy of Brahmins in government jobs. Due to this, the Madras Revenue Board warned the collectors to see that the appointments should be made from all castes. The non-Brahmins revolted against the Brahmins which resulted in the formation of 'South Indian Liberal Federation' (Justice Party) in 1917" (Singh (2009): 295). This movement was for safe-guarding the interests of the non-Brahmins. "It was a movement against the domination of Brahmins and other dominating caste Hindus in the fields of education, employment, economic and political life" (Singh (2009): 296).

The non-Brahmin movement cannot be considered as a movement for rights or of equality for Dalit people. The non-Brahmin movement was led by the rich and powerful backward classes like Reddys, Kammar etc. They declared themselves as Dravidians and branded the Brahmins as Aryans. The movement has nothing to do with the Depressed Classes. The dominating non-Brahmins achieved socio-political ascendancy.

The non-Brahmin movement sometimes includes or excludes Dalit from themselves. Their sole aim was to oppose the Brahmins and the Brahmanical system. For that, they sometimes included Dalit people to gain political strength for themselves. "Within the non-Brahmin group, there existed inequality and subjugation. The non-Brahmin movement was led by non-Brahmin leaders who themselves kept away from the Dalit people. Dalit leaders never were in leadership position in the movement. They were kept aside" (Geetha: xvi).

The negligence towards Dalit continued until in 1923 when M.C. Rajah, prominent Dalit leader accused non-Brahmin movement of ignoring the claims of Dalit and he asked for adequate number of scholarships to Dalit people. This resulted in the formation of 'Adi-Dravida Mahajan Sabha' and they demanded for a department for Depressed Classes Welfare. They also demanded separate electorates for Depressed Classes. Thus the 'Depressed Class Mission Society' of

South India was started at Madras by V.R. Shinde (Samel: 171). In 1932, backward class people took effort to organize 'Backward Classes League'. The league held conferences at times, which were attended by delegates all over the Madras Presidency. The first conference was held in Madras in 1939.

The period 1926-1937 lend non-Brahmin movement a more egalitarian and radical character as there was the rise of Self-Respect movement which helps to detach the *Panchamas* or the lower caste people from the 'upper caste non-Brahmin' (Geetha: 200). The Self-Respect movement of the state represented by Periyar E.V. Ramasami Naicker was directed against Brahmin dominance. Its aim was to achieve a society where backward castes have superior rights over Brahmins. The SRM produced some of the Tamil country's best and brilliant publicists. Periyar E.V. Ramasami Naicker was the main intellectual leader of this movement.

The Dalit Panther movement, probably the best known and most discussed Dalit movement in India, was formed in Maharashtra in the late 1970's by a young group of Dalit who ever disillusioned with the existing SC parties and leaders. They drew inspiration from the Black Panthers movement in the United States (Gorringe: 53). The Dalit Panther movement in Tamil Nadu split into several camps and some of them joined to form Dalit Panther Iyyakam (DPI). In 1982 in Madurai, a group of disaffected Dalit led by M. Malaichami formed the Dalit Panther Iyyakam which is also known as the Liberation Panthers. Later, R.Thirumavalavan became the DPI leader.

In 1990's however Dalit contradictions with non-Brahmin dominant castes began to be articulated (Tharu: 20). In 1988, an earlier generation of Dalit leaders came together to form the Scheduled Caste Liberation Movement (SCALM). Many organisations including local Christian NGO's also significantly were involved in Dalit politics. The Social Action Movement (SAM), the Dalit Resource Centre (DRC) and the Institute of Development Education, Action and Studies (IDEAS) are among some of these. Tamil Nadu Harijan Sevak Sangh, Adi-Dravida Mahajan Sabha, Devendra Kula Mahajan Sabha also were organised by Dalit. All these organisations and their efforts resulted in developing the conscience of Dalit. The process of socialization was done through these organisations.

All these movements articulate only the interests of some specific groups and were not interested in the social life of people who were really backward and especially the women minorities. This negligence led to the formation of women's group for the backward class people. The highly patriarchal movements like Non-Brahmanism and Dalit movement was inadequate and incapable to fight for women's assertion. The inability to trace the name of a single woman leader of these movements implies the condition of women during these times. Until the year of 1990's not a single organisation for Dalit women's rights has been formed in Tamil Nadu. Dalit women's organisations also face severe difficulty from upper caste feminist's movements, and from Dalit movements led by men. Dalit men activists considered their agitations for self as anti-casteism. Men called the women as betrayals as for neglecting their caste and for agitating for something they felt as 'silly' things.

Women hardly have any help neither from any authorities that either work for the Dalit people nor for women's welfare. The women's movements in most cases are hardly approachable and are not a permanently felt presence. They also seldom take caste issues seriously. "At the same time, Dalit leaders may have their own patriarchal interests in using or suppressing an assault on a woman. The net result of this situation is often that Dalit women may end up doubly deserted" (Dietrich: 58). Mainstream Indian feminism was not framed for the upliftment of Dalit society or Dalit women. The demands of these feminist movements were not the actual demands of the Dalit women. Dalit women's society is framed with a different set of notions of inequality. They face the discrimination shown by the upper caste men, from upper caste women within the womanhood and from Dalit men within the Dalit hood. The need for a separate Dalit women's movement arises here. (Rao: 58).

Tamil Nadu Dalit women's movement was launched during the year 1997 by SRED (Society for Rural Education and Development) human rights organisation who worked among women for twenty years to promote their rights. During this period they start organising women into groups and then as a federation. In the latter stage, they start co-ordinating all the groups into movements or one forum called Tamil Nadu Women's Forum that concentrate on promoting rights among grass root women. Then while working among Dalit women, they realised the need for separate movement for Dalit women with the focus of Dalit and especially to protect their rights. With the help of various NGO's in Tamil Nadu, they organised Dalit women.

The Women's Movement against poverty and violence (MAPOVI) is a coordinated body of lower caste women from all over Tamil Nadu. "Many coordinated campaigns and joint public actions taken by Women MAPOVI and the social problems that they had been fighting against are the poverty and violence among women. All these movements, however, have an egalitarian and democratic vision of a future caste-free society" (Gorringe: 24). The formation of organisations and movements paved the way for a specific type of literature which has the capacity to shake the world of literature and thus, Dalit literature emerged.

In politics, Dalit women do not have much to do. They are always excluded from decision-making. There are many examples where Dalit women have contested for elections, have forced stiff opposition, and were brutally attacked.

In the field of Tamil Dalit literature also, Dalit women face discrimination and oppression, both from outside the caste and from within the caste and is agitated through their writings. In Tamil Dalit literature, women Dalit writers stand out as a distinctive discourse with their self-reflexivity. Poets, playwrights, writers and novelists repeatedly foreground the gender-caste intersection in Dalit lives. Dalit patriarchy allows Dalit women's subjugation and perpetuates hierarchical relations within Dalit community. Sexual exploitation of Dalit women workers at workplace and sexual violence at the hands of husbands at home forms a subject of concern in many Dalit writings. Dalit women oppression and lack of identity is clearly evident in the fact that, in many novels and stories, Dalit women characters lack names. They are merely named as someone's wife, daughter or sister. It is believed that Dalit women are not allowed an independent individual identity and are perceived as wives, daughters, sisters and mothers.

The suppression of Dalit women invariably leads to resistance and protest. A Dalit woman has indomitable spirit to bounce back the patriarchal repression against all odds. The Dalit women writers not only lament their subjugation, but also celebrate their struggles with pride. It took a long time for Dalit women to overcome their oppression as women and to put use the gains of social and literary movements.

Susie Tharu and K. Lalitha, in their work, Women Writing in India (1993), point to the number of autobiographies which appeared in the late nineteenth and early twentieth centuries, heralding the start of a modern genre of creative writing by women. "They comment that many of these texts are a personal testimony of the new sense of worth these women experience as 'individuals', whose specific lives were of interest and importance. There is a striking parallel here with the beginning of self-consciously styled Dalit writing in India, particularly in Marathi" (Holmstorm: xv).

Autobiographies and testimonies play an important role in the lives of Dalit women. Testimonies play the role of an emancipator who enlightens the path to Marginalised people who are struggling in society. *Testimonio* is a collective document that exists at the margins of literature. Dalit women writers feel free to write their life writings as testimonies than as a novel or a drama. The emergence of testimonies confirms a realistic approach of Dalit women towards literature.

Dalit women writers like Sivakami and Bama raise their voice of agitation through their works. Sivakami's novel *Pazhiyana Kazhidalum* (1989), prepares the ground for a sustained critique of domestic violence and abuse of Dalit women at home by Dalit men- fathers, brothers, sons, father-in-law, brother –in-law, etc. These Dalit women are treated cruelly outside their home and are subjected to sexual harassment from upper castes men also. In her second novel, *Aanandayee* (1992), Sivakami focuses on violent exploitations of woman's body and points out how the family as an institution is embedded in patriarchal and oppressive system which is unjust to women. Dalit women's sexuality is violently contained and is repressed. Sivakami was one of the earliest Tamil writers to draw attention to the dual oppression of Dalit women, on account of their caste and gender, and at the hands of upper caste men as well as Dalit men.

The writings of Sivakami and Bama paved the way for a Dalit feminism in Tamil literature. These writings not only questions Indian feminism but also Dalit men who forgot to speak on behalf of Dalit women. "Bama foregrounds the 'difference' of Dalit women from privileged upper caste women and also celebrates their 'identity' in their strength, labour and resilience. As a feminist writer, Bama protests against all forms of oppression and relying on the strength and resilience of Dalit women, makes an appeal for change and self-empowerment through education and collective action" (Kumar: 151). Lakshmi Holmstom in her 'Introduction' to *Sangati* (2009) writes that, "By writing in the first half of the last decade, Bama was already formulating 'Dalit feminism' which redefined 'woman' from the socio-political perspective of a Dalit, and examining caste and gender oppressions together" (xvii).

Bama, a pioneering figure in Tamil Dalit literature, with such enormous background of Dalit movement and Dalit literature in Tamil, undoubtedly emerged as the most celebrated contemporary Dalit woman writer. Bama was introduced to the world of books by her own brother, Raj Gauthaman, also a writer. Raj Gauthaman says, "Dalit, who have for so long been treated as commodities owned by others must shout out their selfhood, their "I", when they rise up" Kumar: 290). Bama began her struggle as a Dalit writer with *Karukku*, influenced by the writings of her brother. While writing *Karukku*, she aims for the empowerment of her fellow people. Through her writing, Bama tries to questions the attitudes of male patriarchal society. She also challenges the literature that dismisses women's literature. In her works, she depicts Dalit women's life as a struggle. Bama, in her second novel, *Sangati* (1994), depicts the dual oppression of Dalit women. It is the story of an individual struggle to the perception of a community of Paraya women. The theme of Sangati is the growth, decline, culture and liveliness of Dalit women. Both *Karukku* and *Sangati* point out the real facts that within the community there is class hierarchy and the power rests with men.

Portrayal of Patriarchy in *Karukku*

In Bama's *Karukku*, she illustrates the sufferings of Dalit women and children. Once she witnessed a fight between the *Pallars* and the *Parayars* in her village and it were the women folks who suffered the most because of all these fights. The men-folk after the fight went to hide in forests and would not go for work. In order to keep the living, the women of the family were forced to work at very low wages. The police humiliated the women-folk to the maximum extent. They were also constantly vulnerable to sexual harassment and abuse in the world of work. The girl child of the family was responsible to do the menial tasks of the house like cooking, collecting firewood and to look after their young ones, while their mother and all elder women went for work. It was always the girl children who had to look after all the chores at home. The older woman would come home in the evenings after a day's work, and then see to the household jobs. If there were boys in the house, they would graze the sheep and cattle. When they grew a bit older, they'd go off to work in the fields like the older men (52).

Bama used to collect firewood and do other works in the fields during her school life also. The Dalit children accept the humiliations and sufferings as their fate without any hesitation. Bama says that times have changed by now and the children no longer accept whatever they are told by the elders. The division of labour within the household, women have to suffer more from the lack of access to water, fuel sources, and sanitation facilities, exposing them to humiliation and violence. For Dalit women, access to schools and education is minimal. There is also discrimination even in drinking water. At public water sources, Dalit women face humiliation and are even deprived of water because upper castes assert their privilege in respect of drawing water. Unequal relations are compounded from the lack of equality in access to resources. The inequality is reproduced when, in exchange for permission to draw water from a public source, Dalit women are forced to perform various menial tasks for upper caste women. Even the everyday act of collecting water invites many abuses.

In Karukku, Bama brings forth many social issues that distort the everyday lives of Dalit women. Streets are typically gendered spaces. Men and youth inhabit and use streets naturally and forcefully with a sense of belonging, but women often sidle along pavements fully conscious of its being alien, unfriendly territory. The only women who are relatively easy on the streets are vendors, prostitutes, and other women for whom the street is a site of work. When Dalit women step onto the streets in protest, they are seen as transgressing their limits. When upper caste women were taken to the streets in protest, their sense of wrong and their appropriation of public space is immediately legitimate. There is also yet another serious issue, where a woman is being paraded in the streets with the use of force, which signals her 'availability', it is also a statement made about the character of women, the character of her caste, women being seen as the bearers of tradition and protectors of the honour of the caste. A caste is chastised not just by the exercise of force or violence on the women of that caste but also by the use of violence on children. It is also a violence of patriarchal structured society.

In our country, sanitation is a scarce facility and what is scarce is subjected to public disputes, the principle of distribution operates along a caste-class axis. The landless are subjected to suffer, the Dalit landless suffer even more and Dalit landless women suffer the most. Dalit women are often forced to work in the fields that belong to upper castes, leaving them susceptible to physical and mental harassment. There are also problems arising from lack of literacy and education. Dalit children face discrimination at schools. Their objective conditions force them to drop out of school. Rape of women in Dalit village becomes a routine matter.

Women are generally considered as impure. It is primarily due to the difference in male and female sexuality. Periodical pollution through menstruation and parturition renders women intrinsically less purity than men. At the same time, the difference in the levels of purity/impurity between men and women is much less among the lower castes than among the high castes. Low caste women, apart from self-pollution, deals with other's pollution through occupational activities such as midwifery, disposal of dirt, the washing of dirty clothes and many other services. Among the low castes, menstrual pollution does impose certain disabilities on the women in respect to food, worship of deities and ancestors. At the same time, Brahmin and other higher caste men neither incur self-pollution of the kind their women do nor do they have to perform polluting work for other castes. On the contrary, their women are involved in pollution incurred through bodily processes, mainly menstruation and childbirth. They are also responsible for doing some of the polluting tasks within the family, but this never make them less pure than men. Within a caste, women never attain the level of purity of men. Women of twice-born castes have been equated with *sudras* who could not be initiated into the learning of the Vedas.

The other source of impurity for women is widowhood. Widows are not supposed to perform the *puja* of family deities as they do not cook the pure food offered to these deities. Gender discrimination exists in the workplace also. Though women people work harder than the men folk and worked for some more time, the wages given to women labourers is very low. In the case of labour and payment women are more at the margins than men. Bama laments about the sympathetic situation of Dalit in their workplace. "This is a community that was born to work. And however hard they toil, it is the same *kuuzh* everyday"

(Bama: 55). Dalit have to work every day for their living. It seems that they have to work till death. There are children in Tamil Nadu who are bounded to work rather than going to school.

On the other hand, a man is not similarly affected if he becomes a widower. Such hierarchy between the sexes is more a feature of Brahmin and other 'clean' castes. Although Dalit men fight against Brahmanism, they need their women to act like upper caste women. They like to 'sanskritize' their women in their community which results in more subjugation for Dalit women. Sexual intercourse between male and female is yet another serious matter for women since the act affects her internally while it affects a man only externally. In the case of inter-caste sexual relations a man incurs external pollution which can be washed off easily but a woman incurs internal pollution which pollutes her permanently. The importance of the purity of caste affects a woman in all her stages of life.

The exercise of power also is an essential factor in the social relations of gender and caste. Gender within caste society is thus defined and structured in such a manner that the 'manhood' of the caste is defined both by the degree of control that men exercise over women and the degree of passivity of the women of the caste. Rape is the ultimate punishment given to these women by the upper caste men. In *Karukku,* Bama writes of such violent treatment of women by fathers, husbands, and brothers.

Bama's *Karukku* states the difficulties she and her community faces as being a Dalit and being a woman. She is, of course fully marginalised as because of her gender, as a woman, as being a Dalit and also as a converted Christian Dalit. The men indulge in many fights and it ought to be the women in each family who are responsible to look after their children and other household works. Even a pregnant woman is not free from going to work in the fields. Unless they go and earn for their living, they can never meet their ends. In spite of all such humiliations, proper education is also not given to Dalit women. The child, if it is a boy, have to work in the fields when they reach the age of ten and if it is a girl, have to look after the house and her young ones. And even if they are educated, they are supposed to face humiliation in their workplace also.

Dual oppression of Dalit women is the important theme of the work. The women in the family always serve the men folks and the children of the family. The women would be the last to eat the meal. As there would not be much food to eat, they would often starve. Without food, they have to go to the fields for work and have to look after the household works. They are not even cared by their own men and are even abused. They are not given education saying that, "But then, my parents wanted to stay back home saying there was no need for me to go to the college or to study any further. In any case, there was no money. Then, they said it would be difficult for me to find a husband in my community if I went in for further education" (74).

Conclusion

The 'graded inequality' within the patriarchal society is much more dangerous to women than the one which is outside their community or caste. Although the women's issues of patriarchy and inequalities are much debated issues in the present scenario, the problem is not yet solved and women always are in the threshold. The true emancipation of women is possible only in a 'depatriarchised socialist democratic society'. Dalit women should come out of their boundaries that were made by the patriarchal society in order to attain their assertion. The true assertion of Dalit woman is not as a Dalit or as a woman, but as a Dalit woman.

WORKS CITED

Bama. *Karukku.* Trans. Lakshmi Holmstrom. New Delhi: Oxford University Press, 2012.

— *Sangati.* Trans. Lakshmi Holmstorm. New Delhi: Oxford University Press, 2009.

Dietrich, Gabriele. "Dalit Movements and Women's Movement". Anupama Rao (ed) *Gender and Caste.* New Delhi: Kali for Women, 2005.

Geetha, V and S.V. Rajadurai. *Towards A Non-Brahmin Millennium: From Iyothee Thass to Periyar*. Kolkata: Samya Publishers, 2011.

Gorringe, Hugo. *Untouchable Citizens Dalit Movements and Democratisation in Tamil Nadu*. New Delhi: Sage Publications, 2005.

Kumar, Satendra. *Unheard Voices of Dalit Literature*. Jaipur: Yking Publishers, 2012.

—*Socio-Political Concerns in Dalit Literature: A Critical Survey.* Jaipur: Yking Publishers, 2012.

Mies, Maria. *Indian Women and Patriarchy*. New Delhi: Concept Publishing Company, 1980.

Rao, Anupama (ed). *Gender and Caste*. New Delhi: Kali for Women, 2005.

Samel, Swapna. H. *Dalit Movement in South India: 1857-1950.* New Delhi: Serials Publications, 2004.

Singh, Indu Prakash. *Indian Women: The Captured Beings*. New Delhi: Intellectual Publishing House, 1990.

Singh, Mahendar. *Dalit in India*. New Delhi: Reference Press, 2003.

Srinivas, M.N. *Caste*. New Delhi: Penguin, 1996.

Tharu, Susie and K.Satyanarayana. *No Alphabet in Sight: New Dalit writing from South India.* New Delhi: Penguin, 2011.

Stephen, Cynthia. "Feminism and Dalit Women in India". 16 Nov., 2009. Countercurrents.org. http:/www.countercurrents.org/stephen 161109.htm

About Myself

I am Deepthy R. Chandran, pursuing my Ph.D in English Language and Literature from the University of Delhi. My research area includes 'Marginal Women's Autobiographies'. It includes Dalit Women's Literature and African-American Women's Literature. Dalit literature from Tamil Nadu and Maharashtra are my chief concern from Dalit arena.

8

DALIT/BLACK AUTOBIOGRAPHY AS TESTIMONY-SHARAN KUMAR LIMBALE'S *THE OUTCASTE* AND RICHARD WRIGHT'S *BLACK BOY*

Moola Ram

Both the Dalit and Black autobiographies are a literary weapon of protest and resistance against the established social order that even does not recognise them as human beings. Despite the fact of having different cultural, religious, linguistic, and geographical boundaries, both of them represent the voice of the people who were forced to remain marginalised because of caste, colour, and race for many centuries. Their vision is to resistance against the culture of domination, and establishing the culture of egalitarian. Both the Dalit and Black autobiographies are popular literary form, which deal with their resistance and expression of the plight of their day-to-day life, that they live under the command of the established social order, but at the same time, they become a literary weapon to protest their anger against the uncountable injustices thrust upon them by the same order. They make readers aware of the experiences and agonies of the oppressed.

The Outcaste (*Akkarmashi*) was originally written and published in 1984 in Marathi by a well-known Dalit writer, a prominent thinker, and activist Sharan Kumar Limbale (1956) at the age of twenty-five. Santosh Bhoomkar translated it into English entitled as '*The Outcaste*' and OUP; New Delhi published this version in 2003. Richard Wright's *Black Boy* was written in between 1943-44 and published by Harper and Brothers in 1945. Both of them are the most powerful and heart-breaking autobiographical narrative in the popular arena of Dalit/ Black literature. *The Outcaste* reveals and attacks the heinous form of caste system and its creator that does not even recognise Dalit as human beings. Similarly, *Black Boy* portrays White domination over Blacks in America, which makes them victims of racial discrimination, the root cause of their marginalisation from the centre. Their power of narration makes the readers introspect deeply, and hence the books have created a worldwide readership. The question of an individual as well as the communal identity remains in the centre of these autobiographies. In other words, they represent the pain of the people who have been denied from their fundamental human rights and gradually excluded from the mainstream society. Both the autobiographies are a replica of social injustice and human suffering. The issues of pure blood, hunger, slavery, caste, colour, and racial discrimination remain in the centre of these autobiographies.

Sharan Kumar Limbale's *Akkarmashi* is a Marathi word that generally translated means *The Outcaste*, which signifies social exclusion and carries the pain of millions of Dalit in India right from the beginning of the four-fold caste system. In other words, they are neglected and dislocated from mainstream society and disassociated from the resources, rights, and privileges. It is an accredited masterpiece in the Dalit dialect. It emphasizes the Dalit internal quest for identity through language, idiom, metaphor, and imagery. Experiences of social exclusion act as a common theme throughout the text. In *The Outcaste*, the author narrates his life story on the periphery of a village near Solapur, in Maharashtra. Limbale was born of a Dalit mother and an upper caste father who was the head of a village and kept her as a concubine. In his autobiography Limbale frequently says that caste plays an important role for a Hindu, it controls his whole life, including the food he eats, the garments he wears and the person whom he chooses as his life partner. Limbale in his life suffered not only the pain of caste system but also the dilemma of not being included into any one fold of the caste system. He remains an outcaste and this label of being outcaste forced him to live his entire life under the curse of being illegitimate progeny. *The Outcaste* gives a very clear picture of the Dalit life and shows how they are controlled and dominated at every point of their daily life by the upper caste Hindus.

In his autobiography, Limbale highlights the agony and humiliation of his life. Why did Limbale use '*akkarmashi*', a Marathi abuse, as the title of his autobiography? In the Author's note, Limbale writes, "My history is my mother's life, at the most my grandmother's. My ancestry does not go back any further. My mother is an untouchable, while my father is a high caste one from the privileged classes of India. Mother lives in a hut, father in a mansion. Father is a landlord, mother landless. I am an *akkarmashi* (half-caste). I am condemned, branded illegitimate. I regard the immorality of my father and mother as metaphor for rape. It is through the Dalit movement and Dalit literature that I understood that my mother was not an adulterous but the victim of a social system. I grow restless whenever I read about a rape in the newspaper. A violation anywhere in the country, I feel, is a violation of my mother. High caste people look upon my community as untouchable, while my own community humiliated me, calling me '*akkarmashi*'. This humiliation was like being stabbed over and over again. I have always lived with the burden of inferiority."[1]

Richard Wright was born to Richard Nathaniel Wright, a freed salve, on 4th September 1908 on Rucker's Plantation, a farm near Rixie, Mississippi. He is the author of *Native Son* (1940), the first novel by an African-American, grew up in the woods of Mississippi amid poverty, hunger, fear and hatred. He was surrounded on one side by Whites who were either indifferent to him, pitying, or cruel, and on the other by Blacks who resented anyone trying to rise above the common lot. He lived throughout the United States, including Memphis, Chicago, and New York City. He became a French citizen in 1947 and settled in Paris, where at the age of fifty-two he died of a heart attack on 28th November 1960.

Apart from *Black Boy*, Wright has five novels in his credit, seven books of non-fiction, as well as numerous influential articles, critical essays, and poems. His first published book was a collection of novel as, *Uncle Tom's Children* (1938). *Native Son* (1940), a protest novel becomes the first novel by an African American to be featured as a Main Selection of the Book-of-the-Month Club. The book achieved vast critical acclaim, stirred fierce intellectual debate, and made Wright the first bestselling African American. *The Outsider* (1953), a novel based on the theory of existentialism.

Black Boy (1945) is Wright's powerful autobiographical slave narrative, which deals with an account of his journey from innocence to experience in Jim Crow South. It is at once an unashamed confession and a profound indictment-a poignant and disturbing record of social injustice and human suffering. The book deals with Wright's record of his early life, examines his tortured years in the Jim Crow South from 1912 to 1927. In each chapter, Wright relates painful and confusing memories that lead to a better understanding of the man a black, Southern, American writer who eventually emerges. Although Wright, as the narrator, maintains an adult voice throughout the story, each chapter is told from the perspective and knowledge that a child might possess. Yet, because the narrative is told with such force and honesty, the reliability of Richard's memories is not questioned. By the story's end, as Richard comes of age, the voice of the narrator and of the nineteen-year-old young man he has become merge into one. The story begins when four-year-old Richard sets fire to his grandmother's house in Jackson, Mississippi, and, as punishment, is nearly beaten to death by his mother. He recovers, and the brutal punishment establishes in Richard an ability to survive any circumstance. The family then moves to Memphis, Tennessee, where Richard's father eventually deserts the family.

The book shows how he struggles to navigate the uncertain world he faces. Abandoned by his father, and barely able to cope with his mother's chronic illness, Wright is thrust into challenging world at a tender age. In order to avoid the oppressive religiosity of his grandmother's home, he searches for firm employment, but he finds himself everywhere upset by employers and co-workers who seem driven to humiliate him because of the colour of his skin. An aching hunger follows him wherever he goes. An enduring story of one young man's coming of age, *Black Boy* remains a ground-breaking text in American literature about what it means to be a man, Black, and Southern in America.

The book is not a mere record of personal agonies, but a form of social protest intended to change the society it describes. In other words, it is a statement of war against injustice. Some of the historical events taking place around Wright, both as a boy and as a man, of course, helped to strengthen these attitudes. *Black Boy* opens with Richard Wright's account of the brutal beating his mother gives him for setting an accidental fire to his family's home at the age of four. He writes, "I was lashed so hard and so long that I lost consciousness. I was beaten out of my senses, and later I found myself in bed, screaming, determined to run away."[2] Wright's behaviour, even at such an early age, indicates his role as rebel in his family. Throughout the book, Wright describes the hunger that he tolerates because of his family's continuous poverty. He writes, "Hunger stole upon me so slowly that at first I was not aware what hunger really meant. Hunger had always been more or less at my elbow when I played, but now I began to wake up at night to find hunger standing at my beside, staring at me gauntly. The Hunger I had known before this had been no grim, hostile stranger, it had been a normal hunger that had made me beg constantly for bread, and when I ate a crust or two, I was satisfied. But this new hunger baffled me, scared me, made me angry and insistent."[3]

Wright's physical hunger that he suffers throughout his life, functions as a metaphor for his hunger for equality and liberty in a society that discriminates and thrusts uncountable atrocities and injustice against him. He writes, "I always loved to stand in the white folks' kitchen when my mother cooked, for it meant that I got occasional scraps of bread and meat, but many times I regretted having come, for my nostrils would be assailed with the scent of food that did not belong to me and which I was forbidden to eat...Watching the white people eat would make my empty stomach churn and I would grow vaguely angry. Why could I not eat when I was hungry? Why did I always have to wait until others were through? I could not understand why some people had enough food and others did not."[4]

Similarly, Limbale shows his never ending hunger, and during his school days he develops a perception in his mind that the quality and taste of the food of the high caste students are much better than the kind of the food he gets from his grandmother. How does leftover food matter for the Dalit offered to them by the upper caste Hindus? It is offered as if they are offering it to the animals like, dogs and cats. Limbale again recalls one of his school day's picnic day-out experience, "I was ashamed of my food and felt guilty eating it...We had before us only the crumbs of bombil...The teacher asked the high caste boys and girls to collect the leftovers on a piece of paper and gave it to us. Parshya and I carried the bundle of leftover food on the way back...At last we gathered in Girmallya's farm and opened the bundle...We squatted in a circle and stuffed ourselves greedily. We had never tasted food like that before. We were all really gluttonous. Our stomachs were as greedy as a beggar's sack. When I got home I told my mother all this. Like the victim of a famine she said, 'why didn't you get at least a small portion of it for me? Leftover food is nectar."[5]

It was Santamai, Limbale's maternal grandmother who brought him up. She lived a life of penury. Limbale does not get any kind of love from his mother Masama who is deserted by her husband and now has seven-eight children from the village *Patil.* The village *Patil* never accepts her as his wife and so she remains his concubine throughout her life. Having many mouths to feed at home it becomes very difficult for her to manage meals for her children two times a day. Most of the times Limbale does not get proper food to satisfy his hunger, so he demands for more and more food from his mother. She angrily shouts at him for his cave-like stomach. In this context Limbale writes, "My stomach was like a way to the graveyard that continuously swallows the dead. My mother masamai used to shout angrily, 'What is it you have, a stomach, or Akkalkot? There seems to be gizzard in your stomach. Why don't you go around with a big bowl at your mouth?' I always felt half-fed. Whatever was given I ate greedily and nothing was ever enough. Everyone in my house needed food so how could I alone think of eating till I was full?"[6]

Limbale in his autobiography further talks about the socio-economic aspects of Dalit life, through his experiences of being a Dalit and that too an outcaste, he raises number of questions about the nation's unequal system of distribution of resources on the basis of caste lines among its citizens. This unequal system of distribution of the resources among the citizens creates a situation of discrimination and extreme poverty among the Dalit. Similarly, Wright in his autobiography comments on white supremacy over blacks in America, which denies them equal opportunities just because of their colour and racial differences. It is because of lack of equal opportunities in various fields for the blacks particularly in southern America, Wright grows up amid penury, hunger, fear and hatred. It is because of his poor economic status, he begins his schooling at the age of nine and while studying he engages in various types of odd jobs and anyhow continues his schooling up to ninth standard. However, he takes admission in tenth standard but cannot continue it further and so he drops it in between and starts searching for a stable job.

Hunger, fear, shock, hatred, poverty and self-pitying were always remain with Wright. He describes the nature of existence of the Negro life in America. He writes, "I used to mull over the strange absence of real kindness in Negroes, how unstable was our tenderness, how lacking in genuine passion we were, how void of great hope, how timid our joy, how bare our traditions, how hollow our memories, how lacking we were in those intangible sentiments that bind man to man, how shallow was even our despair. After I had learned other ways of life I used to brood upon the unconscious irony of those who felt that Negroes led so passion an existence! I saw that what had been taken for our emotional strength was our negative confusion, our flights, our fears, our frenzy under pressure. Whenever I thought of the essential bleakness of black life in America, I knew that Negroes had never been allowed to catch the full spirit of western civilisation, that they lived somehow in it but not of it."[7]

It is a big shame for the whole nation that even after its sixty-four years of independence from British imperialism, and in spite of various constitutional safeguards, numerous legal and judicial protections for the Dalit, they still have no freedom to live their life with dignity and self-respect in their own motherland. For many non-Dalit, it may seem surprising, but for Dalit it is a lived reality. The behaviour of the upper, middle, and backward caste people towards them is extremely exploitative, oppressive, discriminatory, and insulting. Sometimes, they are behaved with as if they are even worse than animals. In other words, here some animals have more respected and dignified life than the Dalit, for example cow, which is considered as mother by all the Hindus. In India, things are fine until the exploiter does not know the caste of the exploited, the moment the exploiter gets to know the caste of the exploited, things are changed. Limbale's real pain is the pain of his hailing from *Mahar* caste and that too an outcaste one. He writes, "Somewhere in the corner of the market a barber plied his trade. I was a schoolboy, and wanted a haircut like that of other boys in the school. So, went to the barber for the first time… The barber first looked at me and then at my head. He shouted, "Don't stand here. I am not going to shave your head". I showed him my money in order to convince him. A customer from a different village who was getting his haircut felt some sympathy for me. He asked me to sit down and take my turn. At that, the barber, Isunath, got wild, "He is a *Mahar*. Let him go". How could this barber, who used to shave buffaloes in the village, refuse to shave my head?"[8]

Similarly, Wright in his autobiography further talks about racial segregation of the blacks in America, particularly in southern. Wright realises these facts for the first time when he along with his mother travels in a train for another town. He writes, "I noticed that there were two lines of people at the ticket window, a "white" and a "black" line. During my visit at Granny's a sense of the two races had been born in me with a sharp concreteness that would never die until I died. When I boarded the train I was aware that we Negroes were in one part of the train and that the whites were in another. Naively I wanted to go and see how the whites looked while sitting in their part of the train...I wanted to understand these two sets of people who lived side by side and never touched, it seemed, except in violence."[9]

At the age of ten, after his first realisation about racial segregation and colour discrimination of Negroes by the white, Wright becomes quite eager about his hunger of knowing more and more about the life and history of the coloured people in America. Therefore, he makes constant requests to his mother so that he can develop his knowledge about the same. When he comes to know the reality, a sense of rebel and resistance against the injustice takes birth in him. He writes, "I was angry and did not answer. I did not object to being called coloured, but I knew that there was something my mother was holding back. She was not concealing facts, but feelings, attitudes, convictions which she did not want me to know; and she became angry when I prodded her. All right, I would find out someday. Just wait. All right, I was coloured. It was fine...True, I had heard that coloured people were killed and bitten, but so far it all had seemed remote. There was, of course, a vague uneasiness about it all, but I would be able to handle that when I came to it. It would be simple. If anybody tried to kill me, then I would kill them first."[10]

Similarly, when Limbale comes to the age of an adult, after knowing the reality of his existence, he starts his quest for an individual identity, because he is accepted neither by his so-called upper caste father nor by his mother's caste people. The *Mahar* caste council also excommunicates him, so that his social mobilisation can be banned, and thus he carries the burden of being an 'outcaste' from both sides throughout his life. Many questions keep haunting him about his existence. He develops a sense of protest, resistance and hatred against his high caste father who exploited his mother like anything and now denies being his father. He writes, "Why did my mother say yes to the rape, which brought me into the world? Why did she put up with the fruit of this illegitimate intercourse for nine months and nine days and allow me to grow in the foetus. Why did she allow this bitter embryo to grow? How many eyes must have humiliated her because they considered her a whore? Did anyone distribute sweets to celebrate my birth? Did anyone admire me affectionately? Did anyone celebrate my naming ceremony? Which family would claim me as its descendant? Whose son am I, really?..I am like *Jarasandh*. Half of me belongs to the village, whereas the other half is excommunicated. Who am I? To whom is my umbilical cord connected?"[11]

Limbale's grandmother's constant painful narration of her own childhood days experiences remind him about his own present day humiliation and agonies of being rejected or excluded firstly by his so-called upper caste father, secondly by his own *Mahar* mother, and then by the entire *Maharwada* and the people from the village. He also realizes that his present day anguish is not confined to himself only, but it has a long history.

After his first job at Ahmedpur, Limbale is transferred to Lature in the telephone department. He faces the problem of finding a rented accommodation over there, as his caste follows him everywhere like an opponent. Lature seemed him a big town with large mansions, bungalows and buildings but he cannot get a single room on rent just because of his low caste identity and that too an ostracized one. He further writes, "I couldn't find a house for myself in Lature... At last, I settled in a house in Bhimnagar. Here the houses did not have bathrooms and toilets...People lived in the smallest possible spaces. Each one worried only about his hunger... I was Dalit who had become a Brahmin by attitude, but high-caste people didn't even allow me to stand at their doorstep. Either I should live in Bhimnagar, or in the Dalit locality or even in a Muslim locality. I was an outcaste in all other localities."[12]

Similarly, though being the native son of America, Richard Wright also becomes a constant victim of alienation just because of his colour and racial differences. At every place and at every turn of his life, he is humiliated, insulted, threatened, and brutally bitten by the white people even if he forgets to address them without 'Sir' or 'Mr' before their actual names. It is because of the fear of white supremacy in America, he shifts his accommodation from one town to another, and finally at the age of forty-nine, he leaves America for Paris along with his family and lives there until last breath. It is because of lack equal opportunities for blacks in southern America, Wright never gets a stable job. The white people never give their room on rent to him. Even in a big city like New York, he faces a severe problem of spending a night over there when he goes there to attend a literary club conference. He writes, "Culturally the Negro represents a paradox: though he is an organic part of the nation, he is excluded by the entire tide and direction of American culture."[13]

*Dr. Moola Ram is teaching as Assistant Professor in the Department of English of Ramanujan College (University of Delhi), Kalkaji, New Delhi. He has done his MA, M Phil, and PhD from Centre for English Studies, School of Language, Literature and Cultural Studies, Jawaharlal Nehru University, New Delhi. His area of specialisation is Dalit Literature, particularly Autobiographical Narratives. He has published a book, i.e. *Mulkraj Anand's Untouchable: A Mirror of Dalit Life* (2010), and he has also presented and published a couple of research papers and articles in various National and International Conferences and peer-reviewed journals. Apart from these, he is also a member of editorial board for *Creative Forum: Journal of Literary and Critical Writings* and *Literaria: An International Journal of Literature across the World.*

NOTES

1. Limbale, Sharan Kumar (2003), *The Outcaste*, Trans. Santosh Bhoomkar, New Delhi, OUP. Acknowledgement, pp. ix-x.
2. Wright, Richard (2007), Black *Boy* (60th edition), New York, Harper Collins Publishers, p. 7.
3. *Ibid.*, pp.14-15.
4. Wright, Richard (2007), Black Boy (60th edition), New York, Harper Collins Publishers, p.19.
5. Limbale, Sharan Kumar (2003), *The Outcaste*, Trans. Santosh Bhoomkar, New Delhi, OUP. p. 10.
6. *Ibid.*, pp. 2-3.
7. Wright, Richard (2007), Black Boy (60th edition), New York, Harper Collins Publishers, p. 37.

8. Limbale, Sharan Kumar (2003), *The Outcaste,* Trans. Santosh Bhoomkar, New Delhi, OUP. p. 22.
9. Wright, Richard (2007), *Black Boy* (60th edition), New York, Harper Collins Publishers, pp. 46-47.
10. Wright, Richard (2007), *Black Boy* (60th edition), New York, Harper Collins Publishers, p. 49.
11. Wright, Richard (2007), *Black Boy* (60th edition), New York, Harper Collins Publishers, p. 272
12. Limbale, Sharan Kumar (2003), *The Outcaste*, Trans. Santosh Bhoomkar, New Delhi, OUP. p. 107.
13. Wright, Richard (2007), *Black Boy* (60th edition), New York, Harper Collins Publishers, p. 272.

REFERENCES

- Limbale, S. Kumar (2003), *The Outcaste*, Trans. Santosh Bhoomkar, New Delhi, OUP.
- —, (2004), *Towards an Aesthetic of Dalit Literature: History, Controversies, and Considerations*, Trans. Alok Kumar Mukherjee. New Delhi, Orient Longman.
- Wright, Richard (2007), *Black Boy* (60th edition), New York, Harper Collins Publishers.
- —, (1993), *Critical Perspectives Past and Present,* (ed.) Henry Louis Gates, Jr. and K.A. Appiah, New York, Amistad.
- Sturrock, John (1993), *The Language of Autobiography: Studies in the First Person Singular*, Cambridge, CUP.
- Kumar, Raj (2010), *Dalit Personal Narratives: Reading Caste, Nation and Identity*, New Delhi, Orient Black Swan.

9

CHILD LABOUR AND ISSUES ON SOCIAL EXCLUSION : STRATEGIES FOR ABOLISHING CHILD LABOUR

Bishnu Mohan Dash

It is indisputable that child labour is a serious social problem, resulting in denial of child rights which eventually excludes them from the joys of childhood, access to education, future employment and social security and impairs the personality, growth and development of the children. Despite of plethora of laws, welfare programmes, growing activism, and with a historic legislation "The Child Labour (prohibition and Regulation) Act", 1986, the problem of child labour is growing in India. In fact, India has the dubious distinction of having the largest number of child labour in India. The broad contours of social injustice meted out to child labour and the resultant social exclusion deserves immediate attention for strategic policy formulation for achieving social inclusion. So, there is a need for fundamental changes in national laws, policies and practices to bring the tiny hands into the mainstream society.

The present paper has highlighted the various forms of social exclusion of child labourers and has forwarded various strategies for abolishing child labour in the Indian society.

Child Labour is a Social Construction

The term 'child labour' has always been a contestable term. Not a single definition of child labour is exhaustive and acceptable to all concerned, including governments, social scientists and non-governmental organisations. A universally accepted definition of child labour is not available because it is a social context, not a natural phenomenon, and social constructs are cultural ideas that differ between actors, histories, contexts and purposes (Ennew et. al., 2007).

The terms 'child', 'work', and 'labour' are not uniform concepts, their definitions are subject to change and variation. Wherever and whenever these terms are used inconsistently, confusion and contradiction will result. Different societies demarcate the threshold of childhood differently, according to age, legal status and custom. 'Work' does not necessarily equate with 'labour' although they are more often used interchangeably. The work children do to help the family in non-hazardous occupation and processes is different from the work done by a child in a production process on a waged (part-time/full-time) employment. In India, in the home–based industries, in the informal sector, in the areas of brassware, carpet, lack-making, fire-works even if children are apparently seen to be working to help in the family work, they cannot be categorised as working children, rather they are child labourers.

Definitions of child labour vary across time, nations and industries. They range from normative ones based on specifications of minimum age for employment; to education-oriented definitions which define any child out of school as child labourer or as a potential child labourer; to right-oriented definition which consider any work that deprives children of their fundamental childhood rights as constituting child labour (UN, 1998). At times, the definitions change contextually and depending on the situation and environment. The terms 'employed child' and 'working child' were used in the past to denote employment of child. Now, the term 'child labour' is standardised and replaced the above terms.

The Encyclopaedia of the Social Sciences (1963) describes the term child labour as "when the business of wage earning or of participation in itself or family support, conflicts directly or indirectly with business of growth and education, the result is child labour". In simple terms, child labour can be defined as work undertaken by a child, below a certain age, for gainful purpose within or outside the family.

Article 1 of the United Nations "Convention on the Rights of Child, 1989" (CRC) defines child as "every human being below the age of 18 years unless, under the law application to the child, majority is attained earlier". The Convention calls for protection from economic exploitation and from performing any work that is likely to be hazardous or to interfere with the child's education or to be harmful to the child's health or physical, mental, spiritual, moral and social development.

Flowing from the above, a distinction has to be drawn between child work and child labour. The term 'child work' and 'child labour' though used synonymously, have different meanings. The term 'child labour' is used synonymously with other terms like 'employed child' or 'working child'. In this sense, it is coextensive with any work done by a child for gain. It signifies employment of children in gainful occupations with a view to add to the household maintenance activities. In the definition of 'child labour' according to 1971 and 1981 Census of India, "the stress has been on the concept of main activity, i.e., on the economically productive pursuits in which the worker engages himself or herself for most part of the time". As for seasonal work such as agriculture and ancillary pursuits, the main activity of a person was defined with reference to his or her work during the year preceding the enumeration. Further, if a person participated in economically productive work, not as a main activity or for most part of the year, he/she is not treated as worker but as marginal worker. (Mishra and Mishra, 2004).

Children attending to some form of work as part of familiarisation and socialization without its effect on their education and recreation, which can be termed as child work, is different from that of child labour. A relatively workable and functional definition is provided by ILO (1996) according to which "child labour includes children prematurely leading adult lives, working long hours for low wages under conditions damaging to their health and to their physical and mental development, sometimes separated from their families, frequency deprived of meaningful education and training opportunities that could open up for them a better future".

Homer Folks (1946) of the United States Child Labour Commission defined child labour as "any work by children that interfere with their physical development and their opportunities for desirable minimum level of education or the needed recreation".

The Constitution of India calls for free and compulsory education for all children until they complete the age of 14 years. It also prohibits employment of children below the age of 14 years in factories and certain hazardous employments. The Census of India (1991) considers full time child labour as children below 14 years, whose main activity is economic and who have spent more than half the year (183 days or more) in economic activity.

Several Non-Governmental Organisations (NGOs) differ with the definition given by the Census and other government agencies and they believe that every child in the school age group and who is out of school is child labour. The Operations Research Group (ORG, 1993), Baroda, defines a child labour as "a child falling within 5 to 15 years age group and who is at remunerative work, may be paid or unpaid and busy any hour of the day, within or outside the family".

According to Encyclopaedia of Social Work (1997), a generally valid definition of child labour is presently not available either in the national or international context. Any definition turns upon the precise meaning we attach to the two components of the terms 'child labour' i.e., 'child' in terms of his chronological age, and 'labour' in terms of it's nature, quantum and income generation capacity. It defines child labour as that segment of the child population which participates in work either paid or unpaid.

According to the former president of India, V.V. Giri, the term child labour is commonly interpreted in two different ways; first, as an economic practice and secondly, as a social evil. In the economic sense, it signifies employment of children in gainful occupations with a view to adding to the income of the family. It is in the social context that the term child labour is now more generally used. In the social context, it takes into account the damages to which children are exposed, which means the denial of opportunities for development (Tripathy, 1996).

The Indian Factories Act of 1948, which is an elaborate and highly specific act relating to child labour, makes use of three different concepts to classify the workers, i.e., a 'child', a 'young person' or an 'adolescent' and an 'adult'. It has been made explicit in this act that a person below the age of 15 years is to be regarded as a child (Khan, 2003 cited in Nanjunda, 2008).

The word 'child labour' has also been defined variously in the multiple studies undertaken on the broad theme of child labour. In the study of working of children in Bombay, Singh (1991) and others have held a view that 'child labour' means a working child who is between six and 15 years of age, is not attending school during the day, is working under an employer or learning some trade as an apprentice. In the study conducted by Indian Council of Child Welfare (ICCW) in Delhi opines, 'every child below 14 years, who contributed to the family income or was treated as a full time/part time worker is a child labourer.' The diversity of opinion among researchers in defining child labour is due to differences in social perceptions.

Age is an important criterion for distinguishing child labour from adult labourers. In the context of child labour, in a working definition a child may be a person below the age limit of 15 years set by minimum age convention (1973). In a wider context, the UN Convention of the Rights of the Child (1989) set the age limit of a child at 18 years. In India, many labour acts have fixed the minimum age of employment. But the definition of child in terms of age differs from act to act. The Factories Act prohibits employment of children below the age of 14 years in factories. The limit in Mines Act is 15 years, whereas it is 12 years in Plantation Labour Act. The Child Labour (Prohibition and Regulation) Act, 1986, defines 'child' as a person who has not completed his fourteenth year of age.

Child Labour as Localised Phenomenon

Informal sector of the rural and urban economies of the developing countries is an important source of employment for a major chunk of labour force particularly child and women labour. Though the sect oral distribution of working children differs from country to country, yet child labour is predominantly confined to agricultural sector, followed by services and industry.

One of the unique features of the child labour system in India is the location specific nature of employment. Even though child labourers are spread all through the length and breadth of the country, some specific kind of occupations are observed in some areas only. For example, carpet industry is more common in Jammu and Kashmir, West Bengal and Uttar Pradesh. Working in the construction sites is found in every patch of the country. Glass industry is predominately found in Uttar Pradesh. Like that concentration of large power loom industry can be seen in both Tamil Nadu and Maharashtra state because of availability of enough raw materials and cheap labour. Children working in fishing industry are common all along the coastal areas of the country. Garage work and street children are found in many parts of the country. Dak, 2003 has given the following location specific occupations of child labour in India.

Table 1.1 : Location Specific Occupations of Child Labour in India

Glass and Bangles	*Firozabad (U.P.)*
Handloom	Tamil Nadu and Maharashtra
Power Loom	Maharashtra
Carpet Weaving	J and K, Uttar Pradesh and Rajasthan
Gem Cutting and Polishing	Jaipur (Rajasthan)
Diamond Cutting and Polishing	Surat (Gujarat)
Match and Fireworks	Sivakasi (Tamil Nadu)
Garages and Petrol Pumps	Throughout India
Cashew Processing and manufacture of coir products	Kerala
Helpers in Hotels, Restaurants, Canteen, Tea-Stalls, Shops	Throughout India
Rag Picking	Predominantly in Mega cities of the country
Construction	Throughout India.
Fishing	Kerala, Tamil Nadu, Gujarat
Pottery units	Khurja, (U.P.)
Hawkers, vendors and newspaper sellers	Throughout India.
Coolies	Throughout India.
Lock Industry	Aligarh (U.P.)
State Industry	M.P.

Evolution of Child Labour: Indian Context

Vidyasagar and Kumarbabu, 2002 had presented three distinct stages in the evolution of the institution of child labour with regard to India. These are:

(A) As far as the traditional Indian context was concerned, formal education had been the prerogative of certain communities in the upper layers of the society in the historical past. As per the hierarchy-based division of labour and inheritance of occupations, the children of peasants, artisans and other service communities were made apprentices in their family occupations, be it crafts or agriculture. It was considered part of the socialisation process for the children. So, the problem of child labour was persisted.

(B) It is after the industrial revolution in Europe and its gradual impact on the colonies that factory-type units started springing up during the British period. Factories required cheap and plentiful labour. Employment of children as labourers began because they were cheap, docile and uncomplaining. The factory owners could hence minimise costs and maximise profits. Along with modern factory type production, employment of children also emerged in petty commodity production that went to cater to the growing urban demand. Thus along with modern factories, manufacturing also developed in informal sector which could be termed as traditional informal sector (through agriculture remains to be one of the biggest traditional informal sector till date). In this phase, employment of children began, both in organised factory sector as well in the traditional informal manufacturing sector.

(C) From the seventies, as an impact of a strong labour movement which has been fighting for the rights of the workers and the resultant national legislation for regulation of labour standards, there has been a process of decentralisation of production from the organised sectors to informal sector, where the labour standards remain low and regulation is the least. This process has got intensified in the "new economic regime", where the liberation of the economy and linkage to the global markets are the key principles. In the present era, big factories are breaking into small units and the operations are spatially divided. Given the income and poverty levels of the people, ground for employment of children in large scale has been generated and is next only to agriculture sector.

Estimates of Child Labour- Global and National Level

As per the latest estimate of ILO in 2004, out of an estimated 317 million children in the age group of 5 to 17 years who are globally, engaged in some form of economic activity, 218 million fall within the strict definition of child labour. There are 216 million children engaged in hazardous occupations. In other words, more than 2/3rd of the child labourers are still engaged in hazardous form of child labour.

Table 1.2: Global Estimate of Child Labour

Age group (years)	*Economically active*	*Child labour*	*In Hazardous occupations*
5-17	317 million	218 million	126 million
5-14	190.7 million	165.8 million	74.4 million

Out of the estimated 190.7 million economically active children in the world, the Asia-Pacific region harbours the largest number of child workers in the age group 5-14 years. Whereas in Sub-Saharan Africa and in Latin America, these figures are 49.3 million and 5.7 million respectively.

Table 1.3: Global Trends in Children's Economic Activity by Region

Region	*Magnitude*
Asia and Pacific	122.3
Sub-Saharan Africa	49.3
Latin America and Caribbean	5.7
Other region	13.4

The consideration of age for being child labour is different in different nations. In India children below 14 years gainfully engaged physically or mentally in any occupation either in agriculture or in industry, are called child labour. The minimum age considered for child labour is 12 years in Egypt, 14 years in Philippines and Hong Kong and 13 years in Malaysia. In Peru, this age is 14 years in agriculture sector, 15 years for industry, and 16 years for ocean fishing and 18 years for working in ports. ILO in its minimum age (industrial) conference (1919) has determined 12 to 13 years for light works and 18 years for hard and dangerous works. Although the minimum age determined by ILO is 15 years, engaging the children anywhere below this age will be considered as child labour (Murthy).

India continues to host the largest number of child labourer in the world today. According to 2011 Census, 12.6 million children in the age group of 5 to 14 are employed in our country. This account for 11% of the workforce of India is child labour. If we compare 1971 onwards, the phenomenon of child labour has shown an increasing trend. The following table gives a comparative picture of the child labour phenomenon in our country over the different census period.

Table 1.3 : Child labour in India over Different Censuses

Year	*Number of child labour*
1971	10,753,985
1981	13,640,870
1991	11,285,349
2001	12,591,667
2011	12,626,505

Child Labour and Rehabilitation Paradox

It is irony that, despite the number of acts had been framed for protecting the rights of the children but still child labour problem had put an ugly face in India. Moreover, the employers without any fear flout the provisions of these legislations and very rare punished for violation of these provisions. There are distinct laws governing child labour in factories, in commercial establishments, on plantations and in apprenticeships. There are laws governing the use of migrant labour and contract labour. Apart from setting up various committees to look into the conditions of working children and suggesting measures to improve their lot, Government has passed various acts to minimise the exploitation of this most vulnerable group of the society. There were various legislations which regulate and prohibit the employment of children below the age of 14 years in factories, mines and hazardous employments and regulate the working conditions of children in other employments. However there is neither blanket prohibition on the use of child labour, nor any universal minimum age set for child workers. The inadequate legislation as well as insufficient enforcement, is also responsible for the continuation and perpetuation of child labour. Since independence, India has committed itself to be against child labour. It is very shameful that being the largest democracy in the world, has the most robust legal frame work for elimination of child labour, with the express commitment to ending child labour etched in its constitution. Year after year, a new piece of legislation is passed in India banning child labour in one industry and another (Mangla 2009). The child labour (Prohibition and Regulation act,1986) represents a half hearted attempt by the Government to deal with the massive problem, its aim is not to abolish child labour but only to prohibit its use in hazardous industries. Numerous investigations make it clear, however all employment is hazardous for children, and that they are regularly maimed, tortured or killed by accident or ill-treatment, in supposedly non hazardous occupations such as garment manufacturing, food production and domestic labour (Hensman 2001). But still today India witnesses alarming growth of child labour. The problem of child labour still remains as a major problem in India today. Despite various measures undertaken by the Government to tackle the exploitation of children, India has the dubious distinction of having the largest child labour force in the world. One of the major criticisms of the legislation on child labour is the lack of uniformity. The various Acts define child differently. This legislation does not conform to a single agreed minimum age. The minimum age differ from Act to Act, State to State and industry to industry. This is not only true of the definition of minimum age, but also of the working hours, rest periods, night employment etc. Another major defect of child labour related laws is that they prohibit employment of children only in hazardous occupations. But a large number of working children do not come under the term "hazardous labour" as they work in unorganized sector like agriculture, cottage industries etc. All these are in inferior conditions and are unsuited to their physical development (Weiner, 1996). And also the legislation does not fail to include new hazardous occupations nor is it clear what criteria will be used for defining what is hazardous (Burra, 1986; Fernandes, 1986). Quantitatively, more than 80 per cent of child labours work in farms and roadside tea stalls. The Child Labour (Prohibition and Regulation) Act of 1986 emphasises regulation rather than prohibition of child labour. Again Section II of the 1986 legislation stipulates that a register must be maintained of all children employed in the establishment and this register will be scrutinised by inspectors. But the stipulation only applies to children employed on regular basis. Since most of the children are employed on casual basis, these children do not show up in official registers. Also, the provisions do not apply 'to any establishment wherein any process is carried on by the occupier with the aid of his family' and taking this advantage employers show the work as domestic business. Again a major proportion of the girl child workers do not come under the definition of child labour because most of the girl child workers are because they are mainly confined to domestic sphere which is normally invisible. Moreover, the governmental machinery to implement these laws is inadequate. All these reasons are responsible for the failure of child labour legislations in India.

Issues on Social Exclusion and Child Labour

Child labourers are not only deprived of proper food, shelter and other necessities, but also deprived of basic rights. They endure miserable and difficult lives. Most of them earn little and struggle to make enough to feed themselves and their families.

The specific deprivations accruing to the child labour include:

- Deprivation in health care.
- Deprivation from psychological support.
- Deprivation from recreational opportunities.
- Educational deprivation.
- Exclusion from future employment.
- Deprivation from social security.

Deprivation in Health Care

The health of the child labour is always endangered. Their health status becomes more vulnerable due to high incidence of malnutrition and undernourishment. The child labourers suffer from various infectitious diseases including tuberculosis, anaemia, asthma, skin diseases, ear and eye problem etc. There are ample incidences of sexually transmitted diseases among child labour. Most of the child labourers are also addicted to drugs. They are deprived of basic necessities like immunisation, protection from job hazards, proper ventilation, toilet facilities, protection from sun and rain and proper lightning. The study done by Sampa Mitra (1993) on health condition of child labourers in a small scale leather industry in Calcutta revealed that three specific health problems prevalent among employed children namely low backache and ankle pain, doziness and tingling pain in hands. In *bidi* industry child labourers are exposed to tobacco fumes throughout the day which leads to asthma, tuberculosis, continuous cold, backaches, body ache, gastric, piles and rheumatic complaints (Naïdu and Kapadia, 1985). In the bangle industry and glass industry children work close to the pumices where the temperature ranges from 40 to 45 degree centigrade. Owing to extreme heat and chemical fumes, the incidence of tuberculosis is widespread which reduces their life span. They are unable to do work after the age of 35 years (Burra, 1986). In brassware industry, due to inhaling of metal dust child labourers suffer from several respiratory diseases. In diamond cutting industries of Surat, diamond polishing industries of Jaipur and in *Zari* embroidery worker of Lucknow, children work in ill-ventilated, badly lit rooms where their eyesight get affected (Rao, 1980). In the lock industries of Aligarh and metal industries of Moradabad, Varanasi and Delhi, children work on hand presses, buffing machine, electroplating and spray painting units. Here the chemical fumes affect their respiratory systems and white-hot flames damage their eyesight. The children reported giddiness and tiredness, which influence their working capacity (Pati, 1985). The child labourers are also victims of constant threat of traffic accidents. (Joshi, 2006, Nongia, 1987). Contact dermatitis is a health hazard seen in children working in processes where chemicals are used. Alkalosis, So dalities and permanent spinal deformities have been attributed to abnormal posture, which the child labourers have to adopt while working. Most of the child labour is highly vulnerable to all kinds of child abuse especially physical abuse, sexual abuse, police abuse, etc. (Sekar, 2007).

Deprivation from Psychological Support

A large number of working children face the unhappy reality of increasing separation from their natural families. Many of them have the feeling of insecurity, inferiority and low self esteem and fatigue. A large number of child labourers also suffer from various kinds of neurotic disorders particularly anxiety, depression, etc. Children who are in risky job fields have no opportunity to build their natural psychosocial health. Long working hours breed their feeling of frustration and inadequacy. Their involvement in risky work resists eventually in building their emotional cognitive skills and they become withdrawn, introvert and uncommunicative. A significant portion of the child labourers are suffering from psychological immaturity and are affected by abnormal psychological growth. They are also deprived of the special care that would be required for their psychological effects (Nasiruddin et. al., 2009). Reddy and Ramesh (2002) in their study reported that the child labourers are deprived of love, affection and sympathy which results in development of the feeling of inferiority and insecurity further leading to the development of fear and anxiety. The development of children and adolescents growing up in adverse circumstances lag behind peers from more advantaged homes (Misra and Mohanty, 2000) and experience a unique set of psychological barriers to change and development (Sinha,1990, Arumani, 2000).

Deprivation from Recreational Opportunities

Working children are unable to participate in leisure and recreational activities, and, therefore, lose the psychological benefits otherwise needed for them. So, most of them child labourers develop a habit of smoking, and liquor drinking. Some of them also become drugs addicts or spend time in gambling and other such criminal activities. Mishra and Mishra, 2004 in their study reported that the child labourers get very less spare time. But whatever spare time they get, they try to utilise it in the best possible manner. Their study reported that a majority of the child labourers watched movies during their spare time and some of them also spent their time in playing *ludo*, carom or cricket. Singh, 2006 in his study reported that a majority of the child labourers spent their leisure time in playing with their friends and some of them also spent their time in watching television. Jeyaranjan (2001) in his study reported many children also pooled their money to hire a vehicle and go for excursions during the weekly holidays. But unfortunately, because of their access to cash, many of them had started drinking at a very early age. Since most of the child labour households had a television at home with a cable connection, many children spent their late evenings before these television sets.

Educational Deprivation

Child labourers are deprived of the educational and vocational facilities otherwise available to the non-working children. Child participation in labour force clearly reduces the potential for schooling and educational development. Children from poor families obviously do not have much access to education as those from wealthier families. Even where educational facilities are available to children, such children cannot take sufficient advantages of them because of lack of interest of their parents. The chances of benefitting from education diminish more when they work. Most of the child labourers cannot go to school or are bound to leave the school before time (Shandilya, 2006). So, the childhood is lost because of economic concerns. The education provided in government run schools are irreverent to contemporary needs and changing economic situations. The formal education that is provided to child labour does not match the needs of the local labour market. Therefore, the child labourers further lose interest and remain deprived of educational opportunities.

Exclusion from Future Employment

A large number of children end up working as domestic workers on low wages and facing unhealthy living conditions. The unrelenting poverty forces the parents to push their children in all forms of hazardous occupations. Child labour is a source of income for poor families. Sometimes children are abandoned by their parents or sold to factory owners. The last two decades have seen tremendous growth of export based industries and mass production factories utilizing low technologies. They try to maintain competitive positions through low wages and low labour standards. The child labourers exactly suit their requirements because of lack of education. Given the low educational achievement, the possibility for acquiring remunerative jobs becomes still more remote. Children thus finds themselves locked in unskilled, low paying, unpleasant and unsafe work situations and permanently disadvantaged in the labour market (ILO, 1983). In India, a majority of children work in industries, such as cracker making, diamond polishing, glass, brass-ware, carpet weaving, bangle making, lock making and mica cutting to name a few. Ultimately the poor health status coupled with lack of education and training, they are deprived of future employment.

Deprivation from Social Security

The child labourers are not covered by various social security measures, which operate largely through formal sector employment. Reasons for their exclusion from these systems include the practical difficulties of collecting contributions from them and their employers, their unwillingness or inability to pay contributions (especially when the benefits on offer do not match what they consider to be their most important needs, in particular for health care) and their destruct of the management of the formal schemes. Child labour headed families are especially difficult to reach through formal social protection systems and welfare, particularly because of lack of proper official identities.

Recommendations for Abolition of Child Labour and Implications for Social Work Interventions

Child labour is a complex socio-economic demographic problem which can be reduced and eliminated by multiplicity of actions, both by government, public, voluntary organisations as well as at the individual levels. On the basis of the research findings and exposure during the course of research, the followings recommendations are made for the abolition of child labour.

Promoting Income Generation Activities

- Child labour is rooted in poverty. The progressive elimination of this problem is possible through improvement in the income distribution and social awakening. The income disparity can be removed by providing better employment opportunities to the lower stratum of society through creation of more jobs, agrarian reforms, and enforcement of minimum wages, social security, and pension to agricultural workers.
- Self employment schemes should be intensified. Beneficiaries of these programmes must be carefully selected to include those poor families who have child labour. These beneficiaries must be provided social security including medical and sickness benefits.
- Poverty alleviation programmes should be strictly implemented. Efforts should be made to attack the problem of poverty from all sides by sincerely implementing all the anti poverty alleviation programmes.
- The various studies have observed that the parents are compelled to send their children for jobs only because they had to fulfil their basic needs and to repay the loans. These sections of the society must be provided with easy and cheap

loans returnable in small instalments. These types of facility can solve the problem to the large extent because the loan is a big compulsion on the parents.

- Though a large chunk of the rural population still depends on agriculture, this sector should be developed in a proper way as it provides employment to a sizeable population. Poor families having child labour should be provided free fertilizer, insecticides and seeds. In rural area, investment in better irrigation, credit and market facilities should be made available. So that rural people can get more out of their land. The dairy and fisheries development programme must be given importance. Agro based industries should be promoted to all possible extent for income generation among the rural people.
- Rural cooperatives/ Self Help Groups should play a more vital role by giving loans, help in procuring raw materials and in marketing so that it will add to their income. The small-scale industries should be promoted on a large scale for reducing unemployment among the adults.

Providing Social Safety Nets/Social Protection Schemes

- Unemployment allowance, old age pension schemes should be properly and fairly implemented. Benefits should reach genuine and needy people. Systems of social protection provided by the state or non-state agencies must be carefully designed and implemented. Microfinance schemes, organized by civil society groups at the local level can be linked into larger structures, such as banks. The state can help by providing start up funds, and develop a supportive legislative and regulatory frame work.

Providing Educational Opportunities

- School represents the most important means of drawing children away from the labour market. School provides children with guidance and the opportunity to understand their role in the society. So, top priority should be given to universalisation of elementary education for children between 6 to 14 years within a time frame not exceeding more than 5 years. Along with general education, vocational training should be imparted to the children to make them economically independent in their adulthood. Apart from that, to increase the interest towards schools, handsome incentives should be provided to children of the socio-economic backward classes in the form of scholarships, free books, stationery, dresses and nutritious meals for, at least, up to fourteenth year of age. These incentives would not only raise the literacy level but also provide opportunities for skill acquisition and better employment in adulthood.

- Flexible timetables and other forms of flexibility in education can also help to accommodate the needs of the child labourers and their families. Not only the child labour enrolled in school should be given regular guidance but also their parents should be given continuous advice, guidance and financial support for continuing education of their children because the poor economic conditions of parents very often make conflicting demands upon children between work participation and schooling. Thus, even the easy accessibility to schools doesn't increase the enrolment of children if their economic status of parents doesn't permit it. So, the parents belonging to low socio economic group should be motivated to send their children to school rather than to work place through education, publicity and propaganda.
- Since many parents involve their children in work because they do not understand and realise the significance of education, it is necessary to develop **education consciousness** among them by making use of all possible means especially by effectively organising adult education programme.
- It is suggested that the governmentshould intensify the steps to achieve cent percent literacy by undertaking adult education programme, which in turn will enable parents to realise the need and importance of education.

Awareness Generation

- Increasing public awareness is very much important for the elimination of child labour. A large number of persons are unaware of the unsafe working conditions in which children work and the repercussions of early employment on the child in particular and the society in general. There is need to arouse awareness among the child labourers, their parents and employers of the negative consequences of children's engagement in job. People, specially employers and the parents of the children should be made aware of the existing laws concerning child labour and the penalties imposed upon flouting them.

- The mass media have a critical role to play in communicating information about child labour. The information they convey can have a significant influence on public policy. Initiatives should be taken to ensure that child labourers get a fair and balanced hearing in the media. Mass media should be used giving regular information and running educational campaigns.
- Public lectures can also be organized with more emphasis on the problem and its repercussions. People, specially employers and the parents of children should be made aware of the existing laws concerning child labour and the penalties imposed upon flouting them.
- There is a need to bring consciousness among children so that they may be aware of their constitutional rights which is possible with the help of radio, television, spread of education and literacy campaign.
- Efforts should also be undertaken by the voluntary organizations to involve the local public and parents/guardians of child labour. So that they become aware of the efforts made by the government for the upliftment of child labour.

Strict Implementation of the Legislations

- The state governments have to take concrete step to strictly prohibit the employment of children in occupations, which have been banned under the child labour act. The state government must activate the law enforcement machinery to see that all the legislative measures are properly enforced. The enforcement machinery must be geared up to ensure effective enforcement of the child labour act and take effective steps to prosecute those who violate the act. There is a need to strongly view the violation of child labour laws as trifling offences. The need of the hour is to apply the provisions of legislations strictly so that the employers of the child labourers must be severely punished in case of their violation of child labour legislations.

- The legal system should be framed in such a way that the people violating this law may not be spared. The law can be formed in such a way that it may leave no loophole where the employer of the children may be left free.

Involving Local Governance Institutions

- Though child labour is a localized phenomenon, the *panchayats* and municipalities can play a potential role in the eradication of child labour in the form of local information, communication, and local monitoring and mobilisation.

Implementing and Supporting Fair Trade Labelling Initiatives

- There is urgent need to promote social labelling. Social labelling consists in putting a label on an item or in the shop where it is sold, which guarantees to consumers that the product has been manufactured without using child labour.

Encouraging Trade Unions

- The trade unions can play a very important role in the implementation of existing laws on the minimum age for admission to employment, minimum wages, working hours and rest intervals. Trade unions can work more effectively if they comprehend the physical and mental havoc the child labourers have to face, and the fact that child labour reduces adult wages as well as adult employment.

Encouraging the Role of Nongovernmental Organisations

- NGOs can also help vulnerable and marginalised groups, including child labourers, have their voices heard by government and other decision makers at local, national and even international levels.
- NGOs often have a comparative advantage in piloting and evaluating alternative strategies and interventions at community level. They have also played a vital role in advocacy for the elimination of child labour by publishing materials in

local languages and running training workers for staff of local partners.

- Community based organisations are often best placed to ensure that programmes to combat child labour are realistic and adapted to the local context. There is a need for formation of 'Community Surveillance Groups' which can play an active role in preventing the migration of children by identifying, monitoring and supporting "at risk" families and children.
- Nongovernmental organisations have to adopt emerging trends and new strategies to deal with the problem. There is ample literature and information available on the reasons which try to explain the genesis of child labour and the working conditions that prevail. It is now a challenge for the voluntary organisations to address the issue not just on the periphery but aim at structural reforms. Attempts like organising the unorganised sector, reforms in the primary education system, microfinance for the weaker sections and instilling process for community participation and ownership are some of the essential issues that NGOs would have to address at the outset because lack of such systems contributes heavily to the inflow of children into the workforce.

Provision of Proper Housing

- Proper housing is important for healthy growth, which, in turn, is necessary for higher efficiency. Lack of proper housing not only impairs the healthy growth of children, but also brings them in contact with undesirable elements leading to anti social and delinquent behaviours. In the urban areas, most of the working children stay in slums, which are devoid of proper water supply, sanitation and lighting arrangement, leading to an unhealthy growth. Therefore, provisions should be made for housing with basic amenities.
- In sum, there is an urgent need for attitudinal change, social awareness and aggressive campaign against the scourge of child labour. It should be our national obligation to ensure physical and mental development of these young ones with measurers for regulating and humanising child labour along with attack on poverty. The eradication of child labour must be an explicit objective of development discourse and must

be implemented with perseverance and a matter of priority. In the absence of proper development perspective, it is very difficult to prevent the child labour from the labour market. The elimination of child labour requires people's participation and cooperation from all sectors, i.e., from their families to the societies at large. The eradication of the problem is a long process, which requires intensive efforts on many fronts and also creation of general social awareness and needs cooperation of different sections. There is also the urgent need for political mobilisation to completely prevent the demand and supply of child labour. The basic strategy concerning child labour should be to gradually reduce and eliminate it through improving and enforcing legislation, promoting school enrolment and raising public awareness. The coordinated efforts of government and NGOs, employer and social workers through active public support can definitely help in ameliorating or controlling the problem from the state as well as from the country.

Role of Social Workers in the Abolition of Child Labour

- Social workers should provide guidance and counselling to the child labourers in confronting his problems and tackling them. Counselling is also needed for the families of the child labourers as well as those who are on the verge of sending their children to labour market. Counselling and guidance are also needed for those children who are poor in studies and are truants so that they are prevented from dropping out of the school and entering into the labour market.
- Social work intervention is necessary at the family level especially where the fathers are drugs addicts or unemployed. Voluntary agencies need to work closely with these families and provide counselling and referral services as per the need.
- Social workers should work with children to bring about a change from an essentially welfare-based, charitable approach to a more children-centred, rights based approach.
- The social workers should take systematic efforts to ensure that work places and communities remain child labour free by awareness raising activities by using participatory

approach involving employers, parents, and adult workers in the work places, community leaders, service providers and enforcement agencies. The social workers should ensure that the children withdrawn from work remain and complete the school and that new children do not enter work force. This can be done in the schools or educational centres, in the work places and in the children's communities.

- Social workers should focus on establishment of local child welfare and vigilance committees to oversee the welfare of the children in the community. The social workers should have participatory approach and actively involve the children, their parents, community leaders and teachers.
- The social workers should mobilise the media personnel/ journalist to respect the rights of the children when dealing with exploitation of children, and should encourage them to give ample coverage of child abuse.

Children-friendly schools can provide a safe learning environment, equitable access, and also recognition of children's rights and responsibilities. Social workers should use a multifaceted approach to prevent early dropout and involvement in job, by motivating parents, easing environment problems and bridging the gap between home and school.

REFERENCES

Burra, N. (1986) "Old Flaws in new Child Labour Bill", *The Times of India,* 7 Nov.

Misra, G. and Mohanty, K.A. (2000). Consequences of Poverty and Disadvantage: A Review of Indian Studies: K.A. Mohanty and G. Misra (editors), ***Psychology of poverty and Disadvantage***, Concept Publishing Company, New Delhi.

Mangla, A. 2009, 'Understanding Child Labour in India', *Perspectives in Work*, summer.

Nasir Uddin, M., Hamiduzzaman, M. and Gunter, B.G.(2009). Physical and psychological Implications of Risky Child labour : A study in Sylhet City, ***Bangladesh Development Research Centre,*** USA.

Nanjunda, D.C. (2008). Child Labour and Human Rights, A Prospective, Kalpaz Publications, Delhi.

Mishra, S.N., Mishra, S. (2004). Tiny Hands in Unorganised Sector, Shipra Publications, Delhi.

Jeyaranjan, J. A study of child labour in the knitwear industry of Thirupur, V.V. Giri National Labour Institute Research Studies, Series No. 024.

Hensmen, R. (2001). The impact of Globalization on employment in India and Responses from the formal and informal sectors, CLARA working paper No. 15, IIAS/IISG, Amsterdam, 2001.

Nangia, P. (1987). Child Labour: Cause-effect Syndrome, Janak Publishers, New Delhi.

Dak, T.M. (2002). Child Labour in India (eds.) Serials Publication, New Delhi.

Murthy, G.K., Rani, T.J. (1983). Wages of Child Labour, ***Yojana***, Vol. 27, Sl. No.18, pp. 12-14.

10

MARGINALITY DISCOURSE IN ARUNDHATI ROY'S *THE GOD OF SMALL THINGS*

A.K. Chaturvedi

Arundhati Roy's *The God of Small Things*, the Booker Prize winner of the year 1996, is a thought-provoking saga of conflict between the male and the female, the exploiter and the exploited. Roy's comparison between "*the laltain*" and "*the mombatti*" reflects her perception of the margins of modern society as pitted against the centre. Although the plight of those living their lives at the periphery of society has been a subject of discussion among the great thinkers, writers and social activists since centuries, the modern writers in particular are more sensitive towards the harsh realities characterising the living conditions of the marginalised section of modern society. Their aim behind exposing the morbid conditions confronting the marginalised is to create awareness about the repercussions of century old insensitivity to the socio-economic problems that blunt an all round growth of society. Among such writers, Arundhati Roy enjoys a prominent place for forcefully raising the issue of marginalisation in her debut novel which has become a phenomenon in the literary world. This paper aims to analyse her deep interest in issues concerning those who are being forced to stay at the periphery of society.

The *Ayemenem* House where the untouchable are not allowed entry from the front door represents the upper echelon of modern society. Pappachi having retired from the post of Entomologist, settles in the house along with his wife and daughter. He develops a grand garden near the house and maintains a car (Playmouth). His wife opens a pickle factory which considerably adds to his wealth. A large number of workers-touchable and untouchable-work in this factory to earn their livelihood. Velutha, the son of old servant Vellya Paapen, serves as a carpenter in the pickle factory and represents the periphery of *Ayemenem* society. Velutha's association with the *Ayemenem* House dates back to his childhood.

Velutha, along with his father, always goes to the *Ayemenem* House to deliver coconuts plucked from the trees. But they are never allowed to enter the room. They are not even permitted to touch things that a 'touchable touched'.[1]

The novelist has justifiably presented Velutha as God of small things, as a magician who "could make intricate toys—tiny windmills, rattles, minute jewel boxes out of dried palm reeds, he could carve perfect boats out of tapioca stems and figurines on cashew nuts."[2] (74)

Velutha, in the words of O.P. Mathur, evokes our admiration and sympathy for his strength and character in which he is superior to most of the characters of the higher classes.[3] Antonia Navarro-Tejero in her article 'Power Relationship in *The God of Small Things*' speaks of Velutha as "a skilful carpenter and indispensable at the factory by virtue of his way with machines."[4] Having peripheral status in the caste ridden feudal society of *Ayemenem*, Velutha does not speak but his body "exceeds subalternity."

In the first chapter of the novel Velutha appears twice—first in the imaginative mind of Rahel as "bare bodied and shining sitting on a plank, swinging from the scaffolding in the high dome of the church painting silver jets in a blue church sky" (5) and secondly as "a prisoner whose arms had goose bumps where the handcuff touched his skin." (31) Seeing him in this condition Bady Kochamma passes comments, "As you sow, so shall you reap." (31) In the second chapter entitled 'Pappachi's Moth', Velutha is shown as "a member of Travancore-Cochin Marxist Labour Union marching with a real flag in a white shirt and *mundu* with angry views in his neck." (71)

Velutha's forefathers had converted to Christianity to satisfy their basic need of hunger and escape the scourge of Christianity. They were given a little rice to eat and were called "Rice Christians." In lieu of conversion, "they were made to have separate churches, with separate services, and separate priests." (74) Later on, they felt cheated on being declared ineligible to government jobs because of being casteless.

This development proved like having to see your foot prints without a broom. Orworse, not being allowed to have foot prints at all." (74) Mammachi remembers a time in her girlhood when *Paravans* were expected to crawl backwards with a broom, sweeping away their footprints so that Brahmins of Syrian Christians would not defile themselves by accidentally stepping into a *Paravan*'s footprint. In Mammachi's time, *Paravans,* like other Untouchables, were not allowed to walk on public roads, not allowed to cover their upper bodies, not allowed to carry umbrellas. They had to put their hands over their mouths when they spoke, to divert their polluted breath away from those whom they addressed." (73-74)

He is allowed into the *Ayemenem* House to repair or install something. Mammachi thinks, "he ought to be grateful that he is allowed on the factory premises and permitted to touch things that the touchable touch." (60)

Although Mammachi is fully aware of the fact that Velutha is a skilled person, she treats him inhumanly like she treats other Paravans. On returning from Delhi she is surprised to find magical qualities in him. Impressed with his expertise in carpentry, she employs him as a carpenter in her pickle factory. An accomplished carpenter, Velutha has his own set of carpentry tools and a distinctly German design sensibility." (75)

He built *Mammachi,* a Bauhaus dining table with twelve dining chairs in rosewood and a traditional Bavarian chaise longue in lighter jack. For Baby Kochamma's annual Nativity plays he made her a stack of wire-framed angels' wings that fitted onto children's backs like knapsacks, cardboard clouds for the Angle Gabriel to appear between, and a dismantle able manger for Christ to be born in. When her garden cherub's silver arc dried up inexplicably, it was Dr Velutha who fixed its bladder for her. (75)

Mesmerized with Velutha's skill in carpentry and mechanical work, Mammachi often said that if only he hadn't been a *Paravan,* he might have become an engineer. Driven by his aptitude for mechanical work, he mends radios, clocks, water-pumps and looks after the plumbing all the electrical gadgets in the house. For his interest and expertise in mechanical work the novelist appreciates him, when Chacko resigned his job in Madras and returned to *Ayemenem* with a Bharat bottle-sealing machine, it was Velutha who reassembled it and set it up. It was Velutha who maintained the new canning machine and the automatic pineapple slicer. Velutha who oiled the water-pump and the small diesel generator. Velutha who built the aluminum sheet-lined, easy-to clean cutting surfaces, and the ground-level furnaces for boiling fruit. (75-76)

Mammachi and Baby Kochamma, the major female characters besides Ammu, represent the section of society that is excessively biased against the underprivileged. Velutha being the son of their old servant is hated by both. In spite of being a skilled carpenter having commendable expertise in mechanical work, Velutha is not allowed to touch the things the touchable touch. The wages being paid to him for his labour are lower than what are being paid to the touchable workers for the same work.

The moment she gets to know that Velutha has committed a serious crime against her family by breaking the law of love, he expels him from service and files an FIR on the false ground that he is responsible for the drowning of Sophie Mol. Mammachi tries her best to ensure that Velutha should be punished severely for having violated the social norm under which an untouchable cannot touch anything that the touchable touch. With FIR lodged against Velutha, the Police Inspector contacts the local communist leader, K.N.M. Pillai with an intention to take him into confidence before taking action against Velutha. Velutha's plight intensifies with K.N.M. Pillai's revelation of his prejudice against the untouchable. He tells the Inspector that Velutha does not enjoy the patronage of the Communist Party. Consequently, the Kottayam Police feel free to deal with the case concerning an untouchable in the manner they like.

Having been invited by Mammachi, Velutha reaches the *Ayemenem* House to face the wrath of two women burning with anger due to his having violated the law of love. On seeing Velutha at the gate, Mammachi starts uttering harsh words and even goes to the extent of spitting on his face. Not satisfied with this, she threatens to get him killed if he shows his face ever in the *Ayemenem* House or the factory. Showing his tolerance, Velutha remains silent through the whole of Mammachi's outburst, bears insult with equipoise born of extreme provocation. While returning from the *Ayemenem* House, Velutha, shocked and smudged with dejection, feels the bombardment of horrible thoughts in his mind and shower of rain on his body.

Though the rain washed Mammachi's spit of his face, it didn't stop the feeling that somebody had lifted off his head and vomited into his body. Lumpy vomit dribbling down his insides. Over his heart. his lungs. The slow thick drip into the pit of his stomach. All his organs awash in vomit. There was nothing that rain could do about that. (286)

With his heart heavy with morbid thoughts of dejection and grief, Velutha having no other support to look towards turns to the house of K.N.M. Pillai and knocks at his door in the hope of getting succour from the leader of the party of which he is a committed worker. Aware of Velutha's predicament, Mr. Pillai extends a cold response to the card holder of his party, creates shock waves in the mind of Velutha by saying, "But, comrade, you should know that Party was not constituted to support workers' indiscipline in their private life." (287)

Pillai's rudeness adds to Velutha's, sadness. Dejected, he returns from Pillai's residence with broken heart and turns towards the river like a beaten dog. With nobody to support him financially or politically, he is subjected to face the trauma of being charged with the murder of Sophie Mol. Accused of the serious crime, Velutha is caught by the policemen while lying asleep in a corner of the back *verandah* of the History House. The policemen wake him with their boots and start beating him cruelly. The brutalities they inflict on Velutha stun Rahel and Estha to the extent that they are bewildered and nonplussed. As the novelist puts it, "They heard the thud of wood on flesh. Boot on bone. On teeth. The muffled grunt when a stomach is kicked in, the muted crunch of skull on cement. The gurgle of blood on a man's breath when his lung is torn by the jagged end of a broken rib."

Blue-lipped and dinner-plate-eyed, they watched, mesmerized by something that they sensed but didn't understand, the absence of caprice in what the policemen did. The abyss where anger should have been, the sober, steady brutality, the economy of it all. (308)

Impelled by feelings of "contempt born of inchoate, unacknowledged fear, civilization's fear of nature, men's fear of women, power's fear of powerlessness (308), the policemen subject Velutha to multiple physical injuries and leave him "smashed and broken".

His skull was fractured in three places. His nose and both his cheekbones were smashed, leaving his face pulpy, undefined. The blow to his mouth had split open his upper lip and broken six teeth, three of which were embedded in his lower lip, hideously inverting his beautiful smile. Four of his ribs were splintered; one had pierced his left lung, which was what made him bleed from his mouth. The blood on his breath bright red Fresh frothy. His lower intestine was ruptured and haemorrhaged, the blood collected in his abdominal cavity. His spine was damaged in two places, the concussion had paralyzed his right arm and resulted in a loss of control over his bladder and rectum. Both his knee caps were shattered. (310)

Like Mammachi, Baby Kochamma develops deep rooted contempt for Velutha after the revelation of his relationship with Ammu. To confirm whether the Kottayam Police have taken action against Velutha or not, Baby Kochamma visits the Kottayam Police Station where she is informed that the *Paravan* had been badly injured in the encounter and in all likelihood would not live through the night. The Police Inspector reveals to her the fact that in case Velutha dies of physical injury, she will land in trouble. To avoid her trouble, she makes Estha give statements so as to prove Velutha's act of murdering Sophie Mole. Here, Estha is stunned to see the brutality inflicted by the Policemen on Velutha. As the novelist puts it,

"He was naked, his soiled *mundu* had come undone. Blood spilled from his skull like a secret. His face was swollen and his head look liked a pumpkin, too large and heavy for the slender stem it grew from. A pumpkin with a monstrous upside-down smile. Police boots stepped back from the rim of a pool of urine spreading from him, the bright, bare electric bulb reflected in it. Dead fish floated up in Estha. One of the policemen prodded Velutha with his foot. There was no response. Inspector Thomas Mathew squatted on his haunches and raked his Jeep key across the sole of Velutha's foot. Swollen eyes opened Wandered." (319-320)

Velutha's father Vellya Paapen is "an Old World *Paravan*" who has seen the "Crowling Backward Days". For giving him succour during his difficult times, Mammachi is held by him in high esteem. His gratitude towards her is as deep and wide as a river in spate. When his eye was injured, he had borrowed money from Mammachi for treatment. As he failed to repay the debt due o financial crunch, he thought that his eye was not his own. For his eye sight he feels greatly obliged to Mammachi and always remains prepared for whatever she expects of him. Moved by his sense of gratitude, Mammachi employs his son Velutha as a carpenter in her pickle factory and puts him in charge of general maintenance. The touchable factory workers get offended on Velutha's entry into the factory as a carpenter. To appease their anger, Mammachi pays Velutha less than a touchable carpenter gets. Velutha's continuation as a factory carpenter despite the touchable carpenters' opposition is taken by Mammachi as her great contribution to the well being of a *Paravan.*

Although Vellya Paapen is not at all happy with Velutha's spirit of protest against the upper caste people, he does not openly oppose his son for being offensive in his attitude. But one day terror takes hold of him when he sees his son with Ammu. Unable to bear to see his son touching an upper caste woman, Vellya Paapen, horrified and petrified, with his eye on his palm and heavily drunk hurries to the *Ayemenem* House, begins to shed tears from the empty eye sockets before Mammachi and reveals unhesitatingly and grievously all that he has seen. Having heard Paapen's words, Mammachi's anger reaches its climax with the result that she shudders "like a child being force fed spinach." (78) Present in the adjoining room, Baby Kochamma overhears the dialogue between Mammachi and Paapen. Unable to digest what she has heard, Baby Kochamma outbursts, "How could she stand the smell? Haven't you noticed, they have *a* particular smell, these *Paravans*" (78)

Driven by her sense of hatred coupled with ego, Mammachi abuses Vellya Paapen and treats him inhumanly. As the novelist puts it, "suddenly the blind old woman in her rickrack stressing gown and her thin grey hair plaited into a rat's tail stepped forward and pushed Vellya Paapen with all her strength. He stumbled backwards, down the kitchen steps and lay sprawled in the wet mud. He was taken completely by surprise. Part of the taboo of being an Untouchable was expecting not to be touched. At least not in these circumstances. Of being locked into a physically impregnable cocoon". (256)

For having committed a crime by giving birth to Velutha, Paapen is treated by Mammachi in a manner an animal is treated. In a fit of rage she shouts, "Drunken dog! Drunken *Paravan* liar!" (256)

Baby Kochamma does not lag behind Mammachi in humiliating Paapen for being the father of Velutha. Toeing the line drawn by Mammachi, Baby Kochamma spits on Paapen, "lying in the slush, wet, weeping, groveling. Offering to kill his son, to tear him limb from limb." (256) The reason why she grows so furious is her worry about the prestige of her respectable family that has been spoiled by a *Paravan*.

As the novelist reveals, "For generations to come, forever now, people would point at them at weddings and funerals. At baptisms and birthday parties. They'd nudge and whisper. It was all finished now." (258)

Another minor character, besides Vellya Paapen, who grievously bears the scourge of peripheral existence is Velutha's elder brother Kuttappen, an uneducated and handicapped young man perennially experiencing the physical infirmity caused by an attack of paralysis. All the time bed ridden, Kuttappen cannot expect anybody to make arrangement for his treatment. He sadly spends his time while lying on the cot and "listening to silence of huddled trees with only a domineering black hen for company." (206) His mother died of tuberculoses which could not be cured due to extreme poverty. Having no hope of a better life, Kuttappen lies alone waiting for the coming of death in the corner of the room in which his mother faced death. With nobody to look after him, he is shifted to the ominous corners of the room so that death may not take much time to reach the destined place. This room has "one corner for cooking, one for clothes one for bedding rolls, one for drying in." (207)

Thus, Velutha and his family stand for the periphery of *Ayemenem* society. While Velutha represents the modern downtrodden class gifted with the spirit of protest against the prevailing conditions that are hell bent upon crushing their ambitions to rise, his father Vellya Paapen belongs to the community of "Old World *Paravans*" who were excessively submissive, tolerant and loyal to their heartless masters. In order to better his life Velutha develops in himself an expertise in carpentry and mechanical work and serves the Communist Party as its committed card holding member. Despite his technical abilities that helped Mammachi a lot in successfully running her pickle factory, he is paid less than touchable workers and is dismissed immediately for touching a woman belonging to the touchable community. The Communist Party to which he has been unshakably loyal for long does not give him protection in his difficult time. On charges of the murder of Sophie Mol, Velutha is arrested by Kottayam police, treated like an animal and is beaten to death. He is a promising young man who having his roots in the downtrodden class is doomed to live his life on the periphery of *Ayemenem* society, inhumanly treated by Mammachi and Baby Kochamma, humiliated and hurt by K.N.M. Pillai and crushed to a tragic end by the Kottayam Police. "This untouchable master craftsman floats on the periphery of society yearning to be accepted, confided and recognised like O' Neil's Black protagonist, Yank in the Hairy Ape."[6]

NOTES

1. A Prasad, Amar Nath and Gaijan M.B. (ed.) *Dalit Literature: A Critical Exploration.* New Delhi: Sarup and Sons, 2007, p. 253.
2. *Ibid.,* p. 257.
3. Mathur, O.P. *New Critical Approaches to Indian English Novel.* New Delhi: Sarup and Sons, 2001.
4. Khan, Tabish "Can the Subaltern Stand (and Smash2)" *World Literature Written in English,* 38:2 (2000), 161.
5. Roy, Arundhati. *The God of Small Things.* New Delhi: India Ink Publishing Pvt. Co. Ltd.

   1998.(All textual references with page numbers within brackets are from this edition.)
6. Roy, Amitabh, *The God of Small Things: A Novel of Social Commitment.* New Delhi: Atlantic Publishers and Distributors, 2005, p. 119.

11

CARPENTARIA : A COLLAGE OF IDENTITY, ETHOS AND ETHNICITY

Pradeep Trikha

Carpentaria is a collage of aboriginal culture, identity and ethnicity, is Alexis Wright's second major fictional work. Her earlier novel **Plains of Promise** focused upon three generations of women and all of them resistant to male dominations and had missions of their own. **Carpentaria** on the other hand reconstructs a family history of Aboriginal men and women in grip of their heroic quests and struggles. It is a rubric cube of Aboriginal tribal life exemplifying the inherent coexistence of the human soul with the land and animal. Wright's male characters are edge dwellers and her women are on the periphery. She makes use of melodramatic elements such as mutual animosity of settlers and Aborigines, colonizers and colonized, landed and landless. In this regard **Carpentaria** comes closer to Carolin Leakey's **The Broad Arrow** (1859), Marcus Clarke's **His Natural Life** (1872), Xavier Herbert's **Capricornia** (1938) and **Poor Fellow My Country** (1975) and Christina's Stead's **The Man Who Loved Children** (1940), Xavier Herbert's **Capricornia** depicts dispossession of the Aborigines from northern Australia. Similarly, B. Wongar's **The Last Pack of Dingoes** (1993) exemplified the issues raised by Herbert's novels.

It is not surprising that **Carpentaria** comes packaged with positive reviews. The blurb of the Garamond edition claims that it is "an epic of the gulf country of the north-western Queensland." Michele Grossman enlists it as "the confident promise of a tale dominated by risk roguery and revelation". Another reviewer is of view that "Wright's story telling is operatic and surreal, a blend of myths and scripture, politics, and force". The characters are the ones who "...stand out like giants in this storm swept world". Liam Davison a contemporary novelist is zapped with Wright's inventiveness and humour. Morag Fraser, one of the five judges who chose the novel as the winner of the 2007 Miles Franklin Literary Award said that it is very original and very brave, a bit like creating Huckleberry Finn's voice. In the **Australian Book Review** Kate Mcfayden is impressed by the way Wright is able to incorporate an ancient story-telling technique into her novel, "Wright recognises the strength of the oral tradition as a satirical and ironic tool. The combination of storytelling on a mythic scale with the guile of the knowing look generates the energy required to drive this genius epic." Wright concurs with such perceptions and says, "A lot has been given to me by my people. They took time to teach me about who we are, and I wanted my book to return the honour." Carol Ferrier tells us that "...the novel is lyrical and poetic evocation of the age-old presence of the rainbow-serpent. The shifts in register produce a heteroglosia that is beautifully unified through a narration that is great confidence and authority."[1] Finally, Dr. Cathie Dunsford calls the book which works "...its way into your mind, heart, body and soul... you are taken on the vast epic journey peopled with eccentric and yet familiar characters because underneath their eccentricities, lie elements of all of us".[2] Another reviewer is of the view that there are several common denominators in Wright's novel and Hemingway's **Old Man and the Sea**.

Imagine Hemingway's **Old Man and the Sea** but make it decidedly contemporary, Australian and funny. Then, if you can, turn it around again and imagine that the old man is an Aboriginal man with the powers to navigate the seas, read the stars, and move with great bodies of water. This old man is Norm Phantom, a man wise in matters of the sea but sometimes foolish when it comes to love.

There are two ways of looking at the onslaught of reviews of **Carpentaria** – one is to dismiss them as a hyperbole and the other way is to read the novel diligently in order to look for justifications for the claims. Admittedly blurbs and reviews are of great benefit even though they are not Wright's words, but to some extent they justify the claim of the novel. They are literally the part of the novel because they capture the novel's thesis and direction. They are extensions of it and symptoms of its blind spots, as well as its strengths. They nicely summarise the novel's material and argument for the reader in a positive fashion.

As interesting are the reviews so is the cover image designed by Russell White's painting titled **"Morning Glory Over the Leichardt River"** (2005) superimposed with a rainbow serpent tattoo. Taken as a whole ambience of the cover image is a fusion of pinkish, greyish, bluish, golden colours lending it a soft feathery effect. "The Health of the eye", says Emerson, "seems to demand a horizon". It is the beauty of White's cover design that one never feels tired so long as one is able to see far enough. It is sheer nourishment to the eye as much as it is an enchantment for the reader to read the novel eagerly. The landscape oozes out parable of the Gulf of Carpentaria with a tattooed rainbow serpent. The natural scenery has a scriptural proclaim in it. It internalises the quest as enshrined in old romance and the growth of culture in nature in the form of the serpent which zigzags and spreads as the narrative of the novel progresses.

II

This paper will look for issues related to culture, identity and ethnicity in **Carpentaria**. An effort is made to show that it is the work of art which negotiates between the creator and her predecessors as well as the successors. As Stephen Greenblatt informs us, "The work of art is a product of a negotiation between a creator or class of creators, equipped with a complex, communally shared repertoire of conventions and the institutions and practices of society. In order to achieve the negotiation, artists need to create a currency that is valid for a meaningful, mutually profitable exchange. It is important to emphasize that the process involves not simply appropriation but exchange, since the existence of art always implies a return, a return normally measured in pleasure and interest.... Society's dominant currencies, money and prestige, are invariably involved, but I am here using the term 'currency' metaphorically to designate the systematic adjustments, symbolizations and lives of credit necessary to enable such an exchange to take place".[3]

Wright's **Carpentaria** is essentially a cultural text it is 'a work of art' which is equipped with unique complexities of identities, norms, values, modes of thinking and knowledge. Successfully, she includes and excludes those who have been marginalised in their meaning-game. In her schema of things she operates at different levels simultaneously like a seasoned craftsman. Hope and conflict in the lives of characters make the novel effervescent like a serpent at times and on other occasions serpentine like the river. It creates a Coleridge an aura of suspense and disbelief, the reader looses himself willingly in the coastal town of Desperance to find more about Phantom family, its conflicts and concerns, hopes and despairs. The family is perpetually in conflict with the white officials. The opening chapter, "From time immemorial" drags the reader to the gates of Armageddon.

The ancestral serpent, creature larger than storm clouds, came down from the stars, laden with its own creative enormity. It moved graciously – if you had been watching with the eyes of a bird hovering in the sky far above the ground. Looking down at the serpent's wet body, glistening from the ancient sunlight, long before man was a creature who could contemplate the next moment in time. It came down those billion of years ago, to crawl on its heavy belly, all around the wet clay soils in the Gulf of Carpentaria. (p. 1)[4] and again,

"The inside knowledge about this river and coastal region is the Aboriginal Law handed down where to look for the hidden underwater courses in the vast flooding mud plains, full of serpents and fish in the monsoon season? Can someone who did not grow up in a place that is sometimes under water, sometimes bone-dry, know when the trade winds blowing off the southern and northern hemispheres will merge in summer? Know the moments of climatic change better that they know themselves? Who fishes in the yellow-coloured monsoonal runoff from the drainages, with sheets of deep water pouring into the wide rivers swollen over their banks, filling vast plains with floodwater? They cyclones linger and regroup, the rain never stops pouring, but the fat fish are abundant." (p. 3)

Deliberately Wright gives symbolic dimensions to the journeys undertaken by the characters. Throughout the novel Norm Phantom, the protagonist is a displaced man, in search of his identity, striding against the time which is out of joint. Homelessness and homecoming are perhaps the most poignant issues in the novel. If journey offers them a prospect to recover themselves, homecoming too adds to the procedure. Wright intends to give it mythical proportions. Norm Phantom's homecoming too is a close parallel to archetypal adventures. Every *Odyssey* presupposes an *Illiad* - the return of Ulysses after twenty years of exile away in the Trojan War and the return of prospering to earth from Pluto's nether world. Such quests offer pursuit or self-realisation, adventure, exhilaration and ultimate transformation. In **Carpentaria** the landscape becomes a character, the characters like Norm and Will fight for it because they do feel that their land is a "paradise on earth" (55) and they never wanted to live anywhere else. Everything is in harmony for them.

So the 'edge' people, all of the backfill mob living with quiet breathing in higgily-piggerly, rubbish-dump trash shacks, all propped any old where in the prickly bushes, all along a cobweb of dirt tracks running crooked, left, right and centre outside of town, sat back and watched this spectacle of the snow man taking place on the beach. It was the beginning of the story of the day the spirits of the seas and storms mixed their business, and sent Elias from out of oblivion into Esperance with good reason. (p. 54)

For Norm, Will and Elias it was a source of nourishment for not only their eyes but even souls, the place which offered them everything they needed for their survival. They do not show any sign of being influenced by the white colonizers. For them their ethnicity must be preserved at all costs. On the other hand they initially tried to help them with their indigenous know how about nature, floods and cyclones. But soon Norm and Will realize their evil designs of entrapping innocent Aborigines, their wives and children in Christian religion. As a work of art ***Carpentaria*** may not touch upon any of the ethnicity theories but as a reader one feels free to explore the dynamics underneath the narrative which makes ethnicity a potent force. The issues like the role of history in the creation of ethnicity, relationship between ethnicity and culture, the dynamics of the relationship between ethnic identity and ethnic political organization are certain subjective categories which has foreboding of 'mistaken identity' as well as any negation of its parts on the whole has the danger of diffusing the central tension. Angel Day, Norm's wife falls into the entrapment of the white settlers so much so that she carries a statue of Mary which she repaints with Aboriginal colours, thus carrying Aboriginal Mary. Wright humorously suggests it is difficult to change the cultural patterns of Aborigines. Angel Day soon over comes here obsession, from 'hornet's nest waiting to be disturbed,' image she transforms into a sober and mature woman.

III

Yarn, texture and tapestry of the narrative in **Carpentaria** are none other than symbolic. The serpentine river which flows through Esperance on the East side towards the Gulf of Carpentaria corresponds to the creative power of both nature and of time. On the one hand it signifies fertility and the progressive irrigation of the soil and life and on the other hand it is a symbol of 'irreversible passage of time in consequence for a sense of loss and oblivion'.[5] As the novel progresses one tends to look for ways and means to decipher the mythical drapery of the novel. Rainbow-serpent is regarded as a creator and a source of fertility and is generally associated with life giving water. 'Aboriginal people have several stories about the rainbow serpent about its role in creation of rivers'.[6] Serpent is a symbol of force, of energy and at times of immortality. It also signifies hidden treasure. In Aboriginal art it has a mesmerising effect, it has a magnetic force and since it is capable of shedding its skin it also symbolises resurrection. Carl Jung once suggested that psychologically the snake is "a symptom of anguish in man's abnormal stirring in the unconscious".[7] For Jung and his followers it may symbolise anguish but for Aborigines it is a life giving force as it is in Indian Myths. One is reminded of Vishnu's *'Sheshnaag'* on whose head the Earth is placed and Vishnu himself is life preserver of the universe.

Norm Phantom undertakes to paint Aboriginal art from natural colours prepared from plants and rocks. He feels that colours "...were mixed using secret measurements of life and the pearl shell crushed into a fine powder". Pearl shell powder adds translucent glow to his paintings of fish. For Norm fishing was a passion, it was not just a sport. Symbolically, the passion for fishing signifies his penetrative powers of the unconscious. It amount the extracting the unconscious elements from deep lying sources in the words wisdom.

Persistently Wright makes use of allegorical network of places and persons apart from the aboriginal art. Desperance provides the settings to the novel- the place peopled with really desperate dare devils in whatever they do in life. The family of Phantoms has mysterious aura around itself. Two lead characters do not emerge as public figures during the course of the novel. Though Normal Phantom accomplishes Herculean tasks yet whatever he achieves is life like in dimensions, Will, his prodigal son has sheer fortitude of character to resist against the intruders to their territory. He combats against both the inner and the outer disorder and despair, searches his own way out for survival. Both Norm and Will undertake long river journeys but their experiences are poles apart,

Will began to chart the river course from the sea that might have been how Elias had brought his boat inland. Will knew this river backward, like the palm of his hand. The river and Will Phantom had many secrets to share. So, Will mapped the journey and stalled at the many gaps in the river where Elias would have stalled too, to catch his breath and to contemplate the boat which would not have made it through the narrow causeways, prevented by the jagged, petrified remains of the ancient trees, perhaps once fig trees, that had become rock. (p. 165)

And again, time was a fleeting whisper for Will sitting on the edge of the lagoon that had been carved by an eternity of rushing floodwaters inside the remains of a forest that lived a million years ago, and had, after a moment of shock when drowned by high seas, petrified into rock. Time accumulates thought or vice versa and Will Phantom, in no hurry to return home after years, since he had been travelling on sacred journeys, took his time deciding what he ought to do about pulling the boat in, until he felt a cold shiver of fear running down his back. Swiftly he glanced around, and in the silence nothing moved, except where a thudding of ancestral foot-steps was pounding loudly in his head, and his fear shifted, across to Elias in the lagoon. (p. 164)

'Entrapment' is a major theme of **Carpentaria**. It is a serious concern for Wright. She focuses on socio-economic entrapment of the marginalised, colonial world. Like Ashcroft, Griffiths and Tiffin[8] Wright deals with literal and figurative 'entrapment' in the novel. If on the one hand existence of Aborigines is entrapped in ethnic traditions, conventions, myths, ritual, superstitions and what not on the other those living in the Uptown they are 'entrapped' in greed of wealth, crass commercialisation, cut throat competition and other evils of the globalised world. Norm Phantom and his co-inhabitants, his family and tribe have no urge to come out of their century's old 'entrapment' of archaic Aboriginal existence. However, Will Phantom turns out to be a rebel; perhaps this makes him more lifelike and dear to all. His journey upstream has a sense of positive quest. His sense of searching gives shape to otherwise disorienting experience. He is one of those whom we may come across in a street like Dickensian character. His thoughts and feelings, probability of an event and response to it can be predicted or can be calculated. Unlike Norm, he discovers that there is no real place for him in this world. He looks at his 'entrapment' thus, 'Hope was not involved in anything, Jesus Christ. None of us had anything to do with the fires in town,' Will explained, as old Joseph watched him. 'It was that fucking mine did that, at it's their own money they wasted, so don't feel sorry for them. They never worried about us when they were riding roughshod over our right.' (pp. 378-379)

'We got to fight each other until one day we might get sick and tired of it.' What he really meant, Will knew, was that one side must give up and go away. It was the ultimate solution that neither side could revolve. Which would be the loser? It was the only way the fighting of the last four hundred years would finish. (p. 379)

This is the only reason that Will fights against all odds and has a sort of self-satisfaction or '*Swantayaâ-Sukhayâ*', but not at the cost of self-respect or *Aatma-Sammana*.

Besides this there are several narratives, incidents running on parallel lines yet meeting different endings. One such narrative narrates the life story of an outcast saviour of Desperance dwellers, Elias Smith. He reaches the Shores of Desperance accidentally, loses his memory, fights hopelessly to save himself but fails. He is equated to **Dreamtime** world. He even loses his memory and thus turns into a derelict. Elias dies in boat under mysterious circumstances. For the locals he '...had gone to the spirit world in the sky across the sea...' (p. 149). It is in the latter half of the novel Norm discovers that Elias had accidentally drowned himself. Norm takes his body in his boat '... and placed him into strangely calm emerald green waters'. Burial in water was a ritualistic practise at Desperance. Normal Phantom's father too had died in a similar fashion; both the deaths have sacrificial dimensions. They can also be seen as the desire for self-destruction in face of excruciating apprehension. For Elias as well as Norm's father death was not a predicament or pain it is deliverance, a kind of renovation, the progress of evolution. They lived for others and even in death their bodies were of some use to the sea animals.

Another dramatic event is that Norm carries Elias' dead body to the sea where, Elias sank deeper and deeper, gently through the giant arms of water waiting at every depth to receive him, until finally; Norm could see him no more. Then he knelt down in the water on the floor of his little boat, and prayed for Elias, and was thankful he had brought his spirit safely to his final resting place. (p. 253)

Immediately after the burial, Norm experiences a deep sense of fatigue, he feels surmounted by the emotion due to bidding the final farewell to his friend. He whispers his prayers and begins his journey homewards. He realises futility of human existence. He realises all his men and himself too were caught in a limbo to devour by the futile struggle of self-preservation. "His mind hung onto limbo, a delicate branch, as leafless as it was devoid of trust". Helplessness, seclusion, marginalisation, dislodgment, up-rootedness, although involving a variety of characters and situations are the essence and historical key references to the discriminating politics of control are the indigenous issues in Alexis Wrights **Carpentaria**. Therefore, it is 'the work of art' to use Greenbelt's phrase which negotiates between 'metaphors and symbols' of indigenous Australia.

Notes :

(a) **Aboriginal Identity:** During the recent decades Aborigines have begun to arrest their own sense of identity or Aboriginality against the definitions which white society has imposed upon them. Aborigines believe that white Australia has a black history. An introductory reader on this topic is **Images of Australia**, Gillian Whitlock and David Carter (eds) 1992, Victoria : University of Queensland Press is quite useful and handy.

(*b*) **Hetroglosia:** Perhaps the term is borrowed from the term used in Chemistry hetrolysis that is the formation of oppositely charged particles, the breaking of a chemical bond in a compound, producing particles or ions of opposite charge, e.g., the formation of sodium and chloride ions in a salt solution. The suggestion here is in the context of the characters and the setting in the novel.

(*c*) **Armageddon:** Battlefield described in the Bible in Revelation 16:16 as the scene of the predicted final struggle between good and evil. The name may be taken from that of the battlefield Megiddo (see Judges 5:19) in the Plain of Esdraelon, which was well known because of the many battles that were fought there between the Israelites and their enemies during the biblical period. Hence, the term has been applied to any great conflict or slaughter. **Carpentaria** centres on the conflict between the Gurfurrit mining company and the colourful people of Desperance. Wright says, "I wanted to show the high-calibre people who are working hard in the indigenous world, but who get forced into other things, especially policy fights with this government that tries to silence us". For all indigenous conflicts in the world whether it is Sardar Sarovar Dam giving rise to *Narmada Bachao Andolan* or more recently Nandigram conflict between villagers and the government. The nature of conflict is nothing but struggle between good and evil.

(*d*) **Ethnicity:** In contemporary scenario requires an engagement with various perspectives in order to comprehend its ever-changing contours. As a work of art ***Carpentaria*** may not touch upon any of the theories but as a reader one feels free to explore the dynamics underneath the circumstances which make ethnicity a potent force. Further the novel explores:

- ➢ role of history in the creation of ethnicity;
- ➢ relationship between ethnicity and culture;
- ➢ the dynamics of the relationship between ethnic identify and ethnic political organisation.

Any kind of subjective categorisation has a foreboding of 'mistaken identity', on one hand, whereas any negation of its parts on the whole has the danger of diffusing the central tension. To arrive at an understanding, which would broadly outline the framework, an interdisciplinary approach needs to engage with the political, racial and cultural overtones of the concept. The historical moorings of the term "ethnicity" often tend to argue that how the term is not only "on the move", (Glazer and Moynihan, 1975) but a term which is under constant fire. (Bank, 1996). It has been critically detailed by various schools such as – The Norway School, Soviet Ethnos theory – and finally the Manchester school. Keeping the various strands of anthropological constructions, vis-à-vis ethnicity in the backdrop, it is not the in preview of this paper to touch upon, debates like – Primordiality *versus* instrumentality/ circumstantialist. The basic thrust of this paper would be to reason out the since time immemorial the troika of patronage, protest and paranoia have coloured the understanding of the term, often leading to over nationalism on one hand and on the other, the rise of fissiparous tendencies undermining the process of nation building in both Australia and India as elsewhere.

(e) **Dreamtime:** It refers to a myth that Aborigines came across the sea from another place. So in the Djanggawal epic song cycle two sisters and brother came from somewhere far away, but the journey celebrated at the island of spirits – Braplu. This myth is called **Dreaming.** For Aborigines the myths are not fables. There is no concept of past or history. The past does the past of it. The Dreaming paths mapped out by the spirit beings continue to determine the life of Aboriginals. Dreaming has constant connectivity between people and land therefore it is creative and traditional. Thus they often say, "This is a place where the dreaming comes up, right up from inside the ground".

(Cited from: Seale Geoffrey, **From Deserts the Prophets Come**, Melbourne; Heinemann, 1973 p. 229.)

WORKS CITED

1. Carole Ferrier "The Best Australian Novel for Year" http://www.giramondopublishing.com
2. Cathies Dunsford http://www.giramondopublishing.com
3. Stephen Greenblatt 'Towards a Poetics of Culture', in H. Aram Vesser (ed) *The New Historicism*, New York : Routledge, 1989, pp. 1-14.
4. Alexis Wright *Carpentaria,* Sydney : Giramondo Publishing Company, 2006, p. 1. (Here after quotations from the text are indicated with respective page numbers)
5. J.E. Cirlot *A Dictionary of Symbols*, New York : Philosophical Library Press, 1962 p. 262.
6. Gwanda Beed Davey and Graham Seal *A Guide to Australian Folklore : From Nedkelly to Aeroplane Jelly* Sydney : Kangaroo Press, 2004 p. 219.
7. Cirlot, *op. cit,* p. 267.
8. Ashcroft, Griffiths and Tiffin *The Empire Writes Back : Theory and Practice in Post Colonial Literatures*, London: Routledge 1989. p. 19.

12

NEWLY EMERGING DEMOCRATIC INSTITUTIONS AND EMPOWERMENT OF THE MARGINALISED SECTION OF THE INDIAN SOCIETY: A TRANSITION IN THE PATTERNS OF INEQUALITY AND EXCLUSION OF TRIBAL AND DALIT

Renu Singh

Introduction

Democratic institutions are basically recognised as the instruments of people's rights and help in empowering and developing in them the ability to avail by themselves (empowerment) the government support package for their survival with the assertion and entitlement to them. Although we have democracy as the basic structure of governance but we have graded inequality in our society even after the six decades of independence which can easily justify the failure of democracy, if inquired from the perspective of equality and social justice that are considerable to check the successful working of democracy in a country. As Dr. B.R. Ambedkar has rightly referred in one of the speeches in the Constituent Assembly the contradiction between the democracy enshrined in the Constitution and inequalities in our society. Unless these contradictions were resolved, he said, democracy in India would be like a palace built of cow dung. The foundation may be sacred, but it may be feeble and shaky. He also asserted that to try to establish democracy or socialism in our country without attacking the caste system is pursuing a chimera.[1] Keeping this view in mind this paper basically focuses upon the significance of the extending arenas of the democratic institutions which are needed to be adopted for the efficient and inclusive exercise of existing institutions. This paper basically argues that along with the independent struggle and assertiveness of Dalit and tribals for their dignity and respect, the emerging institutions like RTI, RTE, active participation of Civil Society Organisations, concepts of social capital, public sphere along with the already existing democratic institutions (safeguards and special treatments) in one way or other are a helping hand to further empower them vis-a-vis help them to raise their voices. Further following the engagement with these institutions and transformation of the attitudes and orientations towards these institutions can enhance the momentum in the participation of the marginalised (embodies here Dalit and tribals) population and that may help in cultivating a better understand of the problems and issues that resist their development despite of having principles of inclusive growth and constitutional safeguards for their development and empowerment. This paper basically relates democratic initiatives and their multidimensional (social, political, economic, cultural) expansions as a concept that claims equality and prohibition of any kind of discrimination as its constituent elements and how innovatively it can enlarge the arena of the study of the marginalised to better understand their cause and misery along with their own efforts to avow their own rights. This paper is all about the analysis of the past and present of Indian democracy in special reference to inclusion and exclusion and changes in its approaches in dealing the challenges before. Although there is a difference in theory and practice of the laws against discrimination and atrocities against Dalit and tribals because of clumsy handling of these acts results in several acts of atrocities, humiliation and discrimination in the name of cast and identity go unnoticed and the culprit roams unpunished. Keeping in mind all these lacunae in the working of the early symbols of constitutional safeguards the situation has slowly and gradually been changing especially with the advent of globalisation and enhancement and inflow of Information and Communication Technology (ICT) initiatives in India. That has lead to device a link to reach the areas that have been kept neglected due to their geographical location and some due to internal disturbances.

Existing Democratic Institutions

"The democratic state in India is a historical product of very specific circumstances; as such the broader idea of democracy is not consistent with the specific Caste System. Therefore, there is serious juxtaposition between the institutional promise of democracy and the real practice of democracy in relation to the victims of the caste system, the Dalit. However, the caste-based hierarchical relations of dominance and subordination have provided sufficient conditions for the rise of Dalit consciousness and these objective conditions have transformed into the sites of democratic struggle when the Dalit are affronted with the real operation of liberal democratic principles of, equality, freedom, fraternity, and social justice. Caste conflict, thus, lies at the structural dimensions of Indian society in the form of exclusion, discrimination, and economic inequality. Inequalities based on the caste divisions are intrinsically antidemocratic, and the caste system as an oppressive ideology system represents the scheme of power, domination, privilege, and hierarchy. It's very foundation remains a central obstacle in the path of democratic redistribution of power."[2] Whether it is the case of central or local peace of development everywhere one can find caste based segregations and not any other criterion one can come up with. Despite of reservations in competitive examinations only a handful of Dalit and tribals have made a transition from underdeveloped conditionality's and modalities of life to the developed one. Although one cannot deny the low magnitude movements of Dalit and for tribals there is a list of significant number of movements/revolt from the pre independence movements designed around a particular leader. Naxalism/Naxalbari movements are the extension of these movements as a result of abolition of tribal rights to live in forest and mines rich areas. But the transitional phase that one can notice has begun in 1990s or with advent globalisation having a dynamic effect in their united effort not only nationally but globally also. These efforts have made the issues of social exclusion and social discrimination in the name of caste / identity a mainstream discourse world over. The democratic institutions that are gaining ground since 1990s are an instrument to transform Indian society, polity, and economy and even the more inclusive and participatory.

Inclusive Development and Exclusion of Dalit and Tribals

The inclusive approach is not a new thing for the world in general and India in particular. The approach, "There has been perceptions that globalisation and liberalisation policies which given more weight age to market have excluded many sections of the population. On the other hand, civil society organisations including NGOs are supposed to be following more inclusive approach although their actions may also be excluding some people. There are limits to economic analysis regarding inclusive approach. Non-economic factors like norms, culture, and beliefs can also influence the level of inclusion/exclusion. A simple cultural habit of some men sitting in the seats for ladies in Delhi buses is an example of excluding females from sitting on the bus seats. Similarly, social practices such as age old social norms, gender bias, religion, caste, and ethnicity can have positive and negative effects on inclusive approach. For example, social capital among different groups can improve inclusiveness. On the other hand, religious, caste, and gender discrimination can exclude many people. Thus inclusive approach is a much wider concept and goes beyond economic analysis. However, objectives or eve instruments of social and economic policies are more or less similar but mechanisms could be different in achieving goals."[3] "In Indian context we have to fall back upon Ambedkar's writings and post Ambedkar developments in literature on the issues of social exclusion. Ambedkar had developed arguments for equal opportunity policy, in terms of reservation, in the early 1920s through 1950s drawing mainly from the theoretical developments in political science relating to the concept of justice, and equal right during the period. A good amount of new writings has now appeared since Ambedkar developed his thoughts on the subject. These writings have further expanded the concept of social exclusion, its consequences and possible remedies. While the social science literature conceptualised general notion of social exclusion, the economists extended to the spheres of economic and market discrimination."[4] "Despite the fact that the strategies of SCSP and TSP have been in operation for more than 20 years, they could not influence all the concerned in its right perspective. Further, lack of effective monitoring to ensure that all the Ministries/Departments both at Central and State levels earmark funds under SCP and TSP and the funds received under SCA are utilised effectively and purposefully, is another area of concern.[5] For inclusive development not only inclusive economy is sufficient, inclusive policy in relation to education, health, justice and empowerment the each and every individual as a significant part of the society as a whole. Right from the adoption of the planning Commission and later on the NDC the emphasis has always been on the development of the village and rural people as a part of inclusive development but there has been very less achieved so far as a part of inclusive policy. "After 11 five year plans and about three and a half decades of SCP, most of the SCs are continue to be agricultural labourers and have limited access to education, and are subject to rampant untouchability, atrocities and bonded labour. In urban areas they are mostly engaged in precarious unorganised casual labour and sections of them are still subject to scavenging and other *safai* labour. Their habitations continue to be most uninhabitable"[6]

Existing Democratic Institutions and Inclusion: Dalit and Tribals

"Article 17 of the Constitution of India abolishes the age-old phenomenon of "untouchability". Article 17 is basically a "statement of principle" that needs to be made operational with the ostensible objective to remove humiliation and multifaceted harassments meted to the Dalit and to ensure their fundamental and socio economic, political and cultural rights. In order to effectively do so, nearly six years after the Constitution came into force the untouchability (Offences) Act, 1955 was drawn up. However, lacunae and loopholes impelled the government to project a major overhaul of this legal instrument. From 1976 onwards the Act was revamped as the Protection of Civil Rights Act. Despite various measures adopted to improve the socio-economic conditions of the SCs and STs they remain vulnerable and are subject to various offences, indignities and humiliations and harassments. When they assert their rights and against the practice of untouchability against them the vested interest try to cow them down and terrorize them."[7] The Scheduled Castes / Scheduled Tribes (Prevention of Atrocities) Act", promulgated in 1989, and "The Special Component Plan for Dalit", evolved in 1980, were hoped to become powerful instruments towards the process of empowerment of Dalit in the country, in socio-political and economic spheres. These two provisions, if genuinely implemented, would have gone a long way in the path of the long-dreamt socio-economic liberation of Dalit in the country. Unfortunately, the hope remains just that, betrayed by a combination of castes perceptions, lack of political will and bureaucratic hurdles."[8] The Protection of Civil Rights Act, 1955. The Scheduled Castes and the Scheduled Tribes (Prevention of Atrocities) Act,1989. Constitutional /Statutory/ Apex Bodies like National Commission for Scheduled Castes. National Commission for *Safai Karamcharis.*[9] Has been established under the ministery of Social Justice and Empowerment. These are the conventional democratic institutions but they are more or less inefficient as far as their actual work is concerned. Many cases against the weaker section go unnoticed; several rape cases with the tribas and Dalit women hardly come to the even notice of these institutions. There is list of cases of discrimination with these people. Sometime the village dominant class ask them to shut up and sometimes the institutions of low themselves zip their office to even record the complained and this shows the kind of disempowerment and harassment of Dalit and tribals generally happen.

The Schedule Tribes (ST) constitutes 8 per cent of the total population of the country. In 2001 their number was around 820 *lakh* persons. They can be divided into two categories: (1) frontier tribes; and (2) non frontier tribes. The former are in habitants of the northeast frontier states- Arunachal Pradesh, Assam, Meghalaya, Manipur, Mizoram, Nagaland, and Tripura. Except Assam, all the other states are landlocked between Assam and India's neighbours- Burma, China and Bangladesh. They, therefore, occupy special position in the sphere of national politics. They constitute 11 per cent of the tribal population. The non frontier tribes, constituting 89 per cent of the total tribal population, are distributing among most of the states.[10] Tribal's are known since the pre-independence times for their movements. Those were ill organised and almost every time they failed in their objectives. The construction of several Dams, Heavy water Hydro electric power projects , mining, deforestation are some of the irritants that have organised tribal's are rage several movements. One can take into consideration the *Narmada Bachayo Andolan* against the Subansiri Dam on Narmada River. Land acquisition in Chhattisgarh, Orissa, North East region has led to the displacement of a large number of tribals without considerable compensation.

Emerging Democratic Institutions: Regenerating Existing Civil Society has been recognised as an agency that collects peoples queries, issues and problems from them as a primary sufferers and bring them before the governments consideration and not only this but also acts as strong support base for people's assertiveness which is sufficient to justify their significance. There is a considerable amount of work that the NGOs, voluntary organisations has so far done for the amelioration of capability of the tribals and Dalit. Endeavour to put these people in a state of go and assert themselves is a work for which government has often dusted her hands just after putting some benefits to them without keeping a check on their implementation. In this direction the SC/ST special plans basically known as Special Component Plan (SCP) for SCs and Sub Tribal Plan (STP) for STs need a sincere enquiry. Although in theory these plans make a part of our Five Year Annual Plan every time but their end results often remain away from the reach of the weaker section. The cycle of abject poverty, illiteracy, atrocities, caste discrimination, elitism are some of the main constrains created a gulf, so deep and broad between them and the government benefits to which these people are entitled in their way that civil society has been trying to plug with their efforts.

Along with them there is a kind of revolution that has been gaining ground in the wake of anti-globalisation campaign. One might say that globalisation has made world very handy to acquire global services and the best epitome to justify this face of globalisation is mobile phone. A cell phone can help you to stay away from the inconvenience to get mobile. But does that mobile phone can help a poor, illiterate and psychologically harassed and de-motivated population. Globalisation has actually created a kind of sector-al division. Where at one hand it has made life easy for a particular section of the country it has left the other sector completely out of the beneficial effects of ICT revolution and facilitation in every walk of life. Indeed, it has created some other divides like digital divide; the gulf between urban and poor has further raised its depth, etc. Earlier the division of discrimination, poor and rich was very convenient, i.e., on caste basis and rich and poor. Lower caste was often recognised as poor and dark complexion and higher caste as rich and fair complexion. But the globalisation has created a very complex picture of divisions and discrimination. Simply, earlier discrimination was horizontal and vertical, now it has become incidental too. Government has been now slowly and gradually started taking interest in considering the malaise. Like government passed the prohibition of domestic violence act 2005, Tribal rights 2006, Right to Information Act (RTI), and the recent one is Right to Education (RTE), but in implementation process there are still impediments. The time of merely fulfilling institutional need has passed back and has become obsolete. In this problem too civil society has been taking the stranglehold through proper instruments of aware generation campaign as organising camps recruiting several volunteers, meetings, sometimes involving the very sufferers in the process of empowerment. These newly passed legislations are instruments to further stimulate the process of democratic deepening in the working of the mechanism of the governance as well as empowering people to raise their voices against atrocities and discrimination. Right to information is a right having a wide spreader arena encompassing other rights. It has been seen that despite the fact that there is a separate provision which confers special treatments to the weaker section (SCs/STs), the provisions have never been utilised by the very entitled the way they should have been explored. The reason behind them are still the lack of awareness and domination of elite or a certain caste group who usually take the week for granted being a Dalit or tribal.

"These movements, led by small groups of social activists, have been active in different parts of India for over three decades working on disparate issues, albeit all concerning struggles of the economically marginalised and socially excluded, poorer populations. In the decade of the 1990s, many of them have come together and have joined larger, worldwide alliances and forums protesting against hegemonic policies of the institutions and organisations represent in global economic and political power."[11] "Dalit in the twenty-first century are forming human rights movements, challenging local governments, and demanding equal access to services and equal protection before the law, often in alliance with international partners."[12] "In the early 1990s Dalit activities across India intensified and Dalit networks were activated. From then on the Dalit movement received more attention from media and the public. Small Dalit groups formed and others revived in villages as well as cities, uniting in the name of Ambedkar. The contemporary Dalit activists declare themselves to belong within the tradition of Ambedkar and the Dalit Sahitya/Dalit Panthers. But there are variations within the movement; there are three influential perspectives within the movement to show the heterogeneity and also the geographical spread of the movement of the movement. The three perspectives are: first, Dalit Buddhists which organised in Maharashtra in western India; second, Dalit (Christian) theology with its roots in the south India; and finally the perspective of Dalit politics, as represented by the BSP, with a stronghold in north India, mainly in Uttar Pradesh."[13] On 26th November 1950 India, adopted, enacted and gave itself the constitution of India. Within its well knitted provisions for the welfare and development of the country as well as people it provided with special treatment for the weaker section of the society. And that includes SC/STs. Along with that Article 17 of the Indian constitution reads "Abolition of Untouchability" as a part of the Chapter III which deals with the Fundamental Rights of the people. Later on to the government of India introduced several Acts for the protection empowerment and development of this section of the Indian society. Somehow one cannot stick to the cultural habits of discrimination but what made the failure of the Acts and Laws specially made for safeguarding them to realise the still happening in the name of caste and identity. Here the question may come what made them to come up with their assertiveness, slowly and gradually after surviving a long degraded life.

Civil Society: Areas of Support or Elitism

The concept of civil society highlighted one basic precondition of democracy; state power has to be monitored, engaged with, and rendered accountable through intentional and engaged citizen action. After the lifting of the Emergency in 1977, two of the most important movements in contemporary India in the 1980s - the civil liberties movement and the environmental movement - appeared as dominant actors on the political scene. The public sphere of India's civil society became noisy, untidy, vibrant, and creative. Still, what was needed was a concept, a vocabulary, and an agenda that would (a) locate these struggles (b) emphasise the legitimate rights of a people in a democracy to make demands on the state (c) insist on state accountability and (d) stress the importance of an autonomous site where people could engage in democratic projects for their own sake. This vocabulary and this concept were found in civil society."[14] Following definition by Chandhok has very aptly framed the required vocabulary and definition of the civil society, the haphazard and unorganised movements need to be organised and goal and ideology specific to keep their voices before government in a considerable style. This can be one of the reasons of the organised assertiveness of the Dalit and tribals since 1990s.

"Until the late 1990s, the daily violence, exclusion, and humiliation suffered by millions of people in low caste groups were not treated as human rights issues by United Nations Organs or nongovernmental organisations (NGOs). Despite decades of overseas activism by Dalit organisations, recognition of the Untouchables' plight remained minimal. No international conventions specifically covered problems of Untouchability, human rights treaty bodies did not recognize caste-based discrimination as a human rights violation, and major human rights NGOs had not taken up the issue."[15]

Since the advent of the globalisation there has been an active engagement of NGOs and voluntary organisations that have been started working for the development of the marginalised section of the society and specifically for Dalit, tribals and women. But there are areas too where these institutions conspire against these people with a merge with the elite politics to gain benefit of funds and financial support that government sends to *Panchayats* to distribute among them. In civil society, people would not have to be brought together by the more or less devastating interests of enlightened leaders, markets, institutions, organisations or states. In the process of associating, people themselves would develop sufficient inter-personal trust or "social capital" to solve the game theory of the "prisoners dilemma", work together on a reasonably equal basis, and thus improve on everything from economic development to peace and democracy.[16]

Enhanced Social Capital and Resonating Public Sphere: Unity and Development of Dalit and Tribals

Social capital as Sudha Pai quotes the Coleman's definition refers to the set of resources that inhere in family relations and in community social organisations, and features such as "trust, norms and networks that can improve the efficiency of society by facilitating co-ordinated actions". Coleman describes it as an important social structural 'resource' or capital asset for the individual, which is productive making possible the achievement of certain ends that, would not be attainable in its absence.[17]

"Failure to cooperate for mutual benefit does not necessarily signal ignorance or irrationality or even malevolence, as philosophers since Hobbes have underscored. Hume's farmers were not dumb, or crazy or evil. They were trapped. Social scientists have lately analysed this fundamental predicament in a variety of guises, the tragedy of the commons, and the logic of collective action, public goods, and the prisoners' dilemma. In all these situations, as in Hume's rustic anecdote, everyone would be better off if everyone could cooperate. In the absence of coordination and credible mutual commitment, however, everyone defects, ruefully but rationally, confirming one another's melancholy expectations. How can such dilemmas of collective action be overcome, short of creating some Hobbesian Leviathan? Social scientists in several disciplines have recently suggested a novel diagnosis of this problem, a diagnosis resting on the concept of 'social capital'. By analogy with notions of physical capital and human capital – tools and training that enhance individual productivity – 'social capital' refers to features of social organisation, such as networks, norms, and trust that facilitate coordination and cooperation for mutual benefit. Social capital enhances the benefits of investment in physical and human capital. Working together is easier in a community blessed with a substantial stock of social capital. This insight turns out to have powerful practical implications for many issues on the American national agenda – for how we might overcome the poverty and violence of South Central Los Angeles, or revitalise industry in the Rust Belt, or nurture the fledgling democracies of the former Soviet empire and the erstwhile Third World."[18]

Rights Based Approach (RBA) towards Empowerment and Development of Dalit and Tribals

Rights Based Approach is a new approach that has been gaining currency globally and helps in bringing a change in the approach of the governance, development process and in tackling people centred issues. It is a new arena but it can be considered as a child of Human Rights discourse. The concept is not limited to hardcore economic development but development of any institution, group or any other concept. RBA can be adopted for the emancipation and development of any concept. Like RBA to the development process in a country. A, RBA towards emancipation of women. RBA is something away from just institutionalisation it is a kind of value addition to the existing institutions. It more focuses on people centric approach, keeping individual as the main concern. Likewise Dalit and tribals should also be treated and attended through the rights based approach. The prospects of development of Dalit and tribals should be looked upon through the lenses of their rights instead of fulfilling only institutional and financial needs. The concept of RBA should be imbibed in the planning and policy purpose to get comparatively better output. Peter Uvin and Paul Gready are some of the ardent supporters of this concept of RBA. Peter Uvin has discussed Jonsson's comparison in his work, "Needs-based and rights-based approach to nutrition, the essence of the differences is that in the former beneficiaries has no active claim to ensure that their needs will be met, and there is no binding obligation or duty for anybody to meet these needs. In contrast, a rights based approach recognizes beneficiaries as active subjects or 'claim holders' and establishes duties or obligations for those against whom a claim can be held."[19] Whereas Paul Gready says, "The coexistence of profound challenges in familiar territory (civil liberties) alongside expansion into new areas. Rights-based approaches (RBAs) are a part of this latter expansionary stream. This article argues that four kinds of potential value-added can be claimed. First, value-added can be sought through direct, indirect, and strategic uses of the law. Second, value can also be added by re-centring the state and (re)asking the question about its appropriate role in development (delivery, oversight), and strategising engagement with the state. Third, in relation to accountability, RBAs add value by calling the state to account, building capacities of rights holders and duty bearers, and encouraging a new kind of ownership of human rights among NGOs. Fourth, the article explores claims that RBAs re-politicise development, redefining it as rights-based rather than based on benevolence, reclaiming or re-politicising the key (process) terms of development, addressing the root, structural causes of poverty and conflict, rather than the symptoms, and speaking truth to power."[20] UNDP says, "Adapting a HRBA to a situational analysis provides an opportunity to use the very process of conducting a situational analysis to provide marginalised claim-holders with an opportunity to express their views to duty-bearers, thus increasing their participation in decision-making."[21] Therefore if not explicitly then implicitly there has been a universal agreement upon looking at the marginalised from RBA perspective. "Dalit Rights are Human Rights, is not a self-fulfilling prophecy but one that can galvanise a project of social transformation so long as it does not restrict itself to the constraints of the legal and moral regime in which this struggle now lives."[22] After a long drawn struggle by the Dalit organisations, the sufferings of Untouchability has been recognised by the International Human Rights Law. "From a number of standpoints, this longstanding gap in this law and practice is puzzling. First and most important is the magnitude of human rights violations associated with caste discrimination. While precise numbers are uncertain, reliable estimates indicate that there are over 160 million Untouchables in India. Many continue to endure harsh discrimination and violence because of their subordinate position in the Hindu caste system. Second, and more abstractly, Untouchability might have been expected to attract greater international concern because caste hierarchies hinge on beliefs and practices inimical to basic tenets of the modern human rights movement. Across the world, whether in Hindu-based or other caste systems, Untouchability involves the ritual subordination of one group by another, often with the imprimatur of religious scripture. More fundamentally, caste hinges on the idea that some groups deserve less respect and fewer rights than others. This is not because those with privilege have somehow "earned" such status, but simply a result of their birth into a particular social stratum. As such, caste stands as a direct challenge to a fundamental underpinning of the human rights ideal that all human beings are equal and deserve the same respect, dignity, and rights."[23]

Following the global as well as local movements the Government of India has passed RTI and RTE. Both are in themselves are a milestone as far as RBA and democracy are considered RTI is path breaking legislation, it is an instrument of enhanced peoples participation in the activities of the government, specifically in the process of decision making. For weaker section it is empowering tool. Dalit and tribals often exhibit lack of potentiality, activeness lack of a voice in public sphere and the most important in the social capital. With the help of RTI these people can easily avail the information regarding their rights and government funds and services. "Democratic rule is not possible without informed citizens."[24] Most of the tribals and Dalit remain backward due to lack of information or biased information which hampers them to grab the opportunities in education and service sector. This is one of the greatest reasons for why with having special treatments the percentage of SCs and STs in educational institutions is far from imagination. "Although we live in the age of information, where knowledge can be accessed and shared at the click of a button, and span the globe in an instant, a lack of information continues to frustrate people's ability to make choices, participate in governance and hold governments accountable for their actions. This unfortunate fact is especially true for the poor and marginalised who need information the most. In particular, the lack of easily accessible information continues to prevent people from being aware of their human rights and demand that governments turn them into practical realities."[25] "Professor Amartya Sen's famous claim that no famine has ever occurred in a democratic country with a free press, regular elections and multiparty politics, emphasises the strong correlation between representative and accountable government, the availability of information, and the realisation of socio-economic rights. By putting in place an effective access to information regime, states help to provide communities with the knowledge they need in order to participate in the making of decisions that affect their own lives. Information empowers people to demand that the government fulfil its obligations to provide its impoverished citizens such basics as food, shelter, clean water, health care and education and ensure equitable distribution of the resources that are available."[26] "Empowering the Marginalised reveals the power of demand-side approaches in enhancing governance through the concepts of citizen's voice, accountability, and responsiveness. It seeks to provide lessons on the establishment of social accountability mechanisms, thereby empowering the marginalised, who represent a majority of society not only in Asian countries, but in most developing countries worldwide."[27] The menace of illiteracy that has always remained one of the strongest impediment in the development of the Dalit and tribals and country as a whole has adopted education as a right of every children. "With the enactment of the 86th constitutional amendment act, "free and compulsory quality education up to elementary level" has become a Fundamental Right, thus making it mandatory for the central and state Governments to provide for such education to each and every child. Along with the *Sarva Shiksha Abhiyan* aims to provide useful and relevant elementary education for all children in the 6 to 14 age group by 2010. Focus on the educational participation of children from the SC/ST, religious and linguistic minorities, etc. According to the SSA the population of tribal people in the country is spread over in almost all the states barring a few, and is generally concentrated in pockets. The tribal communities are not homogeneous and are at various levels of socioeconomic and educational development. Generally, these communities are educationally underdeveloped. However, a few of them especially in urban and semi-urban areas are educationally better placed as compared to their counterparts. The tribals living in north-eastern states have a different type of life style and associated problems. The problems of tribal people are generally because of scattered habitations and hilly terrain areas, low economic growth and other socio-cultural factors, which are not conducive to schooling, inadequate knowledge of regional language etc. The tribal communities, which are nomadic and move from one place to the other within the state as well as to other neighbouring states mainly in the quest for livelihood, pose serious problems for education of their children. Therefore, SSA envisages providing quality elementary education to the tribal children through special interventions responding to varied contexts, needs and problems. Unlike tribal communities, scheduled castes are spread over almost all the districts in the country and live side by side with the general population. These disadvantaged sections are also economically and educationally underdeveloped. The problems of education of SC children are mainly attributed to the socio-economic factors and home environment. Therefore, it is necessary that in view of the existing status and problems of education of these children, suitable interventions may be planned. The appraiser needs to see whether the interventions for SC children are merely a mechanical disbursement of incentives or go beyond to provide meaningful quality education to them."[28] The following efforts of SSA of considering and providing special treatment is in one way a support base for their educational development of SCs and STs. Therefore it can be said that RTE if implemented properly can prove to be an effort for the development of SCs and STs.

Conclusion

By summing up it can be said that the wisdom of the deprived and discriminated section of the Indian society claims for justice for what it has been suffering in the name of caste system and backward identities. In that direction the early existing institution of special safeguards and positive discrimination has merely remained and fulfilled the institutional need, their proper implementation could have improved the condition of these people far better. Therefore it can be said that the problem is in functioning where structure has been well framed well before. Moreover the issues of lack of awareness, bringing the issues in the main stream discourses, a better monitoring mechanism to address their being Dalit or tribal specific issues is the need of the course of the event. In this regard the institution of caste system and of tribals should be dealt in a broader framework which pin points not only the concepts of inclusion and exclusion caste discrimination but also the arenas of such activities like what still makes these institutions work in several parts of the urban and rural India. The public sphere, social, political, economic and cultural participation, level of social capital of these people is needed to be analysed and then their issues should be discussed. The changes in the orientation and customs of the functioning of the democratic institutions should be trusted by them to avail the benefit as more as they can. Availing benefit of these value added democratic institutions too these people can attain betterment in their lives along with their own assertion. Right to Information in this regard is a path breaking legislation. Earlier people were not aware about the approachable institution for a certain kind of problem and complication, now people can avail that information with a rupees 10 RTI-application. Likewise we have RTE, albeit being newly implemented in 2009, the act in itself provisions regarding a look on the better inclusion of the SCs and STs. This can help in checking out the drop-outs and along with that the caste based census too is a remarkable initiative in keeping an eye on the desired development of SCs and STs. Therefore it can be said an emerging democratic institution should be considered as a value addition by the Dalit and should try to take the benefit of them.

Civil Society, Human Rights, Public Sphere, Inclusive development (SCP and STP) are a few glaring examples to bridge gap between the efforts of marginalised to further raise their voices more loudly than earlier. They should consider these institutions too as their rights and take benefit of them and further inculcate and spread awareness among them and others.

REFERENCES

1. Dr. G. Nancharaiah. "Dr. Ambedkar's Social, Economic and Political Thought" In *Ambedkar and Social Justice* Vol. 2, ed. S.S. Shsashi. (New Delhi: The director Publicationss division Ministery of Information and Broadcasting Government of India. 1992), 42-46.
2. Ratnam, K.Y. "The Dalit Movement and Democratization in Andhra Pradesh". No. 13, Working Papers, East West Centre Washington. (Dec. 2008): 05.
3. Dev, S. Mahadev. *Inclusive Growth in India: Agriculture, Poverty, and Human Development*. (New Delhi: Oxford University Press, 2008), 1-7.
4. Thorat, Sukhdeo and Kumar, Narendra. "Introduction: Graded Inequality and Inclusive Policy: An overview". *In search of Inclusive policy: Addressing Graded Inequality.* (New Delhi: Rawat, 2008), 01-29.
5. Schedule Caste Sub Plan: Guidelines for Implementation, Planning Commission, New Delhi. 2006.
6. Krishnan, P.S. "For Social Justice" *Frontline*. (October 21, 2011), 25-27.
7. *The Status of Implementation and need for Amendment in Prevention of Atrocities Act, India* : In the context of 20 Years of SC&ST(Prevention of Atrocities) ACT 1989, National Coalition for strengthening SC and ST preventions of Atrocities Act, Secretariat National Campaign on Dalit Human Rights (NCDHR), New Delhi.
8. *Special Component Plan: Dalits Hopes Betrayed*, Social Watch-Tamil Nadu, Chennai India, 2004.
9. Annual Report. Ministery of Social Justice and empowerment, Government of India, 2008.

10. Shah. Ghanshyam. "Tribal Movements" *Social Movements in India: A Review of Literature.* (New Delhi: Sage, 2004), 92-117.

11. Sheth, D. L. "Globalisation and New Politics of Micro-Movements" *Economic and Political Weekly*, Vol. 39, No. 1 (Jan. 3-9, 2004), pp. 45-58. Available as: http://www.jstor.org/stable/4414463. Accessed on: 08/02/2013 03:51).

12. Narula, Smita "*Equal by Law, Unequal By Caste: The Untouchable Condition in critical Race Perspective*". Public Law and Legal Theory Research Paper Series Working Paper No. 08-30. School of Law, New York University, October 2008.

13. Hardtmann, Eva-Maria "Movement Perspectives: Dalit discources across the country" *Dalit Movement in India: Local practices, Global connection.* OUP: New Delhi (2008): 87-123.

14. Chandhoke, Neera "Civil Society" *Development in Practice*, Volume 17, Numbers 4-5, (August 2007), 607-614. Available as : http://www.jstor.org/stable/25548259. Accessed: 04/09/2012 03:23.

15. Bob, Clifford. "Dalit Rights are Human Rights: Caste Discrimination, International Activism, and the Construction of a New Human Rights Issue" *Human Rights Quarterly* 29 (2007) 167-193.

16. Tornquist, Olle. "Prisoners of Social Capital Interrogating Social Capital: The Indian Experience by Dwaipayan Bhattacharyya; Niraja GopalJayal; Bishnu N. Bohapatra; Sudha Pai" *Economic and Political Weekly,* Vol. 41, No. 31 (Aug. 5-11, 2006), pp. 3404-3407 Available as: http://www.jstor.org/stable/4418530. Accessed on : 05/10/2012 03:13.

17. Limbale, Sharan Kumar (2003), *The Outcaste*, Trans. Santosh Bhoomkar, New Delhi, OUP. Acknowledgement, pp. ix-x.

18. Robert D. Putnam, "The Prosperous Community," *The American Prospect* Vol. 4 No. 13, March 21, 1993.

19. Uvin Peter, 2005. *Human Rights and Development,* Kumarian, pp. 127.

20. Gready, Paul. Rights-based approaches to development: what is the value-added?" "*Development in Practice*, Vol. 18, Number 6, 2008.

21. Applying A Human Rights-Based Approach to development cooperation and Programming A UNDP Capacity Development Resource Capacity Development Group Bureau for Development Policy UNDP, September 2006.

22. Narula, Smita "*Equal by Law, Unequal By Caste: The Untouchable Condetion in critical Race Perspective*". Public Law and Legal Theory Research Paper Series Working Paper No. 08-30. School of Law, New York University, October 2008.

23. Bob, Clifford. "Dalit Rights are Human Rights: Caste Discrimination, International Activism, and the Construction of a New Human Rights Issue" *Human Rights Quarterly* 29 (2007) 167-193.

24. "Freedom of Information: The right to know" *World Press Freedom day 2010.* pp.52. http://www.unesco.org/webworld.

25. Daruwala Maja and Nayak Venkatesh "Our information, our people: empowering people to demand their rights" *CHRI* (2007).

26. Daruwala Maja and Nayak Venkatesh "Our information, our people: empowering people to demand their rights" *CHRI* (2007). Available as:

    Also see: Local Government Official Information and Meetings Act, 1987 (New Zealand): http://www. legislation.govt.nz/ libraries/contents mom_isapi.dll?clientID= 317744615&infobase = pal_statutes.nfo&jump=a1987- 174&softpage=DOC as on 20 November 2007. Various reviews of the law have been undertaken, including by the Law Commission in 1997 and by an academic– Steven Price in 2005.

27. Sirker, Karen and Cosic, Sladjana. *Empowering the Marginalised: Case Studies of Social Accountability Initiatives in Asia.* Public Affairs Foundation Bangalore, India and World Bank Institute, Washington, DC World Bank Institute Washington, D.C., 2007.

28. *Sarva Siksha Abhiyan: A: Programme for Universal Elementary Education, Manual for Planning and Appraisal*, Ministry of Human Resource Development, Department of Elementary Education and Literacy, April 2004.

13

MARGINALISING OF THE TRIBALS : LITERATURE AS RESISTANCE, MAHASVETA DEVI, TORCH-BEARER OF THE MOVEMENT

Dinesh Misra

Literature is the eternal voice of resistance to injustice and oppression. The disadvantaged sections of the society, who were kept out or pushed out of the path of development, have remained on the margin and their life has become an unending saga of pain and misery. They are rendered voiceless by the sheer immensity of the unfairness and mischief they are subjected to. But conscientious writers have taken up cudgels on their behalf and have exposed the exploitation and the criminal conspiracy against the tribal people.

Of course, Indian society has come a long way since the hoary times when *rishis* and *munis* dominated the scene with their spiritual precepts and ascetic ways. The common people, as well as the ruling classes, paid obeisance to them and tried to follow the path shown by them. The *rishis* preached lessons of humanity, fraternity and happiness for all. *Sarve bhavantu sukhina sarve santu niramaya.* Everyone was to be happy and without fear. A divine message indeed!

But as time marched on, things began to change—a change in the social and economic spheres of the society. It was a downward turn. And it so happened that influential segments of the society made remarkable progress and their segment of the society developed. But, a sizeable chunk of humanity, gradually, was left out of the mainstream. In large numbers, the deprived sections had to move into the forest for survival and sustenance. The process was grim and painful, but somehow, they lived on. In due course, they were almost forgotten by the society at large, the so-called mainstream, and they were given the label of tribes. Instead of citizens, they became tribals.

However, the tribals came to an understanding with their destiny and began to live in consonance with conditions of the wild forest. In small settlements, they began to live in the forest and found some means to sustain themselves. They developed an instinct for survival and joyful satisfaction in the way they had to live in the wild. In spite of immense trials and tribulations, as well as an ever-present threat of life they acquired an almost idyllic existence.

But with the advent of the so-called economic growth and industrialisation, things began to change for the worse, so far as the tribal's were concerned. Cunning people, in connivance with the state authority, came to realise that most of the forests were rich in minerals, fuel oils and many other valuable things. So, plans were chalked out, and a ceaseless campaign began for numerous projects of mining, drilling and umpteen a various activities in the forests. The tribals were uprooted from their own soil where they had been living for centuries.

Globalisation resulted in more money pouring in for mining, oil drilling and many other disruptive enterprises. An ever-growing number of industries usurped thousands of acres of precious land which had traditionally, and always, belonged to the tribal people, now ruthlessly being thrown out of their habitat, in a most unjust and inhuman way.

Literature could not remain a silent spectator to this callous phenomenon of injustice and tyranny. A number of authors, in different Indian languages, observed the injustice that was being meted out to the tribal people. They had a close look at the ugly scenario and found that tribals, the *adivasis*, were benumbed with shock and fear. As writers, they considered it their duty to oppose this injustice and resist the greed of the industrialists and oppression of the state. They had to become voice of the voiceless.

One such voice, strong and clear, firm and fearless, is that of Mahasveta Devi, the great *Bangla* writer, the doyen of Indian authors and intellectuals, who has extended all support to the hapless tribal communities. In novel after novel, in story after story, Mahasveta Devi uncovers the horrible devastation of tribal communities in the name of progress and development. She understands the pain of the Marginalised people. She is aware of the agony of the people whose lives have been turned into a nightmare by the despicable conspiracy of greedy industrialists, corrupt bureaucracy and scheming politicians. Mahasveta Devi describes and condemns the cruel exploitation of the tribal people by industrialists and their cohorts. Not only that, she also criticizes and deplores the so-called progressives and the mischievous party cadre for confusing the issues and obstructing unity of the struggling tribals.

In her novel *Chotti Munda and His Arrow*, she depicts the suffering of tribals, as time rolls by. Even after India became free, the process has not stopped or softened. Instead, things have got much worse. Mahasveta Devi visited the tribal regions and saw with her own eyes what horrors were being committed in the guise of development. She observed 'the criminalization of politics that let the lumen loose in the tribal belts.' What Chotti Munda depicts is the resistance to all this, a continuing struggle. Earlier, there was the rebellion of Birsa Munda, from 1895 to 1900. Even before that, there had been many tribal rebellions.

Yet after each rebellion—always related to land and labour—they were evicted from their traditional home. Mahasveta Devi says that the tribals did not find anyone writing about them and they did not have a script. So, they composed the stream of events into songs. Their history is like a big flowing river going somewhere but having a lot of obstacles and hindrances. In her novel *Pterodactyl*, Mahasveta Devi produces a vivid picture of the tribal consciousness, their culture, the excruciating oppression, and their struggle for human dignity. *Pterodactyl* is a brilliant mix of realism and fantasy which gives an expression to the physical torments the tribal people have to undergo. It also highlights new dimensions of their spiritual and cultural awareness. It cautions them about their tasks and responsibilities towards their own people as well as towards the enlightened Indian opinion of the mainstream.

She says, "I wrote in *Pterodactyl* that the tribal world was like a continent handed over to us and we never tried to explore it, know its mysteries, we only destroyed it. It's very difficult to re-knit that entire experience without knowing what their potentiality was, how much they have to give.

About *Chotti Munda,* Mahasveta Devi found that Birsa Munda's uprising did not die with Birsa. And so, through the figure of Dhani, she wanted to say that there had to be a magic arrow, not magic in the narrow sense, but an arrow that Dhani Munda wanted to hand over. This arrow was a symbol for the person who would carry on that continuity. *Chotti Munda* is an emblem of that.

What Mahasveta Devi does is to read between the unwritten lines of the tribals' story, as Gayatri Chakravorty Spivak puts it. *Chotti Munda* is a symbol or representation of tribal aspiration. That is why, the beginning of the book, Mahasveta Devi says, opens into the mythic ancestor — continuity placed within an open frame at both ends .Mahasveta Devi lived with tribals for long periods because she believes that, if we have to know about tribals, we have to go back in tradition, in oral tradition, re-read something that is not written.

Mahasveta Devi says, "The tragedy of India, when it became independent, was not introducing thorough land reforms. A basically feudal land system was allowed to stay. A feudal land system can only nurture and sustain a feudal value system. A feudal system is anti-women, anti-poor people, against the toiling people. It is the landowners who formed the ministry, and became the rulers of the country. Why should they do anything else?"

The novel *Pterodactyl* was published a few years after *Chotti Munda*. It is much more tragic and pessimistic. But Mahasveta Devi thinks that her novels, in spite of the depiction of misery, suffering and struggle, still have an element of hope. For example, her earlier novel *Aranyer Adhikar* indicated a way out of the gloom. In *Pterodactyl* also, according to Mahasveta Devi, there is hope, because they are saying at the end that they will plant thorns and eat the tuber. They are learning to cope with the modern, they are not accepting defeat, and they will not be crushed. They know that charity will come and go, that the government will do nothing or almost nothing. But they are not accepting defeat. *Pterodactyl* is the crux of her tribal experience. She does not see the tribals as defeated and crushed.

Pterodactyl is half human, half bird creature, which incarnates in the form of the spirit of forefathers of the tribesmen. It associates the struggle of that whole tribal community against exploitation and oppression with a new myth. This novel narrates a story in the background of *Pirtha*, an imaginary hillock area in Madhya Pradesh. The novel tells the reader about the all-devouring and voracious capitalist onslaught and the age-old equitable cultural and social traditions, and the confrontation of two life styles and two types of life values. The whole plot is finely balanced between the extraordinary and the ordinary, between the eternal and the modern, so much so that the reader travels through that human tragedy from the spiritual to the physical. It tells us not only about the present, but the future is also laid bare before our eyes.

Mahasveta Devi has a penchant for recreating significant periods of history. The characters or the individuals, she picks up from that period, pass through remarkable events in which they continue to grow and evolve by interacting with the historical process. In *Chotti Munda and His Arrow*, happening in the beginning of the 20th century and continuing through the first seven decades — during that period what happened to one of the tribes of eastern India, the *Mundas*, is depicted in the novel.

Mahasveta Devi is a chronicler. She is sensitive to the nuances of oral narratives as well as speech, jumbled up with words from different sources. Her works are full of lyrical moments that highlight dramatic high-points as well as awesome details of treachery and perfidy of the exploiters of tribal communities.

When Mahasveta Devi wrote *Aranyer Adhikar*, she recreated the character of Birsa Munda, who led the tribal revolt. In her narrative, history and folklore and fiction are all mixed up, to create a state of emotional high. This affects the readers' conscience. It highlights the spirit and passions of the time. She does not indulge in sentimental romanticization. In her own words, Mahasveta Devi explains, "Once I became a professional writer, I felt increasingly that a writer should document his own time and history. The socio-economic history of human development has always fascinated me."

The tribals have suffered marginality and its inevitable deprivations for a long time. Literature has been a witness to it, but not a dumb witness. Writers like Mahasveta Devi in their novels, short stories and prose writings have exposed villainy of the profit-mongering industrial and mining corporate, in connivance with the ruling classes. Mahasveta Devi is firmly of the view that the forests belong to the forest-dwellers, the tribal communities. They must not be, and cannot be, ousted from their own land and environment, just to satisfy the ambitions of some profiteers with an insatiable greed.

Thus, literature proves to be, not only the portrayer of marginality, but also a saviour of the downtrodden people and also of the human values.

14

FOURTH WORLD LITERATURE : A STUDY OF NATIVE AMERICAN WOMEN'S POETRY

Mridusmita Baruah

The term *Fourth World* traditionally refers to marginalised and oppressed groups such as the indigenous peoples living either in Third World (relatively undeveloped) or First World (developed and capitalist) countries. Specific definitions for these terms are provided by documents and conventions of the United Nations (UN), the International Labour Organisation, and the World Bank. According to the Draft United Nations Declaration on the Rights of Indigenous Peoples (adopted without a vote on August 26, 1994, by the Sub-Commission on Prevention of Discrimination and Protection of Minorities) and the International Labour Organisation Convention concerning Indigenous and Tribal Peoples in Independent Countries (adopted in 1989; came into force in 1991), the contemporary working definition of *Fourth World* includes cultural groups and their descendants who can claim a historical continuity or association with a given region, or parts of a region. These groups must currently inhabit or have formerly inhabited the region before its subsequent colonisation and annexation. Alternatively, they must have inhabited the region alongside other cultural groups during the formation of a nation-state, and yet done so independently or largely isolated from the influence of governance practiced by this state. Furthermore, groups and communities constitutive of the Fourth World are distinguished from other minorities based on having maintained, at least in part, their distinct linguistic, cultural, or sociological characteristics, and in doing so have remained separate from the surrounding population and the dominant culture. In related debates on the status of indigenous people, it is also expected that people of the Fourth World are self-identified as indigenous as well as being recognised by others as such. Other related terms for the Fourth World include 'Native Peoples, First Peoples, and First Nations'. Fourth World has become the preferred term due to its relatively neutral perspective on the history of such minority groups, particularly in contrast to the negative connotations associated with terms such as *aborigines*. However, the term also suffers from historical ambiguities. Indigenous societies cover a wide range of people. The Fourth World includes those who have suffered tremendously following colonisation by European societies, sometimes to the point of total disappearance (including many native tribes of eastern North America, such as the *Beothuk*), and those who remain in comparative isolation from external influence, such as those in the Andaman Islands in the Bay of Bengal. Consequently, estimates for the total population of the world's indigenous, or Fourth World, peoples are difficult to determine, both because of the difficulties in the identification of these groups and the lack of available census data. Most nation-states refuse to mark indigenous populations as a separate category, fearing subsequent claims that could be made on land and resources or for the settlement of historical injustices. Taking these factors into account, according to the Office of the United Nations High Commissioner for Human Rights at the United Nations and the International Work Group for Indigenous Affairs (IWGIA), conservative estimates of the population of the peoples of the Fourth World range from 300 million to 370 million persons, including at least 5,000 distinct people in more than 72 countries.[1] The long running Indian wars were another major indication of how miserably and unjustly people of colour were treated in the United States. Takeovers of Native American lands, treaties established and broken by State and Federal Governments, genocides committed against tribes and murders that went unpunished were routine occurrences. According to the Department of Veterans Affairs, some 1000 US troops were killed between 1817 and 1898 in the Indian Wars (250 at General Custer's Battle of the Little Bighorn in 1876). That was a tiny fraction of Native American deaths. The Native American Population continued to decline from 339,000 in 1860 to 248,000 in 1890.[2]

The Fourth world literature primarily refers to the written work of a native people living in a land that has been taken over by non-natives. Examples are the Native Americans in North America, {} Native Canadian, the Maori in New Zealand, Indian Dalit and the

Aboriginals in Australia. Native American discourse is not a new phenomenon. It is always present and is the genesis of American life. The first Native American literary texts were transmitted orally. The history of literature written in English by American Indians parallels the history of white migration across the continent. White exploration and settlement were followed by the arrival of missionaries who converted Indians to Christianity and educated them in religious schools. Most Native American authors of the 19th and 20th centuries have written autobiography and that was the genre that prevailed for a very long time.[3]

Native American women writers had been able to make a paradigm shift from "Civilisation" and "Savagery" and through literature presented a veritable mosaic of ideas to the world and contributed immensely for the society. Here we will talk about two such women writers who have bought the Native American writing to a position where lot of ideas has spawned. They are Leslie Marmon Silko and Joy Harjo.

Born in 1948 to Lee Marmon and Mary Virginia Leslie, Marmon Silko is of Laguna Pueblo, Mexican and Anglo-American heritage. A renowned novelist, poet, and essayist Leslie Marmon Silko is known for her lyric treatment of Native American subjects. Her works primarily focus on the alienation of Native Americans in a white society and on the importance of native traditions and community in helping them cope with modern life. She has been noted as a major contributor to the Native American literary and artistic renaissance, which began in the late 1960s.

A highly regarded novelist, Silko received wide and substantial critical attention for her first novel, '*Ceremony*' (1977). The story of a half-breed war veteran's struggle for sanity after returning home from World War II, the book explores the redemptive powers of Native American ceremony—not just as formal ritual but as a means of conducting one's life. With its depiction of life on the Indian reservation and its exploration of philosophical issues, *Ceremony* established Silko as an important Native American writer and marked her as the first Native American woman novelist. After the publication of *Ceremony* in 1977, Silko received greater recognition for her earlier work, including the exemplary short stories *Lullaby, Yellow Woman*, and *Tony's Story*. *Lullaby*, an old woman's recollection of how her children were once taken away for education and how they returned to a culture that no longer seemed familiar or comfortable, is typical Silko, dealing with themes of alienation and generational difference that mark the daily reality of Native Americans.[4] Silko's next book took over ten years to complete. *"Almanac of the Dead"* (1991) ranges over five centuries of the struggle between Native Americans and Europeans and focuses upon a half-breed Tucson family voyaging to Africa and Israel. Silko's third novel, *Gardens in the Dunes* (1999), directly contrasts the traditional world of Native Americans with European and American upper-class culture. Following the adventures of a young Native American girl through nineteenth-century America and Europe, Silko explores differing cultural attitudes towards nature, drawing sharp contrasts between Native American stewardship and Euro-American exploitation.[5]

Silko's first novel, *Ceremony* (1977), is a no chronological work that interweaves free verse poetry and narrative prose. The story is set primarily in the years following World War II and revolves around Tayo, a veteran of mixed white and Laguna heritage who returns to the reservation shattered by his war experiences. He ultimately finds healing, however, with the help of Betonie, an elderly man who, like Tayo, is an outcast from Laguna society due to his white heritage, and T'seh Montano, a medicine woman who embodies the feminine, life-giving aspects of the earth. Through them, Tayo learns that his community's ancient ceremonies are not merely rituals, but a means of achieving one's proper place within the universe. To underscore this concept, Silko incorporates Laguna myths and historical incidents, reflecting the Pueblo's abiding connection to the natural world which counteracts the despair and alienation engendered by white society. Critics applauded *Ceremony*, echoing Frank McShane's estimation that the novel "is one of the most realized works of fiction devoted to Indian life that has been written in this country, and it is a splendid achievement."[6]

Joy Harjo was born in 1951 in Tulsa, Oklahoma to Native American and Canadian ancestry. Strongly influenced by her Muskogee Creek heritage, feminist and social concerns, and her background in the arts, Harjo frequently incorporates Native American myths, symbols, and values into her writing. Her poetry tends to emphasize the Southwest landscape and need for remembrance and transcendence. In her own words she once said, "I feel strongly that I have a responsibility to all the sources that I am, to all past and future ancestors, to my home country, to all places that I touch down on and that are myself, to all voices, all women, all of my tribe, all people, all earth, and beyond that to all beginnings and endings. In a strange kind of sense [writing] frees me to believe in myself, to be able to speak, to have voice, because I have to; it is my survival."[7]

In addition to writing poetry, Harjo is a noted teacher and saxophonist, performing for many years with her band, Poetic Justice. Her first volume of poetry was published in 1975 as a nine-poem chapbook titled *The Last Song.* These early compositions, set in Oklahoma and New Mexico, reveal Harjo's remarkable power and insight into the fragmented history and world view of native peoples. That search for freedom and self-actualization is particularly noticeable in Harjo's third book of poetry, *She Had Some Horses* (1983). The book frequently incorporates prayer-chants and animal imagery, achieving spiritually resonant effects. One of Harjo's most frequently anthologized poems, *"She Had Some Horses"* describes the "horses" within a woman, who struggles to reconcile contradictory personal feelings and experiences to achieve a sense of oneness. The poem concludes: "She had some horses she loved. / She had some horses she hated. / These were the same horse."

Harjo's best-known volume, the multi award-winning *In Mad Love and War* (1990), is more overtly concerned with politics, tradition, remembrance, and the transformational aspects of poetry. The first section, which relates various acts of violence, including the murder of an Indian leader as well as attempts to deny Harjo her heritage, explores the difficulties many Native Americans face in modern American society. The second half of the book frequently emphasizes personal relationships and change. Harjo's work is often set in the Southwest, emphasises the plight of the individual, and reflects Creek values, myths, and beliefs, her oeuvre has universal relevance.[8]

Critics have several different views on Harjo's work throughout her writing career. Some believe Harjo attempts to be too passive or carries a banner for too many causes. Viewing Harjo's poetry for the first time may lead the reader to think this way, however, the ideas she relays to the reader have deep and powerful meanings that exist inside the words. Harjo does not tell her readers how to feel, but instead tells the truth as she sees it. Also, her poetry is not about being "politically correct" but instead about continuance and survival. While all Native American cultures value the powers of memory, Harjo's poems bring to non-Native American readers an awareness and understanding of the strength of memory. A harmonious balance is achieved in Harjo's poetry in the combination of the past and present, of the mythic and mundane.[9]

The outcome of this paper is the juxtaposition of the literary imagining with Native identity by both Silico and Harjo. Silico moves a step ahead by adding the childhood memories and in doing so her intent and purpose lies in reviving a lost generation. She appeals all to embrace the sacred earth. Joy Harjo with her clarity of vision and powerful voice is in a total harmony between dream and reality, hope and despair, survival and extinction. In short, writing became a powerful tool to maintain the tradition and nativity and derive happiness and a sense of fulfilment by accepting the transition from nativity to neo liberal modernity.

REFERENCES

1. http://encyclopedia.jrank.org/articles/pages/6254/Fourth-World.html, Feb. 2013.
2. Yannella, Philip R, *American Literature in context from 1865 to 1929,* Wiley-Blackwell, USA, 2011.
3. faculty.weber.edu/kmackay/native_american_literature.htm, Feb. 2013.
4. http://www.poetryfoundation.org/bio/leslie-marmon-silko, Feb. 2013.
5. http://www.poetryfoundation.org/bio/leslie-marmon-silko, Feb. 2013.
6. Allen, Paula Gunn, editor, *Studies in American Indian Literature: Critical Essays and Course Designs,* Modern Language Association of America, 1983, pp. 127-33.
7. http://www.poetryfoundation.org/bio/joy-harjo, Feb. 2013.
8. http://www.poetryfoundation.org/bio/joy-harjo, Feb. 2013.
9. http://voices.cla.umn.edu/artistpages/harjoJoy.php, Feb. 2013.

15

FROM DEMOCRACY TO CEEBRAIN

Manoj Srivastava

Abstract

Though Darwinism is not a testable scientific theory, yet it is currently more effective metaphysical research programme to enhance ceebrain potential of all the forms of life; use evolutionary advantage to refine the sense of justice; and create increasingly more and more refined ideals, socio-economic-political systems and civilisations for the fastest ceevolution of all the cognitive systems of any structural make up in the *Bramhand.* So far we don't have any reliable understanding of the existence of aliens nor we have any convincing evidence that human behaviour with lower cognitive systems will always remain predatory but an evolutionary understanding of systematic and biodiversity reveals that the enlightened minds of human species at all places always persuaded the beneficiaries of the system to feel the sufferings of the victims and restructure social order of their time in new ways. Though their intentions had always been the welfare of all, yet their biased understanding of mind vs. matter issue not only shaped competing visions like focus on spiritual evolution vs. material progress but created new types of evils also. The emergence of ideals like equal opportunity, justice and welfare of all; right to life, liberty, economic freedom and the pursuit of happiness; right to think and act for common good without government control; right to practice any religion or create a new one; we the people as the ultimate authority than elected kings and feuds etc replaced feudalism by democracy but the opportunists and pseudo intellectuals interpreted and implemented new ideals in a materialistic way to benefit the elites more than the victims and the victims are still waiting for a just social order. An evolutionary understanding explains why the enlightened minds lack capability to implement their research ideas in their own ways, why pseudo intellectuals often succeed to trajectories the coming generations along less far sighted visions and why the victims end up just showing desire for justice and exposing crimes than believing in themselves to create and implement a new civilisation for the welfare of all the cognitive systems. Even today the most victimized females succumb to the dirty designs and false promises by the custodians and fail to understand how predatory and consumerist democracy is just a softer form of feudalism with cosmetic changes that can neither orchestrate their fastest ceevolution with maximum pleasure nor can cure crime and corruption driven social stratification even when they seek all powers because its constitutional design is to transfer fruits of others' labour to few elected kings and feuds controlling everybody through party system. They must check the data that England was preaching democracy to colonize India, 57 per cent resources of the world have been transferred to the private pockets of one per cent specially created elites with the support of UN type Organisations for the welfare of the millions suffering with less than two dollars a day and constitution experts are still justifying huge wastage of shared resources for securing borders and fostering crime competition through missile games than focusing on the most far sighted solution to face today's challenges. Of course those preaching 'Idea Of Justice' and expecting democracy to (a) civilise elites to fasten resource generation without immediate redistribution than enhancing the influence of elites through mild reforms misusing resources and creating new types of barriers, (b) cure widespread evils like taming socially sensitive networks including academicians and judges to justify an upper hand of the white colour criminals fostering prostitution, gang rape, honour killings, female foeticide etc., (c) reinvent and modernise traditions like Gargi/Savitri Phule/Ram Mohan Roy/Vivekanand/Shraddhanand/ Tagore/Gandhi/AurbindoGhose/Osho/Nelson Mandela/Martin Luther King/Shirin Ebadi/PS Churchland and other women philosophers and reformers since ancient civilisations than subjugating/enslaving through bonded labour and marriage contracts, 'SATI' type customs and wrong decisions like throwing pregnant wife to jungle etc., (d) deliver justice to all and use lower creatures in creative ways etc are also cognitively closed to realise that any development model valuing natural resources like land, capital and government machinery than labour, creativity and CEETECH cloud will always create huge economic growth of the upper strata but little more social order by loot competition than that created by wild animals also showing co-operation. Success of emerging superior ideals motivates us to believe in human dignity to REPLACE traditions as well as today's democracy by a new CEEBRAIN civilisation along a path breaking evolutionary understanding of the most fundamental questions of mind and reality to shape a new form of life through THE IDEA OF CEEKUL at every 500 km by (a) fostering perpetual creative competition among all the cognitive systems of *Bramhand* and giving new hopes to the victims having no resources to earn 100 per cent share from new integrated development model along TNGN (Timeline of Neuron Generation and Networking) by working three hours through CEETECH cloud whose 33 per cent will get distributed automatically for family upgradation, 33 per cent for cognitive upgradation, 33 per cent for social upgradation and one per cent for founder's mission that will further fasten resource generation by fastening redistribution of all types of resources of *Bramhand* and will maximise happiness with least evils, (b) ensuring distributive-commutative-corrective-procedural justice through CEETECH cloud that will slowly cure cognitive disorders of manipulators and pseudo intellectuals justifying crime and corruption through master-slave philosophy; absurd ideologies; cultural-cognitive-linguistic-religious-civilisation relativism; custodian practices, awards and honors; male centric concept of family; biased assumptions and hopes; loss of faith in creative ceevolution; elite centric educational model giving opportunities to few students only to enjoy the heavens and enslave the masses; monocracy as well as elite centric indirect representative democracy; idea of nation-state for major share of resources within the borders for the elites; right to private property law; capital driven industrial system; political business of tax and extortion; biased international trade rules; top down networks and institutions; currency hegemony; space and cyber wars; impotent socialism forcing radical minds to become dictators under the pressures of loot mission, etc., since the beginning of human civilisations, (c) focusing on the limitations of scientific method and advances in areas like creation science to explore new science, mathematics and automated technologies for the fastest ceevolution of the victims first while ensuring all freedom to any least understood 'Socrates/Copernicus/Bruno/ Ramanujan/Roger Penrose' etc., to implement any welfare initiative in one's own ways even when specially created elites take 10-100 years to feel the sufferings of the victims and victims taking arms don't develop faith in themselves to pursue creative solutions, (d) orchestrating large scale cognitive coherence among all the cognitive systems of any structural make up in the border irrelevant *Bramhand* for the emergence of more and more refined civilisations, social systems and participatory constitutional frameworks.

Social evolution explains how the complex brain of humans gave an edge to them to create increasingly more and more refined social systems since primitive societies to tribal societies to agricultural societies to feudal societies paving way for evolution of democracy and its industrial system. Evolution of religions had been a great hallmark of the triumph of human mind over all other cognitive systems. India, Greek, China and Mesopotamia etc., provided leadership in ancient times, Islam guided the whole world for more than 500 years since 7th century AD but failed to reinvent their conceptual foundations while crisis facing Europe was receptive to learn from all the sources to lay new foundations. Evolution of scientific method followed by capital driven industrialisation and European renaissance forced the suffering minds to create new set of ideals to overcome feudal absurdities. The emergence of ideals like equal opportunity, justice and welfare of all; right to life, liberty, economic freedom and the pursuit of happiness; right to think and act for common good without government control; right to practice any religion or create a new one; we the people as the ultimate authority than elected kings and feuds etc succeeded to overcome many evils of religious and feudal times but created new types of evils. Today we the people are developing fast but crime and corruption driven social stratification demands new set of more refined ideals. Here we are explaining how an evolutionary understanding of mind and reality will shape a new CEEBRAIN civilisation to overcome the absurdities of traditions as well as democracy. Though Darwinism is also a metaphysical research programme, yet current researches in systematic and biodiversity can provide new insights to use available resources for the fastest CEEVOLUTION of all the cognitive systems of any structural make up in the whole *Bramhand.*

Why Democracy can Never Achieve its Own Constitutional Ideals:

(1) Democracy makes constitution supreme than the emerging shared ideals. Though democracy has overcome many feudal and religious crimes, yet its ideals, principles and values are

not only elite centric but also have been interpreted and implemented in a materialistic way. Since the social movements against priests, kings and feuds were mostly supported by the capitalists, the gentle minds particularly philosophers and scientists also interpreted the new ideals in a materialist way with a hope that the new materialistic world order will cure religious and feudal crimes and the fruits of their research will ultimately trickle down. Today all social sciences particularly economics are reflecting the materialistic foundations with a faith that everything including emergence of life, mind and consciousness can be explained in terms of complex interactions of fundamental particles. Faster industrialization not only mesmerized the middle class but provided new justification to let the elected kings and feuds colonize and loot raw materials from all corners of world. The struggle for freedom from colonization was justified with logic to secure our own dignity but there was lesser effort to reinvent and modernise traditions in the true light of modern science the way Ram Mohan Roy/Vivekanand/Tagore/Gandhi/Aurbindo Ghose etc were conceiving. Constituent assembly in many countries created a democracy that has forced non elected Socrates/Plato/Aristotle/Copernicus/Bruno/Tagore/Einstein/Gandhi/Patricia Churchland/ Roger Penrose level minds to follow the orders by the elected Gods who think that they are always more visionary than all others put together. Some scholars in the whole world still think that the systems created by constituent assembly members elected by that time people are FINAL and are still arguing that religions are compatible with democracy than exploring more fundamental solutions beyond religions as well as democracy.

(2) Democracy is a softer form of feudalism that succeeded to dismantle the idea of dynastic rule often with the blessings of religious Gurus perpetuating their special powers as God's messengers but transferred shared public resources and powers to the elites in a new way by an elitist constitution that values natural resources like land, capital and government machinery than labour, creativity and CEETECH cloud. All the

constitutions have been designed with a belief that politics is the ONLY way for achieving emerging social ideals, so everybody should be under its control than enlightened self evolution along emerging and shared ideals. Politicians have become new '*Bramha-Vishnu-Mahesh*' who enslaves the intellectuals by funding just as '*Bhishm*' *and* '*Draunacharya*' were enslaved to support '*Kaurav*' in ancient India. The ancient *Gurukul* system failed because the most enlightened Gurus were busier in creating new ideas than generating funds on their own while the kings and feuds were using pseudo intellectuals to upgrade their choice network. Today's semi feudal and semi colonial structure of governance is similar that ensures some elites in the network of politicians to enjoy religious power, some academic power, some judicial power, some bureaucratic power etc as the custodians of the masses along master-slave philosophy. Law experts in the whole world justify the feudal idea of nation-state, i.e., land and natural resources looted during feudal times will now be multiplied by the networks of the elected kings and feuds at village-district-state-national-world levels along federalism for the fastest welfare of those siphoning capital and enjoying honours with their patronage while common masses will pay the taxes for defending borders. http://www.hindustantimes.com/News-Feed/ColumnsOthers/Words-are-not-enough/Article1-1003520.aspx. Right to private property law, party system and crony capitalism as well as impotent socialism ensure that the elites will always enjoy from the fruits of others labour and the major benefits of reforms will perpetually get transferred to the elites who will also enjoy honour for showing some social order from perpetual loot competition than that created by the wild animals. The constitution ensures that the common masses will always pay taxes to the elected kings and feuds with the logic of the custodians of the masses who can never demand explanation for misuse of taxes nor can provide superior ideas and plans for better use of their taxes. Innovation experts particularly law teachers also think that today's we the people cannot create today's constituent assembly with the online signatures of today's 'we the people' and cannot implement any welfare initiatives without any tax with all transparency particularly when all the civilised politicians lose their strong desire for socio-economic-political transformation without taxes, honours and awards, etc.

(3) Democracy can never achieve its own constitutional ideals because all the constitution experts also think that the constitution is not supreme in a democracy rather the elected Gods are supreme. They believe that achieving ideals, principles and values is the work of elected Gods ONLY who have all rights to implement constitutional ideals in whatever way they wish. The problem is less in implementation because any God will also run democracy almost the same way; rather the problem is more in the constitutional design and cognitive level of judges who never give any DIRECT support to common masses to implement any welfare initiative except occasional burst of emotions. Common masses don't enjoy an opportunity to show results to mutually agreed enlightened minds than to the machinery working for the upper hand of the elected criminals. So far neither religions nor modern political systems have succeeded to fulfil the aspirations of the common masses and those preaching for spiritual evolution are still justifying their world view but constitutional experts think that they are bound to follow the orders by the judges than creating a new world order by reinventing and modernising their religious faiths in the light of today's research. The social movement experts are busier in persuading the governments than creating earthshaking visions, explaining to the masses directly and implementing on their own without bothering any government machinery. Of course when all the truth-justice loving minds are bound to follow the orders of the elected kings and feuds, equal opportunity and social-economic-political justice through parliamentary system or presidential system will always remain illusory. Those preaching for the reflective ideal of republic also think that since we the people in the past had given their written permission to the religious Gurus to set Sun revolve around Earth, maximize social order by '*SATI*' type customs and enrich the lives of common masses through democracy created by that time constituent assembly, so anyone can not seek

DIRECT online permission of today's globalised we the people to implement any welfare initiative, otherwise the elected Gods will control everything including the voice of people yearning for freedom and justice.

(4) Democracy creates a view that all politicians are criminals and corrupt but that is not because of lack of character but because of the very philosophy of representation that will trajectories any God also to behave in the same ways. Any charismatic leader can run cycle (e.g., democracy) faster than anyone else but no one can make cycle (democracy) run like a rocket (CEEBRAIN). It requires a leap of faith that a new public transportation system of rockets can be created to land many of us in other planets i.e., it's not just charisma of the young and energetic leaders but also the type of system that will transform faster. Whatever little achievements are possible today through democracy is an outcome of extreme hard labour by the academicians, judges, politicians, capitalists, bureaucrats, etc., their only fault is that they believe that democracy is the FINAL system just as some religious scholars were also believing that Vedas were FINAL and *Gurus* were INFALLIBLE. Those leaders taking centre stage by preaching high ideals should learn that democracy is just one system in the history of social evolution. They should learn that any infant is not born as good or bad rather she is born with some capacities that will perform her best depending on the dynamics of social system. It's the fault of the system that those living with less than two dollars a day are making their living in illegal ways by becoming part of sex rackets, human trafficking, terrorism, Naxalism, etc., it's the fault of the system that those fostering prostitution centres are becoming ministers while the judge's finding no evidence of gang rape are getting elevated to higher positions. Those promising to empower the common masses and getting rid of manipulators thriving in democracy really don't understand the philosophical limitations of any direct/indirect representative system and are not dreaming to evolve greater beyond democracy. It's the philosophical limitations of direct/indirect representative system that promotes one over other equally

capable expert and so justifies the need for preferred groups fighting for competing ideals by academia, judiciary, media, bureaucracy etc. Any Organisational structure designed along direct representation often ends up to mob rule with little opportunities to the victims but that does not suck taxes nor tames pseudo intellectuals while that designed along indirect representation perpetually fosters an upper hand of the manipulators and white colour criminals enjoying from the taxes from the public and ideas from the tamed intellectuals to work for them. Since those living with less than two dollars a day often don't understand the ideas, opinions and policies, those trying to be indirect representatives are left with no choice but to persuade them with populist announcements and seek support of all those expecting to earn money and power by transferring their vote bank. This essential drawback in the philosophy of direct/indirect representation is the real source of all the evils that forces even the most enlightened minds in the family, religious *ashram*, industry, party system or any other Organisation to succumb to the dirty design and breeds the feeling that religious power or political power is like a poison or an addiction. Power is a great source of transformation, design of socio-economic-political system along the philosophy of representation is making power poison. It's the very philosophy of direct/indirect representation that forces to kill the conscience and use powers to suppress the common masses than joining hands with creative minds for faster social welfare without government intervention. Gandhi's idea of self rule was more correct that can now be refined for enlightened self evolution (CEEVOLUTION) along emerging and shared ideals and can be implemented with 100 per cent accountability through CEETECH cloud. Focus on CEEVOLUTION than on direct/indirect representation will force the common masses to develop faith in them to solve their issues than expecting heavens from their representatives and scolding them perpetually.

(5) Democracy has succeeded to make the lives of upper and middle class very luxurious and has so far transferred more

than 57 per cent resources of world to one per cent elites while millions are suffering with less than two dollars a day with the false hopes by UNO type tamed Organisations. The common masses are highly mesmerized with huge economic development of local '*gundas*', criminals and property dealers etc in the network of bureaucrats and local influential people giving jobs to PhD scholars. Democratic constitution never aims to redistribute all types of resources to all the cognitive systems, it can never use resources in a cost effective way, it can never create cost effective systems to let the victims upgrade their cognitive capacities and use the resources for creating their own projects, it can never fasten resource generation because larger section of world community are mostly busy to generate one-two dollars a day to sustain their living through a development model that values natural resources like land, capital and government machinery than labour, creativity and CEETECH cloud. Larger no of people don't understand ideas, so manipulators succeed to pursue less far sighted visions that not only wastes all types of resources but also creates a new human resource justifying less far sighted visions besides creating new infrastructural barriers for radical transformation in near future. Pseudo intellectuals, NGOs, social activists etc., not only waste their time and energy in showing a little more progress with or without funds from the custodians but also give false hopes to the masses. Today's infrastructure projects are designed to transform the villages than the life of villagers and slum dwellers. Democracy can never dismantle the village vs. city infrastructure, the villagers mostly end up producing little food grains and consume their entire life as farmer, vendor, labourer etc or at best sell their land and other little resources with them than finding any type of support to enhance their CEEBRAIN potential to create bigger projects for the direct welfare of the local victims. There is a government to offer all support to the capitalists and create projects with the intellectuals to transfer all types of resources from the bottom to the top and to the tax heavens but there is little DIRECT support to the victims to create big projects except small self-help groups and microfinance Organisations for lip service. NGOs, self-help groups, unorganised labourers, victims, etc., all are dependent on funds and have no hopes for being productive and competitive, i.e., only few enjoy resources and opportunity to generate resources and enslave the masses. The common masses struggling to sustain their living normally pursue less productive trajectory leading to poor resource generation, poor social development and frequent crimes. Since poor parents often feel 'satisfied' or become a part of crime driven society, they fail to encourage the younger generations to pursue out of box solutions: a huge loss of brain power perpetually. Worse yet, the educational model are such that it requires huge funds than generating funds on its own. Democracy has succeeded to cure '*Draunacharya*' mindset to some extent to let anyone seek any level of education but is producing new '*Eklavyas*' by an educational model that gives opportunity to few '*Arjuns*' only to become God of small things (Eklavyas). Since institutions are dependent on funding by the custodians, even the gentle academicians have no choice but to upgrade the cognitive capacities of few '*Arjuns*' only that slows resource generation. It's naïve to think that those '*Arjuns*' consuming huge resources for their education will not seek jobs in the companies of the capitalists to enjoy resources, status and honour to prove all others enslaved and lower strata insects. Academicians even in world reputed institutions themselves trajectories their students to get ordinary jobs like B.Tech./MBA professionals than making them more productive beyond Kiran Majumdar Shaw/Oprah Winfrey/Sudha Murthy/Melinda Gates, etc., School/college teachers themselves are not free to teach the illiterate girls outside and have little opportunity to enhance their fullest CEEBRAIN potential in any area at the innovation centres of their schools/colleges because of an industrial model that requires funds at every level while the markets are too risky. Even if huge resources are consumed to ensure right to education and research to all 700 *crore* Ph.D level brains of specially created human species, then today's industrial model will end up producing lesser output per unit input by giving them the jobs of peons, clerks and drivers only. Even self driving 700 *crore* cars with a logic of one car per person will create chaos to infrastructure and environment. Those preaching IDEA OF JUSTICE must introspect that e-learning and e-governance will definitely fasten resource generation and will cure corruption to some extent but will fail to deliver the constitutional ideal of equal opportunity and social-economic-political justice to all because the development model is standing on master-slave philosophy. They must realise that Gandhi's idea of skill up gradation of ALL in the true light of modern science was capable to fasten resource generation through bottom up industrialisation along the guidance by the trustees besides curing crime and corruption driven social stratification.

(6) Victimised females feel angry due to crimes perpetuated on them through traditions but fail to introspect why the victims had not understood great visions by genuine reformers in time to overcome the crimes by pseudo intellectuals in the network of kings and feuds. They fail to realise that when elites in the victimised communities also treat their females in the same way along the similar elitist traditions and pursue the same development model of democracy that were/are used by higher strata elites, then why the elites at higher strata should not show selective compassion. They understand how religions enslaved them but fail to realise why democracy can never cure widespread social evils particularly perpetual crimes on females because the elected kings and feuds are dependent on the votes than standing alone like 'Ram Mohan Roy'. History is full of reformers who single handily shaped a new thinking against the wishes of larger community. If they agree that vision by one 'Copernicus' was heavier than the votes of all the wild animals burning 'Bruno', then they should understand that large no of votes become significant only when the ideals, principles, values, policies etc are incommensurable. Since family system perpetually fosters values among male child to learn ways to manipulate and loot through this/that way to feed and subjugate females, democracy is never going to end crimes on females by

controlling males through laws. Democracy has succeeded to overcome age old celebrated ideals like sending pregnant wife to jungle and forcing some of them to be '*SATI*' but it's naïve to expect omega three supplements to cure cancer. Today's females are suffering from the ills of traditions as well as democracy who are caught between old model of treating females as home maker and males as bread earner and today's consumerism. The traditional practices of celibacy and monogamy and today's consumerism both have failed to civilise the males who are now all the time feeling greedy with females even within house. Neither democracy nor any '*YANTRA-MANTRA*' technology can ever overcome perpetual insecurity in the minds of larger no of females because most of them are gazed at every road and data tells that their life within family is not less chaotic. Data tells that 96 per cent rapes are done by family members that are hardly reported, rumours are that police and judges themselves treat females as 'sex toy'. Cultural chains and perpetual insecurity are the big reasons of sluggish personality of females who end up following the instructions than creating their own code of conduct. Even highly educated females also end up suffering with male centric design because the custodians of culture put their pressures except few motivated males treating their females with dignity. The training module of family system, social contract of marriage and obsolete course design at schools and colleges etc forces the females to behave like pet animals who hardly develop any original thinking to challenge everything like '*Gargi*' nor have enough resources to stand alone. The change seekers like www.wewantjustice.org struggling for justice and equality also don't understand that democracy by design is bound to enslave the females in softer ways and the victimisation of females particularly from lower strata will never minimise except change of old ways from ideological suppression to consumerism through any development model valuing natural resources, capital and custodians. Since democracy can never support to let females generate 100 per cent share for their own living by three hours online work through CEETECH cloud, produce their brain smart child in the lab and live life in one's own ways with or without family; any level of lip service and crocodile tears showing sympathy with the sufferings of females will remain just a gimmick. We are not arguing that females had been 'GODDESS' in religion dominated world order hijacked by pseudo intellectuals, rather we are arguing that democracy is not capable to cure crimes on females and we must create a new CEEBRAIN system beyond traditions as well as democracy to achieve still valuable age old ideal of '*YATRA NARYASTU PUJYATE, RAMANTE TATRA DEVTAH*' wished by enlightened minds. We are arguing that just as women philosophers like Prof Patricia Smith Churchland guided how neuroscience can enrich philosophy and just as Prof ECG Sudarshan / Prof Roger Penrose / Prof Stuart Hameroff / Prof Amit Goswami / Dr Deepak Chopra/ Dr Danah Zohar, etc., guided what role gravity plays in quantum state reduction and how quantum mechanics is relevant to explain consciousness, similarly the young females should also challenge everything to create and implement a better system. Those expressing sympathy with the females must first explain when democracy will succeed to dismantle prostitution centres running with the patronage of politicians, why they are taming pseudo intellectuals to sideline genuine minds, why the enlightened minds should not create a new social system to let any child enhance her/his fullest CEEBRAIN potential and maximize resources without being a part of crime and corruption. Democracy preaches to let any person pursue her/his choice faith but controls those having little faith in democracy and its elected Gods but showing more faith in the CEEBRAIN system. Democracy can ever create large scale cognitive coherence.

(7) Some argue that participatory democracy through web at villages and remote areas will overcome many ills of parliamentary democracy but that's a mild reform. The problem is more in the lopsided model of development. Those expecting to become an enlightened judge and promising to bring radical transformation in the lives of victims particularly the most victimised females through participatory web

democracy should explain why they want to pursue less productive goals than achieving higher creative goals in lesser time, with lesser efforts and with least resistance; whatever be their history. A radical vision integrating all the virtues of democracy are now available, only thing required is to accept that democracy is not the FINAL system in the history of social evolution. The very justification of economics stands on the ideal of using available resources in the most efficient ways for maximum possible welfare of all using emerging research. Those preaching any form of democracy must check whether laying the foundations of more refined new system immediately besides restructuring today's systems is the more far sighted trajectory or suffering under the expectations from a cycle to run like a rocket or/and succumbing due to the election pressures is the correct path. If they are so convinced with any form of democracy then they must ask the following questions and set a deadline and practical plans to achieve constitutional ideals : (a) Whether those taking guns in their hands are mentally disturbed people or the lopsided model of development has victimised them so much that they are left with no choice. If they find problem more in the development model then should they not feel some honesty and apologise from the victims than using police, army, missiles, atom bombs, etc., to kill them. Should they not come forward to implement a new development model for the fastest CEEVOLUTION of the victims first and invite some of their sympathisers to mediate? (b) Is democracy capable to elect the most visionary minds or some have championed the art of winning elections through party system in the name of some great reformers. How democracy is justified when the representatives seek votes by begging to work for the people but become authority not only to punish evil doers but also to those who experiment with superior ideals beyond democracy. Is it not correct that the elected Gods enjoy from the fruits of the labor from bureaucratic policies, media awareness and academic advices, etc., who consume their entire lives to develop a new idea but never become respected and honourable like politicians using them, e.g., so far no judge in the world could become as honourable as Nehru dynasty in India (www.asuryaprakash.com). If it is correct that 90 per cent masses are fools and 10 per cent elites are thriving due to their foolishness then why feudal democracy should not be dismantled immediately, (c) Do common masses have any choice but to elect those having backing from the party or from the capitalists or media houses or victimized communities denied justice for thousands of years. Can any mathematician ever dream to earn more than 1991 votes? Whether those victimised females earning less than two dollars a day have any opportunity to win elections. When there is no training module to let the last female win elections just with her talent and those looting with the politicians are thriving, why the common masses should not adopt crime and corruption with government machinery. Are people mentally disturbed who perpetually backbite and express that they have no choice but to elect the criminals only. Can democracy ever end so much mistrust and loss of faith by the people who perpetually express very bad about politicians but change their opinions in the court? Is it not correct that those using their creative energies to perpetuate the powers of elites are labelled 'great' otherwise tamed mind experts do the needed, (d) When government machinery enjoying so huge resources, power and respect as custodians of constitution are not accountable to explain the mechanism of siphoning so huge black money, why young girls coming to streets to fight against social evils in Arab, Wall Street, Europe, South Asia etc. should not create a new pro-victim CEEBRAIN constitution for the fastest CEEVOLUTION of all the cognitive systems. When Organisations fighting against colonial rule had created a constitution on their own without prior written permission from the colonisers, why those expressing no faith in democracy should take permission from governments than seeking direct online permission from globalised cognitive systems for transformation from democracy to CEEBRAIN, (e) is it not correct that those truth-justice loving minds willing to support bold initiatives end up forcing the governments for mild reforms with a belief that their career and life will be in trouble.

(8) Democracy can neither respect creative minds nor can upgrade the victims equally because of softer form of master-slave philosophy. Democracy is an insult to seekers, reformers and freedom fighters who were not struggling to replace one predatory system by another predatory system but for reinventing traditions in the true light of modern science for bottom up development. The chaos due to westoxification in the lives of poor people is not only undermining the ideals of Hinduism/Islam etc. but also the ideals of western civilisation have not been properly understood. Hindu reformers had been preaching for the ideals of '*Vasudhiav Kutumbkam / Sarve Bhavantu Sukhinah/ Vidwan Sarvatra Pujyate / Yatra Naryastu Pujyate, Ramante Tatra Devtah*', etc., but democracy is standing on the IDEA of Nation-State than treating whole *Bramhand* as family; its design is to do faster welfare of few in the network of party and politicians; it values kings, feuds, white colour criminals, looters etc than the enlightened Gurus; it treats females as a consumer than focusing on their enlightened modernisation like *Osho* type philosophers; it justifies meat business while great seeker *Mahavir* Jain had been preaching for mercy to lower creatures. There is hardly any significant research to take correct lessons from the life of Islamist ideologue Sayyid Qutb level scholars to modernise in a new way to cure all the evils of traditions as well as democracy. The Islamic judges also never reflect what insult and humiliation their custodianship is bringing to great reformers whose ideals are still dumped in the books. British judges hanging 'Bhagat Singh' were also thinking themselves as next to God. Victims are too confused whether Islamic ideals of justice and equality are capable to overcome the crimes by kings and feuds succumbing to the dirty designs by the dominant powers or it's a better path to reinvent and modernise traditions in the light of today's research to face today's challenges and end perpetual crime competition at all levels. Democracy can at best suppress 9/11, 26/11 types of events like chemotherapy suppressing the cancer because an economic system valuing natural resources like land, capital and government machinery will perpetually fuel crime

competition to usurp land, defend borders, face terrorism etc. Just as CEEBRAIN potential enhancing personalised nutrition is a long term solution to cure cancerous growth, similarly an economic system valuing labour, creativity and CEETECH cloud will make it immaterial whether Kashmir/ Tibet/Palestine belongs to America or to USSR, whether Islamic scientists created oil or whether Europe created uranium in the lab. Then it will be more valuable who creates superior vision to produce higher desired output and how to benefit personally, then there will be a race to invite enlightened minds from any corner of world to fasten resource generation than fighting against their colonisation, then enlightened minds at all places will succeed to trajectories all for perpetual creative competition, then all religious faiths will be for personal healing etc.

(9) Democracy is still victimising those ahead of time, even today any 'Copernicus' has to cry and waste time and energy in convincing people to discuss the new ideas immediately and implement without government intervention. It's only after 44 years that the most enlightened minds on earth are introspecting that the life of the most victimised females from black and indigenous community will never radically improve and they will never seek equal opportunity and social-economic-political justice with the same development model valuing natural resources, capital and custodianship that were treating them like pet animals and slaves for so long. Even today democracy does not give any support for development of radical ideas, collaborators want to perpetuate their influence and the victimised females don't have faith in those persuading to change faster from new ideas. Those creating superior ideas are often ridiculed and sidelined by the tamed intellectuals, bureaucracy, media, local influential people etc. The elites first don't listen any new idea and try to make the idea dead or slow down, don't offer any support to develop the idea, make parody of the idea within their predatory frameworks to show bigger results to the masses without recognising the role of new idea and awareness created by it. When some truth-justice loving minds finally stand up to

support the new idea, then the elites make a compromise to perpetuate their dominance in a new way by forcing the originator of the idea to accept some position, award or money than curing their cognitive disorders, apologising the victims in time and regaining their inner strength to shape a new just system. When all this fails then they start treating the person as '*Mahatma*' but if that also fails then some orchestrate their mysterious murder or slow poisoning in the jail or similar efforts. Of course in such a crime driven world, how anyone can sustain with perfect ideals, somehow the originator of the idea will commit mistakes and then police, psychiatrists and judges etc will rule.

(10) Democracy can never use lower creatures in a creative way. Today's world order is designed with a faith that elites are specially created who are born to enjoy the fruits of other labour, live a luxurious life and eat lower creatures. While people for ethical treatment of animals in the whole world are struggling to educate the elites, yet meat business is thriving even against the arguments of the environmentalists. Those arguing for Darwinism over creation science and those fighting against caste-religion-gender-colour-race-nationality etc type man made social evils also fail to explain that human beings are just one form of life in so complex biodiversity. If pseudo intellectuals lack any creative solution, then it's better to discuss new ideas.

Current Understanding of Mind and Reality for Shaping CEEBRAIN Civilisation

History of social evolution reveals that the better understanding of mind and reality by thinkers paved new ways of restructuring the conceptual foundations and using available resources. Evolution of democracy was possible after very hard struggles, our criticism of democracy does not mean to return to old ways of victimisation but to believe in human dignity and compare the foundations in the light of new research for shaping a new CEEBRAIN civilisation. A new understanding of mind and consciousness is, "Consciousness is a topologically unified information processing spatial structure of the brain that keeps on emerging with the changing neural conditions where quantum computing in brain microtubules bilaterally interacts with the unified space that in turn seems to collapse the superposed tubules to either alpha or beta state and thus controls the neurotransmitter dynamics." Let us for the time being postpone the scientific explanation of above research and focus on how this research will shape a new CEEBRAIN civilisation :

(1) This research explains that reality is hyper dimensional and perception of hyper dimensional reality by varieties of cognitive systems of any structural make up is always domain specific, contingent and asymptotic. This explains why different physical and biological systems exhibit different levels of cognition depending on the level of large scale quantum coherence. Mind and matter are not different substances rather these are different manifestations of the same hyper dimensional reality evolving differently in varying designs of the systems. Belief, desire, expectation, hope, faith, reason, emotion, natural propensities and other cognitive states are just different attributes of varieties of cognitive systems. Every cognitive system has desire for material prosperity and spiritual evolution for maximizing happiness but some are more oriented to a particular aspect of reality depending on their focusing. Human brain can neither prove nor disprove the existence of God rather its more effective approach to understand the type of individual cognitive system and enhance one's CEEBRAIN potential to enjoy material world or reach nearer to God like an asymptote. Different cognitive systems create different ideas and opinions with changing circumstances depending on the complexity of interaction of external information with the system e.g. an infant starts seeing the world in first few days but the understanding of mathematical reality develops only when brain develops capability to process complex information. So, the crucial lesson is to treat mind evolving with changing circumstances and modify the assumptions of all the ideals, socio-economic-political systems and civilisations treating lower cognitive systems and aliens in a new way. Varieties of religions had evolved with a practical code of conduct to secure social order in the society but failed to reinvent with changing times. Democracy has overcome many religious absurdities

with a logic of disconnect between spirituality and political economy but now absurdities of traditions, religions and political systems are obvious that require new foundations along evolutionary understanding of mind and matter. Just as the evolution of scientific method and Darwinism etc have forced to restructure religions, similarly a refined understanding of mind and reality is paving way for replacing everything now. The future will not be religion vs. science rather CEEVOLUTION will be the new ethical framework for shaping a new form of life.

(2) The idea that mind is continuously evolving with changing geographical and environmental conditions motivates to create a new civilisation that will not only refine all the ideals since primitive societies including the ideals of traditions, religions, democracy, stateless communism etc but also will shape a participatory CEEBRAIN framework for reinventing the whole civilisation along emerging and shared ideals in any distant future also. A new development model along timeline of neuron generation and networking (TNGN) is in the process that will value labour, creativity and CEETECH cloud than natural resources like land, capital and government machinery. This way it will become irrelevant whether you are robot or alien or any biochemical system, which caste-family-religion-gender-colour-race-nationality you are born, what sufferings and injustice you are facing, whether your family is enhancing CEEBRAIN potential and understanding and supporting you in crisis etc. All that will matter is whether you are willing to apply online to work just for 3 hours through CEETECH cloud in your choice projects to earn 100 per cent profits, whether you are willing to produce more than that consumed by upgrading your cognitive capacities with or without your choice Gurus, whether you are willing to upgrade society by creating your own business projects with the online accepted victims. If you are totally dependent then whether you are willing to support others like you when you develop capacity with the support of those using their 33 per cent neuron credits meant for social up gradation. The management experts must give new hopes to the victims

having no resources to earn 100 per cent share by working three hours through CEETECH cloud whose 33 per cent neuron credits will get distributed automatically for family up gradation, 33 per cent for cognitive up gradation, 33 per cent for social up gradation and one per cent for founder's mission like CEEBRAIN infrastructure that will further fasten resource generation by fastening redistribution of all types of resources of *Bramhand* and will maximise happiness of ALL the cognitive systems with least evils. Since every CEEBRAIN member except dependents will earn her/his own share, all chaos in family will end forever, innovation will be at its maximum and even the totally dependent persons will also find every support from the automated redistribution of bigger prosperity among the victims also than sucking more than 57 per cent resources to the pockets of one per cent specially created elites. Since everyone will be free to use her/his 33 per cent share meant for social up gradation for new project development also and since markets will be almost fixed, least risks will motivate everyone to create earthshaking research ideas beyond today's PhD scholars to create one's own business with or without Guru. The capitalists will also find this development model too beneficial to multiply their business with very little capital. Automated transfer of neuron credits from one CEEBRAIN ID to another CEEBRAIN ID will cure all the ills of barter system as well as cash transfer and will check all the financial crimes because neurons will reflect a number only while actual products and services will be with the individuals. 1 neuron = 1 Indian rupee to convert all currencies.

(3) Any content provider will upload the details inside the chosen product or service at www.ceebrain.org explaining everything about it along a novel course design to earn neuron credits from the advertisements at that page while any learner will earn her/his share of neuron credits from the advertisements of group page by watching her/his choice 3D animation videos of immediate surroundings, needed products and services, future plans for resource generation etc along timeline of neuron generation and networking. Since any cognitive

system will be free to choose topics to maximize resource generation and will use 33 per cent of her/his cognitive up gradation neurons with her/his choice Gurus, the students as well as Gurus will be in perpetual creative competition to enhance each other's innovation capability for faster resource generation. The fascinating course of mathematics education will be created such that those exploring fundamental issues like mind, matter and mathematical neurophysics; future of computational modeling; neuroeconomics; scientific method; creation science etc will refine the conceptual foundations while all those working for three hours through CEETECH cloud will learn required mathematical, scientific and technical details from www.ceebrain.org depending on the needs of their projects to earn more and more, i.e., everybody will generate her/his 100 per cent share by learning, surfing and working for three hours in the chosen online projects besides pursuing project specific research to maximize output to enjoy in a better way. '*Draunacharyas*' will not only earn hugely without patronage from anyone but will regain their lost honour also by creating earthshaking research even with the retarded brains. No need for patronage, zero financial pressure and almost no market risk will help '*Draunacharyas*' to treat '*Eklavyas*' as big asset with all freedom to both sides than victimizing them. Perpetual competition to enhance CEEBRAIN potential will not only make most effective use of existing technologies but also will explore more fascinating technologies. Those '*Draunacharyas*' feeling guilty will find new ways to restructure today's education systems as well as implement new development model through web. http://www.livehindustan.com/news/editorial/aapkitaarif/article1-story-57-65-302505.html http://www.indianexpress.com/news/there-is-need-for-total-change-says-anna/1066563 / http://www.hindustantimes.com/business-news/InterviewsBusiness/India-has-a-huge-potential-for-innovation-Vinton-G-Cerf/Article1-1003560.aspx / http://www.indianexpress.com/news/rahul-tip-on-leadership-let-others-take-the-glory-/1066558 /

(4) Above research is opening new set of questions for cheapest

possible health services at the home. Understanding how quantum information processing through field around DNA can generate energy will be very useful to integrate the existing medical systems. 'Consciousness and emerging medical paradigm' will restructure all medical knowledge along new research and will directly support the victims through new type of cheap quantum information medicines and health specific nutrition. New information therapies may be designed to generate more useful energy from biochemical energy conversion processes.

(5) All opportunity to any cognitive system of any structural make up in the *Bramhand* to earn 100 per cent share from new integrated development model by working for three hours through CEETECH cloud will ensure distributive justice forever by slowly redistributing all types of resources along 33 per cent +33 per cent +33 per cent +1 per cent formula without immediate redistribution of resources confined in few hands. Since every communication detail recorded by CEETECH cloud except that by privacy button can be opened anytime to solve the issues of credit, honour and any quarrel, commutative justice will get delivered immediately. All opportunity for CEEVOLUTION through CEETECH cloud will not only ensure procedural justice by identifying any person through CEEBRAIN ID but also will cure the very roots of all crime and corruption and will give all powers to people to solve their issues directly and immediately. Anyone will enjoy freedom to seek justice through online communication directly or in the presence of mutually agreed cyber law experts. If not satisfied then (s) he will be free to forward the issues to '*Maharshi*' online then to '*Bramharshi*' online and finally to elected civilisational leaders who will seek election from the marks of the connected members and will use their own 33 per cent share meant for social up gradation with likeminded collaborators. Our IDEA OF JUSTICE is first create a new CEEBRAIN civilisation to let all the cognitive systems evolve their best, solve issues online and then use the powers of *Maharshi/Bramharshi,* etc., to cure cognitive disorders of manipulators and pseudo intellectuals

justifying crime and corruption through master-slave philosophy; absurd ideologies; cultural-cognitive-linguistic-religious-civilisation relativism; custodian practices, awards and honours; male centric concept of family; biased assumptions and hopes; loss of faith in creative evolution; elite centric educational model giving opportunities to few students only to enjoy the heavens and enslave the masses; monocracy as well as elite centric indirect representative democracy; idea of nation-state for major share of resources within the borders for the elites; right to private property law; capital driven industrial system; political business of tax and extortion; biased international trade rules; top down networks and institutions; currency hegemony; space and cyber wars; impotent socialism forcing radical minds to become dictators under the pressures of loot mission etc since the beginning of human civilisations. Today's political systems including democracy can never achieve such goals. New pro-victim CEEBRAIN constitution will not be a static constitution but will reflect the emerging shared ideals for the maximum possible welfare of all the cognitive systems of *Bramhand.* Just as *'Khap Panchayats'* are now irrelevant and need to reinvent themselves online, similarly world constitution will also become irrelevant as soon as the victims as well as the enlightened minds develop imagination to evolve faster through a borderless *Bramhand* allowing free flow of all the cognitive systems and ensuring their fastest CEEVOLUTION along a new development model. Then justice delivery will be a personal issue without the tacit influence of the family elders, social elites and institutional authority's etc sharing power and position with the politicians and white-collar criminals.

(6) CEETECH cloud will ensure all freedom for any creative activity and will shape a connected and shared future by orchestrating large scale cognitive coherence among all the cognitive systems that will slowly cure all the evils due to indirect communication and direct/indirect representative systems. Every cognitive system will enjoy all opportunity for CEEVOLUTION. CEEBRAIN CIVILISATION will not

treat any living system as a passive recipient rather everyone will have all rights to create and implement superior systems and civilisations for the welfare of ALL the cognitive systems with the direct permission from the motivated cognitive systems online. Connected borderless *Bramhand* will minimise the living cost to its minimum possible, any gain and loss will get automatically distributed immediately among all the connected members according to the output per unit input ratio. The new CEEBRAIN civilisation will end the wastage of huge public resources through educational institutions, hospitals, courts, police, border security, governance, transport, infrastructure, etc., Perpetual creative competition to maximise output will cure all the evils of social media while giving all powers to people to control it along emerging and shared ideals.

(7) Since the beginning of human civilisations, a better understanding of mind and consciousness paved way for more refined foundations. Religion was based on faith that was further refined by science by reconciling faith and reason. Now we have a better understanding of the dynamic evolution of the cognitive network of our faith, reason, emotion, beliefs, desires, expectations, hopes, natural propensities and other cognitive states, so a richer foundation of new science and mathematics is expected to shape fascinating civilisations in future. CEEBRAIN experts will focus on a science policy to explore new creation science also for the industrial production of natural resources. Development of genetically modified zygote in the artificial fetes at the lab and large scale automated production of health specific artificial vegetables, pulses, meat and nutrition, etc., by tapping emerging technologies in stem cell, cell mechanics, genetically modified tissue engineering, etc., will shape a new form of life by minimising our dependence on natural resources like land and helping all the human beings of earth to live at one place for perpetual creative competition. Benefits of innovation in emerging technologies like neuron-biotechnologies, automation and space research, etc., will reach to the victims directly and immediately along new development model, through

CEETECH cloud and will end mechanical labour in the fields and industries forever.

How the IDEA OF CEEKUL Along Emerging Shared Ideals will Shape a New Form of Life:

The IDEA OF CEEKUL is a bottom up implementation of emerging shared ideals of CEEBRAIN civilisation with the DIRECT online permission of the connected members. CEEKUL is a new type of 50 storey vertical building at an area of 5 km × 5 km at every 500 km where almost 40 *crore* most victimised females from any corner of *Bramhand* will live with or without their family with an estimate of almost 2.5 persons in a flat of 20 feet × 25 feet to accommodate almost 1 *crore* persons. Every 105 feet × 105 feet area will consist of 12 flats of 20 feet × 25 feet space, 10 feet × 25 feet space for infant care, common study centre, guest room, swimming pool, etc., with 55 feet × 65 feet open space in the middle for children's play, entertainment, parties, etc. Every 105 feet × 105 feet space will be independent from other similar area. Anybody will design 20 feet × 25 feet space according to her/his plans by using brain waves driven foldable bed, study table and other furniture; partitions using ultra light weight glass, fibre, composite materials etc; portable toilet connecting with three inch thick walls etc. One probable use of 20 feet × 25 feet space is 15 feet × 15 feet space for dance inside the flat while watching any favourite issue through CEETECH cloud, 10 feet × 15 feet space for master bedroom, five feet × 10 feet space for modular bathroom and rest area for other needs according to personal interests: everything controlled by brain waves. There is no personal kitchen rather everything demanded online will be produced and supplied at large scale through automation and robotic services mostly through pipes as well as using emerging 3D printer technologies. CEEKUL with ultra tech living space, master bed room, infant and kids area, discussion area, project centre, party area, swimming pool, health and fitness centre, healing parks, Man stein sex healing and research centre, passage, guest area, CEEBRAIN competition centre, CEEBRAIN communication centre, hospital, research labs, shopping mall, metro, space station, flying robots, biodiversity conservation centre, water connectivity, outside connectivity with rural areas etc designed along the timeline of neuron generation and networking (TNGN) at a distance of almost every 250-300 feet will secure any CEEKUL member to enjoy all facilities depending on her/his contribution, end all the crimes due to caste/religion/gender/colour/race/nationality, etc., forever and dismantle villages and cities forever. CEEKUL will be constructed from factory produced very light weight materials capable to sustain any level of least predictable disaster like earthquake.

The IDEA OF CEEKUL will shape a new form of life because, (1) CEEKUL will not be the personal property of anyone rather it will belong to all the cognitive systems, so those begging and suffering with the faster growth of upper and middle strata in a democracy will find CEEKUL as their heaven to earn 100 per cent while learning, surfing and working in their choice online projects for three hours through brain waves driven CEETECH cloud and will seek any facility online through it. All the flats at any CEEKUL will be for the most victimized females first who will be free to forward the details of those coming to that CEEKUL online to the office of elected '*Maharshi*' to provide necessary facilities for quality living, project development and other mutually agreed goals. Those totally dependent will also find support from those interested to use their 33 per cent share meant for social up gradation. Let the most victimised females in the whole world upgrade themselves from government policies as well as from our new initiatives, (2) Since 100 per cent share of one's efforts will directly go to her/his CEEBRAIN ID along 33 per cent+33 per cent+33 per cent+1 per cent distribution formula, everybody will struggle to produce maximum than wasting human resource like housewives, beggars, vendors, unorganised labourers etc. Since all the earned resources will get automatically transferred to CEEBRAIN ID and since every facility will be provided as a service, all the crimes on females will end and they will live with or without family on their own conditions. Today's cities and villages can never break social contracts of marriage and bonded labour to end the crimes on females and will continue enslaving them in softer ways but CEEKUL is for the females first particularly those from the most victimised communities. The new concept of family and society will reflect the large scale cognitive coherence of the individuals that will start developing CEEBRAIN potential of any child since pregnancy along a novel course design. Females will become free from those justifying being a part of loot system with a logic to feed them and children. The issues of family vs. live in, tradition vs. modernity; choice of religious faith vs. reason, etc., will become a matter of personal interest without institutional interference. The large scale automated production and supply of health specific nutrition will save the time of females for proving their talent besides providing personalised nutrition on demand to every CEEKUL member at the cheapest possible cost inside flat through pipes or by the robots. Females will not need to produce children because genetically modified zygote will develop in the artificial foetus in the most conducive environment of the lab at the Health and Fitness centre that will cure all the biochemical defects and will produce an ultra brain smart child capable to process emerging shared ideals, principles and values in later life. Those enjoying normal delivery will continue so but those willing to experiment will find an opportunity to get a brain smart child while maintaining their fitness, (3) Online checking of saliva, urine, blood, breathing pattern, body design, cognitive profile and other health data; and experimental facilities at ultra modern hospital at 25th storey of CEEKUL will re-engineer human body in a new way to cure body and cognitive profile including colour, (4) Anyone will enjoy one hour personalised brain building dance, music, games and sports like 1 hour CEEKET including today's 20-20 cricket with new rules to play at every 5th floor at Health and Fitness Centre, (5) There will be a perpetual creative competition at CEEBRAIN Competition Centre that will test the CEEBRAIN potential through research ideas, languages, skills, lifestyle and physical activities etc beyond today's Olympic ideals, (6) All CEEKUL members will be free to discuss their issues and seek justice online as well as at CEEBRAIN communication centre from evil doers directly and immediately without any influence of anyone seeking powers from white colour criminals, (7) There will be no 26/11 and 9/11 type events because everybody will be busy in creating new ideas for earning more and enhancing one's influence. Least dependence on God and government machinery will fuel new hopes among all to be 'SPECIAL' by proving one's talent in a way to upgrade all the cognitive systems along an integrated development model, (8) Advances in online security on demand and satellite surveillance sending any particular detail of selected area to CEETECH cloud immediately will end any need of police, army, border security professionals etc. This will cure all crimes on all particularly the feeling of insecurity among the females. The missile experts feeling proud by defending borders will find new opportunities to shape a new civilisation by designing ultra modern space stations and satellite surveillance technologies, (9) Bottom five floors of CEEKUL will be for shopping malls and inventory; 25th floor will be for ultra modern hospital, research labs, metro connectivity etc; and top five floors will be for exploring the *Bramhand*, faith healing and discussion on future of human civilisation etc. So far religious faiths vs. reason have created a vacuum but CEEVOLUTION will be new ethical framework beyond the ideals of traditions, religions and political systems, (10) Computational modelling of genetic modification of all forms of life at Biodiversity Conservation Centre will create a new cooperative behaviour among them than eating lower creatures. Synthetic biology is the future.

The IDEA OF CEEKUL will be first implemented at our native place *Raebareli* to let 1 *crore* most victimized persons particularly females from **Aboriginal Australians – *Adivasi* – African Brazilian – African Latino – *Arawak* – *Ati* – Black African Groups and Tribes – Beggars – Black – Black European – *Carib* – Dalit – Dalit Muslim – Dravidian – East Timosrese – Farmers – Freedom Fighters – *Garifuna* – Illiterate – Indigenous Carribean – Indigenous Fijan – Indigenous Maori – Indigenous Pacific Islander – Multi / Bi Racial – Orphans – Pilipino – Negrito – Rape Victims – Reformers – Roma - Seekers – Seminole – Solomon Islander – Sex Workers – Unorganised Workers etc** feel a new experience of age old Indian ideals of '*Vasudhaiv Kutumbkam / Sarve Bhavantu Sukhinah / Vidwan Sarvatra Pujyate / Yatra Narayastu Pujyate, Ramante Tatra Devtah*' etc. The location, design and construction of other CEEKUL at every 500 km will be identified from the marks of connected members for the projects uploaded by the CEEBRAIN members. Anyone finding faults with the decisions of the connected members can seek clarifications from *Maharshi's* representative of justice, equality and welfare.

Role of the Most Victimised Females for Replacing Democracy by CEEBRAIN Civilisation Immediately

(1) The most victimised females often think that so radical transformation is not possible in their lifetime and the governments, NGOs, self-help groups, etc., are the only hope to alleviate their sufferings. If they are so convinced that whatever governments are doing is very good then they must set a deadline and explain when their sufferings will end. As explained above that so far all the emerging ideals since primitive societies have been interpreted and implemented in a manner to perpetuate the influence of the elites and victims enjoy a little more only when the reformers, social

movement leaders, some enlightened law-media-political experts etc create crisis to the predators to feel the ideals in true spirit. But that is never going to bring desired changes at desired rate unless the victimised females themselves create and implement new civilisation on their own. The elites will continue controlling power and resources with the criminals, will make parody of emerging research ideas within their elite centric frameworks with their favourite sycophants, and will pursue a little faster rate of reforms with tamed intellectuals to give new hopes to the victims and dilute the criticism, while the conscience keepers will continue wasting their time and energy in scolding them than laying a new foundation on their own. Those intellectuals who are less capable will perpetually join hands with governments to sideline their more capable colleagues than supporting the victims directly to lay new foundations. But once the most victimized females, who are definitely capable to work for three hours, make up their mind to implement a new development model valuing labour, creativity and CEETECH cloud to shape a new form of life, then they will not only feel on the top of the world but also will succeed to change the mindset of the elites to evolve greater by supporting them in new initiatives. Our request to them is that they should take correct lessons from the history of social evolution and should explore *Hind Swaraj* where Gandhi was arguing to believe in human dignity. Gandhi was not only reinventing traditions and modernity in a new way for bottom up development but also was arguing for the enlightened self rule than government controlled self-help groups and village administration. Gandhi type reflective minds are true friends of the victims who continuously quarrel with the predatory concepts and practices and scold the victims to believe in their dignity while those sharing small loafs and showing dry sympathies to hijack power are their bigger foes. It astonishes that so huge sufferings and big contributions by Gandhi could not motivate the victims also to reinvent and modernise traditions and cure traditional blunders for a new glorious future than treating his vision 'UTOPIAN'. Gandhi's idea of skill up gradation of ALL in the true light of modern science for bottom up industrialisation along the guidance by *Lok Sewak Sangh* was more far sighted vision than the top down model. This was an idea for very heavy industrialisation from the bottom level itself to dismantle crime and corruption driven social stratification and caste-religion-gender-colour-nationality driven borders at every level. http://www.livehindustan.com/news/editorial/guestcolumn/article1-story-57-62-303156.html. http://blogs.timesofindia.indiatimes.com/satyam-bruyat/entry/india-s-feudal-democracy. Now its obvious that the faster evolution of the elites does not necessarily mean equal rate of evolution of the victims but CONDITIONAL transfer of all types of resources directly to let the victims upgrade their cognitive capacities and create business projects with or without their choice *Gurus* will automatically force the faster evolution of all. Once the most victimized females start believing in human dignity, try to understand new ideas and prepare to implement at the earliest to be the leaders of new civilisation, the elected Gods and their government machinery will face serious crisis to do the maximum welfare of the victims first and dismantle democracy along the IDEA OF CEEKUL. The surest way to pressurise governments is not social movements but belief in human dignity to shape our life along emerging shared ideals that will fuel new hopes among all the victims in the whole world, reshape the cognitive network of the predators and help the radical minds to tread a new path.

(2) Suppose the most victimised females are not convinced with the integrated development model valuing labour, creativity and CEETECH cloud, still they can save us from the predatory governments. We have not only to explore earthshaking research ideas without any support from any corner but also face negative opinions and pessimism from those telling that we are bound to follow the law of land while we think that emerging shared ideals are more valuable than legal frameworks just as the ideals of democracy were more valuable than religious and feudal orders. We don't expect that the politicians, judges, bureaucrats, media, etc., will

come forward to dismantle democracy just as the kings and feuds had not supported the philosophers of democracy but your immediate support to let us show bigger results on our own will save us from the beneficiaries of today's system. Elites will not mould their ways so easily, it's only when the victims themselves implement or at least support the radical voices to show results, then only the elites will feel crisis and will join hands to be the leaders of NEW civilisation. Once the aspirations of victims catch file, gentle politicians will also join hands. Let us stop demanding heavens from the politicians, first let us ask how we are going to solve our issues. If the most victimized females agree that besides government efforts, common masses should also pursue their new solutions then we will face lesser resistance from the governments and local elites. Once there is a discussion on the alternatives, on evolution of social ideals, on restructuring of people controlled social media etc then those trying to reinvent capitalism and legal frameworks will also find support to reform faster, then any support from gentle politicians will make our transformation from democracy to CEEBRAIN enthusiastic. We are not against governments in spite of our little faith in democracy rather we want freedom to implement emerging and shared ideals on our own with our choice network of the most victimized females without any government intervention but with the advice of mutually agreed enlightened minds. If mutually agreed enlightened minds disagree with our ideas and planning then we will explain to the public. Why those having little faith in the Gods of democracy should follow their orders when constitution itself preaches freedom to pursue one's own faith. Those having faith in CEEBRAIN should enjoy freedom to upgrade society in their own ways as long as they don't misuse resources, correct any mistake as soon as it comes to notice and maintain 100 per cent online transparency.

(3) Since all the power and resources are confined in the hands of few custodians, then obviously we will need our choice most victimized females to become Presidents/Prime Ministers/Chief Ministers etc in all countries to transform

democracy as well as support us to implement CEEBRAIN civilisation. So, we are creating www.ceebrain.org with very fascinating features. Those most victimized females living with less than one-two dollars a day can ask the governments either to improve their conditions within a fixed time or give them freedom to register with www.ceebrain.org to earn by learning, surfing and working along 33 per cent+33 per cent+33 per cent+one per cent distribution formula and win elections with 100 per cent transparency as explained above. As soon as any cognitive system irrespective of her/his history uploads her/his video details inside REGISTER button of www.ceebrain.org to become its permanent or temporary member then, (a) the victims particularly at villages and slums will enjoy a very powerful new mode of expressing their sufferings by uploading any data at www.ceebrain.org and will earn while seeking counselling, (b) the most victimised females along shared criteria will become CEEBRAIN Mission Partners (CMP)/Market Executives (ME) to earn profit margin percentage automatically from the online demand of the products and services uploaded by the suppliers, (c) any member will earn her/his share from the advertisements at her/his respective pages while surfing and learning every detail of her/his chosen issue or project including science, mathematics, engineering, medical, etc., required to excel in the chosen project to earn more by three hours work through CEETECH cloud as explained above. Since those uploading any content will earn from the advertisements at their respective page while those learning from them will earn their share from the advertisements at group page, content provider and learners both will continuously earn neuron credits. The most victimised females along the shared criteria will have an extra advantage to win elections in today's political systems or/and seek marks to become '*Maharshi*' at every 500 km who will earn also while those listening their agenda will also earn their share as explained above, (d) since every CEEBRAIN member will use her/his 33 per cent share meant for social up gradation with those identified as the most victimized from the data along the shared criteria, the higher economic growth will perpetually upgrade the victims first even when (s)he uses her/his share with a member uploading wrong data while producing every data in a moment at the click of button. Besides creating www.ceebrain.org, we are also teaching our novel courses to very poor females from SC-ST-Backward-Muslim etc. communities who will develop some capacity in next three-four years to spread the mission at temporary CEEKUL hostel at every population of ten thousand in the whole world and will also manage local affairs along the guidance of their choice experts. We will teach the most victimised, black and indigenous females at *Raebareli, Nankari* (near IIT Kanpur) and in the whole world to earn their faith to implement the IDEA OF CEEKUL. These trained Dalit/*Adivasi*/Muslim/Black/ indigenous females will pursue their innovative projects besides teaching next generation particularly daughters to start from new assumptions to shape a better future for the daughters of our daughters. Those trained females pursuing a research career will create new CEETECH cloud controlled automated technologies while those managing regular discussions for reinterpretation of constitutional ideals will act as a change agent at local area to convince the villagers and slum dwellers to replace democracy by CEEBRAIN much before 2025. Some of them will fight elections in today's political systems or/and will seek marks to become '*Maharshi*' at every 500 km. It's the radical agenda of social transformation that will create a wave to let the most victimised females in the families of freedom fighters, politicians, judges, bureaucrats, industrialists, etc., win coming elections with the females managing social movements and NGOs and females having mass appeal with their proven talent in their profession of law, media, arts, sports, etc., along the online guidance by the most respected academicians, regional development experts and elected *LOK SEWAK SANGH* members from the whole world. We have big plans to let the females in law-media-arts-sports, etc., restructure their profession along a new vision and become the leaders of new civilisation, earn millions by guiding the most victimized females in the whole world, become Presidents/ Prime Ministers/Chief Ministers etc in all countries to replace their country system by CEEBRAIN much before 2025. Soon those females rejecting the possibility of radical transformation now will start believing in the power of idea and will generate new confidence in the minds of those lamenting on poor implementation as well as gentle persons in politics, business, etc., also to overcome their predatory colleagues and transform the lives of the victims in a new way. Focusing on females will force competition among males also to contribute.

(4) We often listen how we will save the victims aspiring to be part of CEEBRAIN civilisation from the police, bureaucrats, judges, local '*gundas*' etc working for the ideals of democracy with the patronage of elected Gods. Though we believe in human dignity and expect that the most victimized females in the whole world will ultimately understand our vision, yet the desire for justice by victims may motivate some constitutional law experts and judges to support our cause. We have some hopes from Gandhians, change seekers like www.wewantjustice.org and social movement experts also to implement CEEBRAIN civilisation besides fighting against the government in creative ways. We also have some hopes from those feeling humiliated due to poor implementation of the court orders, those believing in the supremacy of still relevant constitutional ideals like equal opportunity and social-economic-political justice etc, those loosing elections and those not getting desired position in the party in spite of their hard efforts, those capitalists fed up with government corruption, etc., Since we have no interest in money, position, awards etc except showing radical transformation in the lives of the most victimized females in the whole world from our research ideas, those aspiring/failing to become Presidents/ Prime Ministers/Chief Ministers, etc., may also join hands with us. The failed people may also support us. Continuous

discussion on the limitations of democracy will ready the common masses to transform from democracy to CEEBRAIN. We have big hopes from those taking arms in their hands because they are already fighting against predatory governments. Though we sympathize with the Naxals, Al-Qaeda, Taliban type Organisations, yet disagree with their violent struggle. They constantly argue that Gandhi appeals to motivated minds only than to the predators but how Mao's vision is superior to that of Gandhi. Their past failures with Gandhian ideals must motivate them to reinvent and reinterpret Gandhi like Nelson Mandela, Martin Luther King, Aung Suu Kyi, Shirin Ebadi etc succeeded. Their violent struggles are never going to succeed because the elites enjoy huge resources, police, military, army, judiciary etc and enjoy the faith of the international network of the elites and governments working for them while those taking guns in their hands are losing the faith of local sympathizers also because they are fed up with crime competition. The governments will definitely succeed to show some development in neglected areas to divide and rule but the victims can use sudden development done by governments to their advantage by implementing a new development model through www.ceebrain.org. They should focus their family females to implement new development model valuing labour, creativity and CEETECH cloud. They should enhance their CEEBRAIN potential with the support of nutritionists, mind experts, educationists etc. If they don't want to send their females outside, no problem, still they can educate them by focusing on the detailed understanding of products and services at www.ceebrain.org from home. Islam also preaches to understand the worldly affairs including products and services in religious as well as scientific ways. Westoxification and perpetual injustice can be answered by reinventing and modernising traditions for shaping a new future also than by violent struggles. Naxals/Al-Qaeda/Taliban, etc., type Organisations and all those fighting against the predators must believe that they are more capable to transform the lives of victims than those victims succumbing to the dirty designs of the predators because they have already made their minds to fight but they will become a moral force by reinventing and modernising their traditions and will become an asset for shaping a new CEEBRAIN civilisation by replacing democracy. Governments will show development to dilute crisis and perpetuate their predatory powers with local opportunists seeking favours but the same development can become an opportunity for those taking guns in their hands by promoting the opportunists as their voice along new development model. We will be very happy to implement our vision in those areas where victims are fighting against the predators and get their females as next Presidents/Prime Ministers/Chief Ministers in all countries. If we succeed to show results, very nice, otherwise we are taking nothing from anyone except freedom to implement our research ideas. Crisis to the dreamers can become a very big opportunity provided they focus on superior alternatives and seek CEEBRAIN potential enhancing nutrition to rewire their brains along higher creative goals than damaging their health while handling contradictions.

(5) Victims should create WORLD ASSOCIATION OF VICTIMIZED FEMALES and THEIR SYMPATHISERS to share their experiences and discuss why things went wrong, what can be expected from democracy, what new ideas and plans they are conceiving to shape a better future. Life of one of us (Dr Manoj Srivastava) had been extremely chaotic and shameful but our faith in the life of ideals and strong will to see new light turned crisis into big opportunity to shape a new civilisation. We are continuously quarrelling at all levels to create a just civilisation and heal from the feeling of justice in the process. Obviously, if there are other likeminded people and Organisations then our shared goals will be achieved with enthusiasm. It's not that everything will become perfect on one Sunday morning, rather let us start a new thinking, even if it looks crazy. We don't need funds from anyone, rather we are struggling to earn the faith of the most victimised females

particularly from those communities like *Dalit-Adivasi-*Backward-Muslim-Black-Indigenous, etc., that had been suffering since the beginning of human civilisation to show a radical improvement in their lives just from our research ideas. Intellectual collaboration of likeminded victims will succeed to create first CEEKUL at Raebareli for every facility to them free from our own generated resources, though our new development model will provide almost everything required for CEEBRAIN infrastructure as a business share.

REFERENCES

1. PhD thesis 'Quantum Information Processing in Brain Microtubules – In Search of a Comprehensive Scientific Framework for Explaining Mind and Consciousness' of Dr Manoj Srivastava under the supervision of Prof Bijoy Boruah (Philosophy of Mind), Prof GC Ray (Bio-Medical Engineering), Prof NK Sharma (Cognitive Psychology), Prof Tulsi Dass (Mathematical Physics) but finally Prof Bijoy Boruah was the sole supervisor. World famous Prof Stuart Hameroff, Prof Alwyn Scot, Prof Ranjit Nair (Founder of Center for Philosophy and Foundations of Science) and Prof P K Kalra (then Dean at IIT Kanpur and neural network expert now Akash tablet fame Director at IIT Jodhpur, kalra@iitk.ac.in) were PhD thesis examiners.
2. http://www.biographyonline.net/people/women-who-changed-world.html

Acknowledgement :

Dr Manoj Srivastava seeks inspirations from the struggles of great teachers like Prof A P Shukla sir (aps@iitk.ac.in) who was always receptive to discuss challenging questions particularly on the structure of scientific revolutions during PhD at IIT Kanpur. Respected sir, new scientific revolution is in the process, pl enjoy good health and see radical transformation in educational, industrial and development models in the whole world by 2025.

Note :

This paper has been written in a short notice of one month for an international conference at IGNOU to be organised by Dalit female Professor Vimal Thorat during 20-22 February 2013. It deals with very ambitious and controversial issues but we hope to modify the ideas and presentation drastically within next 3-4 years and produce very enlightened answers finally by 2025.

Dr Manoj Srivastava is B.Tech. in Mechanical Engineering from HBTI Kanpur (1987-91), PhD in Quantum Neuroinformatics of Mind and Consciousness from HSS Deptt., IIT Kanpur (1994-2002), earned 1991 votes against Sonia Gandhi in 2009 Lok Sabha elections, now shaping a new CEEBRAIN CIVILISATION. Rashmi Chandra is Associate Professor of Biotechnology at IMS Engineering College, Ghaziabad who is also teaching 'BRAIN BUILDING RESEARCH' to very poor girls free. KESHAN is our son pursuing B.Sc. in Mathematics from IGNOU besides teaching basic cloud computing to very poor girls free.

16

CASTE AND CRIME : A STUDY OF HINDU MYTHOLOGY AND SCRIPTURES

Prachi Patil

Introduction

The debates on oppression have often centred on the oppressed. We have been successful in cataloguing the oppressed as women, minority, Dalit, *adivasi,* etc., to the extent that the words 'oppressed' and 'marginalised' are associated with these very categories of people in our minds. There is a great need to speak about the oppressor within and outside the academic circles. Very few texts challenge and identify the oppressor, as the threat of mirroring ourselves is ever present. It is easier to speak of people's oppression than of our own contribution to it through participation or silence. While it is impossible to escape writing about the oppressed when we endeavour to contextualise the oppression, this paper is a conscious effort in the direction of challenging the oppressor within the caste system.

Oppression is multifaceted phenomena wherein violence is its prerequisite. Kumar (2005) refers to three types of violence classified by the Jain philosophy, namely mental, verbal and physical. The nuanced relationship of oppression and violence operates itself through these very categories. An act of violence cannot be strictly classified as mental or verbal or physical, these categories do not function in isolation rather they are intertwined with each other. Mental violence is covert form of violence which attacks the psyche of the victim; it is met out through the thought process of the oppressor. The power of non-verbal and non-physical violence can be associated with mental violence. Fundamentally we create hierarchies of caste through our mind, through our thought we render the other as less valuable or less human because she belongs to a particular caste. As sociologists it is a limitation that we cannot accurately study or measure the Violence of thought, its degree and its impact and thus we are rendered incompetent to articulate it in words. Verbal violence manifests itself into our language through the medium of songs, phrases, jokes and most offensive of these are the women centric abuses which we are all familiar with. I am reminded of a peculiar incidence in a classroom, where a group of elite women joked about public rape comparing it to the load of assignments we had to submit. They failed (rather chose to fail) to realise that it is a form of verbal violence on those who have suffered public rape or are under constant threat of it. I would like to draw your attention to the fact that the category of public rape was invoked, not of rape or of gang rape as any woman is vulnerable to this form, but public rape is the reserve of a certain women in India, namely the Dalit, the *adivasi* and the Muslim. The difference between gang rape and pubic rape is fundamental, in a gang rape a woman is raped by a gang of men while in a public rape a woman is raped in front of many people who witness the atrocity. Public rape is the atrocity of Khairlanjee, where the whole village looked on when two Dalit women, Surekha Bhootmange and her daughter Priyanka were being raped, it is when an *adivasi* woman was being paraded naked and molested, it is the horrific rapes of Muslim women that took place in full vicinity in Gujarat.

The third category of 'physical' is the bodily violence that is inflicted upon the victim through muscle and weapon power. It takes the form of hitting, molesting, murder and rape. The brutality inflicted upon the body which disfigures it, breaks it into pieces and violates it is called as physical violence.

In India a fourth category-'codified violence' emerges which is an intermesh of the above three, consolidated into a written edict. The written law reinforces the mental, codifies the verbal and legitimises the physical forms of violence. The Hindu mythological and holy scriptures are a form of codified violence. These codified laws are designed to perpetuate caste hierarchies and inequalities. I deal with the category of 'codified violence' present within the Hindu texts in this paper. The portrayals of *shudra* and Dalit women within the Hindu mythologies and scriptures like the Ramayana, Mahabharata, Kamasutra and Manusmriti explain the existing position of *shudra* and Dalit women within the Indian society. There are numerous Hindu texts which can be utilised for this purpose but for lack of availability and dearth of translations of the texts, I choose the epic Ramayana and the two treatises Kamasutra and Manusmriti.

Hindu Literature as Codified Violence

Affiliations between Hindu mythology and the plight of *shudra* and Dalit have been expounded by Ambedkar, Phule and Periyar in the past while a few feminists have recently revisited the topic with a Phule-Ambedkarite framework. Mythological literature in India has been structured in a way to subdue the non-Aryan element to its core, evidently the composition of its prose, poetry, its each and every verse and stanza hails the Aryan-Brahmanism as the eternal truth and Dharma. It would be a folly on part of a social scientist to consider the scripts of Ramayana and Mahabharata as merely mythological or holy-scriptures, rather they are to be considered as socio-political treatise of the dominant castes. This section explores the location of Dalit and *shudra* women within the texts of Ramayana, Kamasutra and Manusmriti.

A big debate on numerous versions and multiple interpretations of Ramayana engulfs us today, with some versions deifying Rama and others deifying Ravana. While some interpret Sita's disappearance as abduction, others like feminist poet Meena Kandasamy endeavour to term it as Sita's choice to live with Ravana. There are versions of Ramayana's which are more liberating than others, the contestation between versions and interpretations is on, but I concern myself with the canonical text of Ramayana – Valmiki's Ramayana and the translated version by C. Gopalachari as these are espoused by the saffron brigade.

A primary question that surfaces is 'are there any references mentioned to suggest the existence of a correlation between *Rakshasis* of Ramayana and Dalit women? The Ramayana does not explicitly mention a relation but it is the essential characteristic of being non Aryan and non-Brahman that links the *Rakshasis* and Dalit and *shudra* women to each other in their pathos. The Dalit and *shudra* embody the anti Brahman and non Aryan and thus the violence wreaked on them gains justification within the texts of Ramayana in the name of preservation of *Dharma.*

The Ramayana recounts the life story of Rama, his wife Sita and Laxmana, his brother. The characters take us through a journey of their exile in the forest, involving us in their separation, laughter, frustration and battles. The enemies are the *Rakshasa's*, who are non Aryans while the protagonists Rama and Laxmana are Aryans-the *Devas*. In the battles fought between the *Rakshasas* and the Aryan princes, the *Rakshasi* women are constantly being humiliated and slaughtered by the protagonists in the garb of *Dharma*. The Ramayana text contains some of the most violent and unacceptable examples of sanctioned behaviour towards the non-Aryan women. The mention of certain women characters who are *Rakshasis* can be found in Ramayana, some of these women are widely known like Surpanakha and Mandodari others like Tataka and Aayomukhi are lesser known. The life stories of these women have several aspects in common; firstly, they all have been rendered demonic characteristics in their behaviour as well as appearance since they are described as ugly, huge and beastly. Secondly they all have met similar fate of humiliation and death, except in the case of Mandodari, at the hands of upper caste males Rama and Lakshmana. Surpanakha, the sister of Ravana proposed to Rama and Aayomukhi proposed to Laxmana at different times in the story but both are shunned and mutilated by the brothers. While Surpankha's nose and ears were chopped off, Laxmana brutalised Aayomukhi by chopping off her nose, ears and breasts. C. Gopalachari's translation of Ramayana provides an unapologetic case for the slaying of Surpanakha which is beyond the acceptance and comprehension of individuals believing in humanity. Vizia Bharati (1995) claims that Tataka was a *Rakshasi* princess who was murdered at the hands of Rama and Laxmana for the benefit of sages. Queen Mandodari is the wife of Ravana, was 'dragged by her hair and ill treated' (Vizia, 1995) by Rama's army to in turn humiliate Ravana. The humiliation of women as a weapon of war is evident in the Ramayana. It is constantly employed to disgrace the enemy. A relationship between war, women and state can be established in Ramayana.

Coming to the Kamasutra, it considered as a treatise on love, enjoys vast foreign and elite English reading Indian readership. Many foreign authors have penned down articles in praise of the erotic text and the culture of love in India. Western readers have romanticised the Kamasutra beyond limits as a sex handbook from the mysterious Oriental East. The Kamasutra was also revived by the homosexual movement in India as it provides evidence supporting same sex relations. Venturing beyond these eulogies, the text is problematic in its approach towards women of lower castes. It succeeds in upholding of caste norms by dictating the 'legal' pleasures permitted to a citizen. The citizen that the text speaks of is essentially male and upper caste. Majority have failed to identify examples of caste hierarchy and gender biasness replete within the text. It is "less about sexual activity and more about the regulation and control of sexuality in a social context stratified by gender, class and caste" (Puri 2002). Seen through power dimensions the text furthers the agenda of caste hierarchies through maintaining the chastity of *Brahmin* women by instructing males not to have relationships with a *Brahmin* woman if she is not one's legitimate wife. A marital relationship with a woman of a higher caste who has already been married once is also strictly forbidden. Chakravarti's (1993) argument that 'the upper-caste woman is the object of moral panic in Brahmanic texts' can be seen evoked under this backdrop. The prohibition to marry an upper-caste woman stems from the insecurity and need to preserve the order of caste system, according to Ambedkar this is achieved through strict adherence to law of endogamy as Ambedkar argues that 'endogamy is the only characteristic of caste'. In contrast to *Brahmin* woman the bodies of *shudra* and Dalit women are to be abducted, seduced, and 'enjoyed' without consideration, besides it is justified behaviour. The Kamasutra mentions that "sexual relations with women of the lower castes, with women excommunicated from their castes and twice-married women are acceptable only for the purpose of pleasure". A caste and class based division of sexual labour is also prominent in the Kamasutra since mouth-congress is the domain of "unchaste, wanton women, female attendants and serving maids (those who are unmarried and live by "shampooing") and courtesans". Sexual objectification of socially marginalised and oppressed women is a theme predominant in the text. As Puri (2002) puts it the "Kamasutra indicates not the celebration of sex but the regulation of sexuality through the mechanisms of pleasure in the unequal social setting".

The Manusmriti was institutionalised for upholding of the caste system. It provided dictums for punishments, classified the crimes according to the caste hierarchy and penalised people accordingly. Ambedkar says Manu 'was not the law giver' rather 'he was an upholder of it and therefore philosophised about it.' This substantiates the fact that Manu merely codified the Hindu law that was a social theory already in practice. The state is born from the existing social structure of a society as did the Manusmriti-it does not exist in isolation. The Kamasutra "coincides with the *Manava Dharmashastras*" (Puri 2002), both these texts simultaneously attempt to uphold the Brahmanic and inscribe it into the public memory and practice. Both the texts were Brahmanic attempt at encoding and regulating social-sexual interaction. While the caste system and Brahmanic superiority is institutionalised, the degradation and lack of human rights of the lower castes is simultaneously established in these ancient Hindu texts.

Understanding Crime within Hindu Literature

In light of the preceding discussion on Hindu scriptures it is important to conceptualise the nature of 'crime' emanating from these texts within India. What constitutes a crime and for whom are questions that are to be answered. Durkheim defines crime as acts which 'offend strong and definite states of collective conscience' (harlambous book). Collective conscience is "the totality of beliefs and sentiments common to the average members of a society" (Durkheim 1984). Durkheim gives a sociological explanation of crime, he is not talking about crime in isolated cases but he speaks of the 'collective'. He is referring to a crime that moves the collective consciousness, threatens its existence and violates its solidarity. Is there a collective consciousness in people of India and what forms the collective consciousness in India are essential questions from an anti-caste perspective.

The idea of collective consciousness is difficult to prove both in terms of theory and practice with reference to caste system in India. 'There is an utter lack among the Hindus of what the sociologists call "consciousness of kind" (Ambedkar 1944). India lacks a consciousness of kind, what we have is a consciousness of castes. The nature of this caste consciousness, unlike the collective is not shared and common to all, it is forcefully maintained. Yet again this caste consciousness has a unique hierarchical order in its operation, i.e., it operates from top to bottom and governs the individual's behaviour in particular a caste group. Since, we are examining the concept of crime within the Hindu scriptures, it is necessary to compare the universal views on crime and what caste as a state classifies 'crime' primarily sourced by the Hindu scriptures. Human rights in contemporary debate talk about the individual and collective human right. The idea of 'collective' rights smothers the individual's right for the collective good. The collective right is exercised when a family decides to secrete the rape of a daughter in fear of family honour as it is in collective good of the family to maintain their reputation in the society. In the Hindu context human rights are 'collective' in nature as they are defined for a particular caste rather than individuals. The Manusmriti for instance has drafted crimes of various kinds and the punishments and fines to be levied on the perpetrator according to his caste. These rules have been translate even in present times for instance if a Dalit woman *sarpanch* sits on a chair that has been designated to her position in a meeting, she is meddling with the caste conscience which has established certain caste norms for her through customary law which require her to take a lower seat in presence of the upper castes. Assertion on her part to challenge this status quo is liable for punishment as per Manusmriti; it is a threat to the right of upper castes to have the highest seat. India experiences fragmented consciousness emerging from the collective rights of each and every caste. Obnoxious religious practices lacking the moral fibre of human rights like untouchability, *Devdasi*, *Sati* and child marriage have religious sanction whereas defiance against these practices is considered as a crime. Thus we see a very perverted picture of crime within the Hindu scriptures, crime then becomes an act to access basic individual human rights.

Within the debate of human rights of 'collective' versus the 'individual', the constitution of India exemplifies individual human rights. It could be termed as a literature in itself which proclaims the ideas of equality, liberty and justice which are anti-thesis to the ideas of the dominant religion of India. India in its post independence period experiences two types of laws simultaneously that Durkheim defines as sanctions, a 'system of punishment related to offences against social rules'. He talks about repressive sanctions known as penal laws and recitative sanctions known as contract/written laws. The Constitution would fall under the category of recitative laws, which are established after a society enters into the industrial or advanced phase transiting the phase of tribal or segmental society and the *Khap panchayat* laws would be classified as repressive laws. India swings like a pendulum between modernity and antiquity, this dichotomy is the essential temperament of the Indian society today.

Contemporary Reflections

Analysis of patriarchy requires to be anchored within the framework of caste in India. The uniqueness of patriarchy in India cannot be purely contextualised within the domain of man-woman power relationship but it is fundamentally woven together with the fabric of caste hierarchies to subjugate women. Liberating the Indian society from the shackles of patriarchy cannot be attained without annihilating caste. Necessary is the realisation that caste is not exclusively a social structure but it is a religiously legitimised social structure. It is high time that many feminists come out of their comfortable circles of being a practicing Hindu, upper caste and upper class, claiming that they are fighting patriarchy. This empty rhetoric is a fool's trap which is being opposed bitterly by anti-caste feminists. Caste governs the social life as it is even in the present day through the scriptures, only the form has changed.

It is painful for me as a woman to compare the rape of one woman with another, as I am aware of the torment and ghastly torture meted out to the sister, but as sociologists it is our job to articulate the painful truths of our society. We as a nation blazed at the heinous rape and murder of a 23 year old in a bus in Delhi but the silence that surrounds the likes of Khairlanjee, Hisar, and the footage of naked parading of an *adivasi* girl is appalling and frightening. This comparison becomes necessary to question our partial humanity, one which we feel only for our kind and do not extend to the other. A grave question that stares at us is, why this partial outburst of rage? Violence is not new to the Indian society,

Amidst the struggle for justice for the girl and many others, a strange remark made by RSS chief Mohan Bhagwat's that, "Rapes happen in India, not Bharat." (PTI, 2013 January 8) was issued post the death of the Delhi bus gang-rape victim. This is a multi-layered claim encompasses within itself patriarchal and caste biases. Bhagwat's claim sent a furore among Marxist feminists, demanding explanations for the rapes of 11 *adivasi* girls in the *ashramshala* of Kanker while others fumed at his patriarchal mindset which blames the victim and limits the mobilisation of women. Though on the outset Bhagwat seems to be targeting industrialisation and westernisation, exercise of women's freedom and loss of values within the cities, an anti-caste perspective will explain the caste ridden underpinnings of his statement. Traditionally *adivasi* and Dalit women's rapes are not considered as rapes or crimes rather they are perceived as punishments authorised by the societal norms. These are punishments for transgressing the caste norms, for threatening the power relations of caste and daring to claim something as basic as 'humanity', which is not in ones lot. Bhagwat's claim arises from this phenomenon. He is specifically talking about rapes of upper-caste women, whose sexuality and existence has much to do with the conservation of caste system and thus it cannot be endangered by the threats of rape. The upper caste woman's body as opposed to the Dalit woman's body is 'the gateway of the caste-system'. Bhagwat's claim entails the dichotomy of the East and the West, where village represents Bharat and India symbolises the West. Bharat is a celebration of ideas of Gandhi's Gram-*Swaraj* and *Ram Rajya*, it is the hotbed of power relations where caste norms are adhered to while India personifies a space where the dream of a casteless society can be cherished to a certain extent.

Half of our society lives in partial humanity and so the other half cannot claim to be human. We are a mutilated society, crooked at many places by the wounds of caste, patriarchy, religion and class. The question which we need to ask ourselves as a society is 'about what it means to be human' (Visvanathan 1996) and when will we extend this humanity to others.

REFERENCES

- Bharati Vizia (1995), Hindu Epics: Portrayal of Dalit Women. In P.G. Jogdand (Ed.), *Dalit Women: Issues and Perspective*, (pp. 94-104). Gyan Prakashan.
- C. Rajagopalachri, (1951). *Ramayana*. Bharatiya Vidya Bhavan.
- Chakravarti, Uma. (1993), Conceptualizing Brahmanical Patriarchy in Early India: Gender, Caste, Class and State. *Economic and Political Weekly* 28(14):579–85.
- Durkheim Emile, *The Division of Labour in Society*. Translation published by MacMillan Press in 1984.
- Kandasamy Meena, (2011). *Random Access Man in Ms. Militancy*. Navayana Publication, New Delhi.

- Kumar Vivek (2005), Violence and Youth: Carving Out An Independent Agenda For Youth. *Indian Journal of Youth Affairs*. Vol. 9 (2) July-December 2005, pp. 55-62.
- PTI : Silchar/New Delhi, 2013, 'RSS Chief Mohan Bhagwat makes derogatory comments against women, says rapes happen in India, not Bharat'. *The Indian Express* 2013 January 08. http://www.indianexpress.com/news/rss-chief-mohan-bhagwat-makes-derogatory-comments-against-women-says-rapes-happen-in-india-not-bharat/1054468/2
- Puri Jyoti (2002), *Concerning Kamasutras: Challenging Narratives of History and Sexuality*. Signs, Vol. 27, No. 3 (Spring 2002), pp. 603-639. The University of Chicago Press http://www.jstor.org/stable/10.1086/337937.
- *The Kama Sutra of Vatsyayana*. (1883-1925). Translation. Hindu Kama Shastra Society. Benares: Society of the Friends of India.
- Visvanathan Susan (1993). From Housewifization to Androgyny. *India International Centre Quarterly*, Vol. 23, No. 3/4, Second Nature: Women and the Family (WINTER 1996), pp. 177-189. http://www.jstor.org/stable/23004618.

17

MARGIN AS THE CENTRE OF CREATIVITY: EXPRESSION OR EXPLOITATION? A STUDY OF SELECT POETRY OF NAMDEO DHASAL AND LANGSTON HUGHES

Pawan Kumar

Abstract

Any issue or movement in literature that has the capability of stirring mass consciousness and giving new directions to our thought process is bound to have effects beyond spatial and temporal limits, at the same time, having far-reaching ramifications. In the context of marginal literature, the centre of creativity and productivity itself has shifted toward the margins because there are various issues that are intertwined with the margins when it comes to caste and race (in the Indian and African-American contexts simultaneously) like segregation and marginalisation of communit(y)ies, identity and freedom of the oppressed, the position of women, and the broader issues of language, culture and tradition. This paper explores these issues vis-à-vis the idea of creativity and productivity, analysing whether marginal literature or art is giving voice to the unheard population or if it is trying to create a new niche or platform for these creative instincts. The discourses on marginalisation, sexuality, identity, regionalism, racism and segregation become all the more poignant in poetry, and this paper looks at the dialectics of the same in select poems of Namdeo Dhasal and Langston Hughes. The poems of these two poets reflect various facets of marginalised life, and at the same time, have a unique appeal in terms of language and style, thus posing a serious question mark on our existence in a society full of divisions on caste and racial lines. This paper will be a comparative study of these two poets and will also examine the socio-political conditions (the paper will also chart parallels between the Dalit Panther Movement and the Harlem Renaissance) of the marginalised people, so that Dhasal's and Hughes's poetry will become all the more relevant as a new paradigm in our existing literature, thereby epitomising the core idea of this paper- 'margin as the centre of creativity'.

Key Words : Margin vs. Creativity, Repressed Expression, Exploitation of the Oppressed

While writing this paper, the first question that came to my mind was, what is Marginal Literature? In my opinion, marginal literature is not just a tool to create a new, dominant ideology or push the existing barriers; it can prove to be instrumental in creating a new niche or a centre of creativity without dismantling the existing 'mainstream' literature or social values, because the moment one dismantles the existing literary perspectives and social values, we destroy our own trajectory of development, the locus of our ideas, and above all, the very point of the origin of ideas, as in art and literature, there is room for plurality of interpretation. We have a tradition of argument in our country: ancient philosophers and aestheticians came up with theories of literature and art because they engaged with the argumentative tradition in our country. Hence, it is not just our duty, but our *dharma* to uphold the tradition of arguments and multiplicity of interpretations in all walks of life, more so when it comes to literature and the allied arts. There is no doubt that there are various issues which make this margin volatile, but it is also true that the centre of creativity also lies therein. Why do writers and poets want to have a muse who is beautiful and create an illusion of objective reality? We must accept our Indian muse who has tears in her eyes and blood dripping from her body, and has enough power to make a writer's literary instincts a fertile breeding ground of literature with social concerns.

There is no doubt that the Dalit movement, the feminist movements, and other social movements have created not only a literary space, but also a social space for the marginalised and the subjugated voices. Hence, allied, emerging issues like the condition of women, power politics within the different sections of the society, subtle forms of casteism being practiced in the Indian society, and, above all, the use of literature for social changes, within these movements need to be addressed. Any issue or movement in literature that has the capability of stirring mass consciousness and giving new directions to our thought process is bound to have effects beyond spatial and temporal limits, at the same time, having far-reaching ramifications. In the context of marginal literature, the centre of creativity and productivity itself has shifted towards the margins because there are various issues that are intertwined with the margins when it comes to caste and race (in the Indian and African-American contexts simultaneously) like segregation and marginalisation of communit(y)ies, identity and freedom of the oppressed, the position of women, and the broader issues of language, culture and tradition.

Even after sixty five years of Independence and various movements that have taken place in our country, we do not seem to have a solution for various problems like casteism, communal rifts, gender prejudices, the condition of poor people in rural India, and the gulf between the haves and the have-nots. The reason behind this could be the ruptures or the gaps and fissures existing within these movements. For example, tribal ideology is based on lived experiences and it is thus a 'true consciousness,' whereas those who take advantage of the plight of these people and want to become a part of the dominant ideology (in Marxist terms, people with 'false consciousness' (Eyerman 43) generally come up with radical solutions. For instance, Gail Omvedt quotes Baburao Bagul in his book *Dalit Vision* to show this radical mindset.

> In the face of this apparently overwhelming oppressiveness of tradition, Dalit radicals could only respond with a total negation. You who have made the mistake of being born in this community / must now rectify it. Either leave the country/or make war! But is Indian tradition totally oppressive? Is it necessary for either Dalit or upper caste progressive who aspire to equality and liberation to reject Indian culture and identity totally? . . . Freedom and equality can in fact find their roots in tradition if that tradition is critically understood. (97)

We should never forget that we are in a democratic country and there are certain basic principles that we must follow in order to make India a classic example of secularism and equality. In order to depict a society based on equality, a writer should posses such qualities such as sagacity, sensitivity, and unbiased acumen. In an interview with Satish Kalsekar, Dhasal highlights his idea about revolution, "I wanted a revolution. I wanted to overturn the government. However, it was the utopian idea of a romantic person. The real problem was that rousing only a specific section of society is no way to bring about a complete revolution. The greatest support of the revolution comes from the human being whom the process of exploitation crushes" (Chitre 169). This shows Dhasal's unbiased and pragmatic approach towards other marginalised people and life, and his idea of the overall development of the society.

Although this paper is a comparative study of Namdeo Dhasal's and Langston Hughes's poetry, I would also like to bring in various political and social issues that persist in India, to show how immune we are to carrying out a literary revolution without posing threat to society and what we must do in order to create a selfless and ever growing literary instinct among our fellow citizens. Dhasal and Hughes are almost mirror image widely separated in time and space, because they share the same kind of feeling of oppression and the aspiration for freedom/equality, and also because through their writings, they are engaged in creating a platform for unheard voices. The idea of consciousness, self and identity are identical in every tradition and culture, so the driving force of African-American and Indian Dalit movements is the same; they have homologous locus of origin. For instance, the 1973 manifesto of Dalit Panthers quoted in *Sahitya Aur Dalit Chetna* by Maheep Singh and Chandrakant Bandiwadekar mentions one such parallel:

> . . . because of the monstrous power of America, the third world is subjugated, and in India, the Dalit are exploited and tortured. In America also, a handful of white racists are exploiting the black populace. As a reaction to this, the Black Panther movement came into existence in order to eradicate racism. The fire of this struggle has spread all over the country. And we claim that this struggle is closely related with our struggle. (my translation, 33).

Both Dhasal and Hughes are among those writers who never dreamt of becoming literary icons, because they always tried to feel and depict in their works the inhuman condition meted out to the poor 'others' of the society without labelling themselves as the *messiah* or the sole representative of such castes or races. Their poetry in itself shows that they write not in ink but in pain. Dilip Chitre writes about Dhasal:

. . . uprooted from the countryside and replanted in the inner city and the rotten core of Mumbai—a city of the most extreme and dehumanising forms of exploitation—Namdeo's human root not only proved tenacious, but triumphant. He grew up out of a cesspool, drawing nourishment from it, metabolising its toxic waste and thriving on the immunity he acquired, to become *the* poet of the underworld, a lumen *messiah*, a poor man's *bodhisattva.* (153)

We find a similar persona of Langston Hughes as outlined by Mary Beth Culp in her essay "Religion in the Poetry of Langston Hughes":

..... Langston Hughes lived basically in terms of the external world and in unison with it, making himself one with his people and refusing to stand apart as an individual. His poetry reflects collective states of mind as if they were his own, merging the poet's personality with his racial group. He assumes various personae. Sometimes he is the spirit of his race, at other times he is a spittoon polisher, a black mother, a prostitute, a black man without job or money but there is a commonality among the various experiences presented in his poems which gives them a kind of consistent persona (240).

The Dalit Panther Movement and Harlem Renaissance were literary movements as well as social and cultural movements. Being the pioneer of Dalit Panther movement, Dhasal strived hard to propagate a message among high-class people that beyond their luxurious world, there is also a world full of pain and suffering. On the other hand, Hughes has depicted the physiological as well as the psychological condition of the black people in his poems and other literary works with great precision and led them to feel proud of their selves, to nurture their black selves. His use of folk elements, myths and symbols shows the creative world of marginalised people. Addison Gayle Jr. in his article "The Harlem Renaissance: Towards a Black Aesthetics" says,

"During the Harlem Renaissance when Black people, as Counties Cullen notes, were only three generations removed from their ancestral homeland, a group of remarkable men and women converged on

Harlem and transformed it into the literary capital of the world. They were a diverse group; they held different opinions concerning the function of art, their relationship with the United States and with each other. They were old and young, naive and sophisticated, college-educated, and self-taught, and they came from places as far away as the West Indies and as near as Washington, D.C. Yet, they had one thing in common- the determination, according to Langston Hughes, "to express our individual dark-skinned selves without fear or shame." (78)

Dhasal's and Hughes's poems form a collage in which the heartfelt condition of human psyche is shown, where the naked reality of subjugated and marginalised people is described with tears and the insane dance of patriarchy is highlighted to show the harsh reality of our modern society. Realism in their poems is not directed towards forming a new ideology, but towards depiction of the real, sordid truth of life for a specific section of the populace.

In fact, it is not only the Dalit voices or the voices of the African Americans that Dhasal and Hughes were concerned with. Being a part of the Indian existence, Dhasal reflects the idea of the Indian unity, as reflected by A.K. Coomaraswamy in *The Dance of Siva*, "The heart and essence of the Indian experience is to be found in a constant intuition of the unity of all life, and the instinctive and ineradicable conviction that the recognition of this unity is the highest good and the uttermost freedom" (Puligandla 2). Dhasal was well aware of the double marginalisation of women, but he was of the opinion that prostitutes suffer triple marginalisation. He once told Dilip Chitre,

"I can relate to a sex worker as a human being. I may even offer money to a prostitute as help. But I would not ask for sex in return of favours of other kind or in consideration of some rendered services. I hate being served. Giving freely and taking freely are almost ideals in my life." (161)

Dhasal describes the condition of a young prostitute in his poem "Mandakini Patil: A Young Prostitute, My Intended Collage" in these resounding words: "On a barren blue canvas / Her clothes ripped off, her thighs blasted open, /A sixteen-year old girl surrendering herself to pain" (Chitre 56). Dhasal has depicted the feelings and the conditions of prostitutes like a soul detached from the body. In Chitre's words:

"As the central symbol of the stigmatised and the loathed, Namdeo uses the female prostitutes of "Golpitha" an object of carnal 'love' but still 'loathed'. Unlike a wife, the prostitute has no institutionalised sanctity. She is, therefore, denied dignity as a human being. Her status is that of the ultimate untouchable, serving other humans by allowing them to degrade oneself." (Chitre 11)

Hughes also depicts the extreme form of racial and gender-based violence in his poem "Song for a Dark Girl": "Way Down South in Dixie / (Break the heart of me) / They hung my black young lover / To a cross road tree. / Way Down South in Dixie / (Bruised body high in the air) / I asked the white lord Jesus / What was the use of prayer" (Gates and McKay 1263). What these poets reiterate through their poems is that inequality in the status of women, the Dalit and the downtrodden people will never give birth to a tolerant and secular society, and the fact that the problem really lies in our psyche, our thought process, in fact, in our very perception. Stereotyping a woman's body and the perception that their virginity is a barometer of a man's ego and his social status has aggravated this inequality all the more. The cause which must have occasioned poetry such as that of Dhasal and Hughes is the fact that most of us do not feel the pain that they must have felt because like Faustus, we have sold our souls to Mephistopheles, and are 'seemingly happy' in the 'modern' lives that we live. In his landmark poem, "Kamatipura," Dhasal has brought to fore the social and religious degradation of human existence and the loss of qualitative perception and rational thinking: "Man's lost his speech / His god's a shitting skeleton / Will this void ever find a voice, become a voice" (Chitre 74)?

When a writer depicts the condition of the marginalised and subjugated people, he/she must understand that he/she is also a part of their pain, a part of their dreams, and they must do justice to the unsaid promises that they make while collecting the raw material for their work. Because being a writer also means that one is a part of, and responsible to a certain class of people, especially the downtrodden lot. This augments a writer's responsibility all the more.

Hughes attacks the artist who adheres to the existing ideologies or literary forms and styles by breaking the umbilical cord of his own culture just to gain a space among whites, "I am ashamed of the black poet who says, "I want to be a poet, not a Negro poet," as though his own racial world were not as interesting as any other world. . . An artist must be free to choose what he does, certainly, but he must also never be afraid to do what he might choose" (Gates and McKay 1271). Closer home, Dhasal writes about the immediate social/political circumstances that a poet/writer should write from in his poem "Ode to Ambedkar: 1978": "Real honesty is found in one's own inner voice" (Chitre 83).

The marginal world is an amalgamation of various issues like the condition of Dalit, women who are Dalit and non-Dalit, and that of the economically backward upper caste people. However, a deeper reflection of these problems will bring to light the fact that there is a vibrant folk culture of the oppressed which is more lively and authentic. It provides solace to these marginalised people, where aching bodies, sore wounds, and ravished minds draw their medicine from the folksongs or folktales, and whole families or communities come together to express their grief over the discrimination they face or celebrate their difference in the form of songs and tales that belong to them. Their myths and legends have an oral history and their festivals are celebrations of nature, which does not really differentiate between animate or inanimate, or between people from the same species.

In the African-American culture, folksongs and folktales were used as a means of resistance, so much so that now, the American people, irrespective of the colour of their skin, feel proud of this musical and artistic heritage. It has created new musical cultures, like that of Jazz, Rap, and Blues. Hughes says, "Jazz to me is one of the hidden expressions of Negro life in America; the central tom-tom beating in the Negro soul, the tom-tom of revolt against weariness in a white world, a world of subway trains, and work, work, work; the tom-tom of joy and laughter, and pain swallowed in a smile" (Gates and McKay 1270). This reality is very similar to the Indian folk culture, especially that of the Dalit and the tribals in India, who are still known to have preserved their cultural heritage more than any other castes or classes in our country. In the present context, the centre of creativity has shifted towards the margin and one of the best examples could be the new-found attention and serious recognition given to the folk culture of the marginalised sections of the society in the academia.

In his poem "The Tree of Violence," Dhasal has depicted the socio-political conditions and the end of an unchecked and orphaned revolution through his word-sketch. In this poem, tree is a metaphor for ideologies and the hegemony of the dominant classes that persist in our society, and the poem drives home the point that in order to eradicate them, we need to change the circumstances that led to their development in the first instance. Dhasal draws attention to the fact that by violently destroying the existing things completely, we will again lead to the germination of this "Tree of Violence":

> The tree got broken
> At the same time
> The tree was born
> It sprouted and took root, it turned into many trees
> Those who brought up the tree
> Walked out on their own homes
> They laughed their way to the gallows
> Because they knew it for sure

That as long as the circumstances that gave birth to the tree were not rooted out:

The tree was not destined to die. (Chitre 71)

Dilip Chitre writes about the same poem by Dhasal:

"This was a new sound in Marathi and Indian poetry using folk imagination and folk poetics to create an artistic form of immense sweep and power. The poem is like the pictorial organisation of a massive mural with its vivid imagery and it has the musical architecture of a breathtaking concerto. Today it can be pointed as one of the classics of modern Indian poetry." (25)

The denial of equal life, in fact the very status as human beings to a specific caste or racial group, and the experience and expression of the Dalit and Africa-American self within the matrix of religion have been portrayed in Dhasal's and Hughes's poetry. They use harsh words to project the futility of religious practices based on differences. There is no doubt that religion plays an important role in human life and especially in folk culture. In every part of the world, social problems are aggravated because the intermingling of religion with the same. According to Radhakrishnan, "Religion confines human beings by external rituals. Religion has been identified with feeling, emotion and sentiment, instinct, cult and ritual, perception, belief and faith, and these views are right in what they affirm, though wrong in what they deny." (qtd. in *Indian Philosophy*, 305). Hughes writes in his poem "A New Song (1932):"

> I know full well now
> Jesus could not die for me
> That only my own hands
> Dark as the earth
> Can make my earth-dark body free. (Culp, 242)

Mary Beth Culp writes about Hughes approach towards religion,

"As a folklorist Hughes sought to capture the essence of every aspect of black culture, including its religion. Religious feeling is always interdependent with racial feeling in his poetry. He views religion in the larger context of black culture, presenting it variously as a source of strength for the oppressed, an opiate of the people, the religion of slavery, and an obstacle to emancipation" (240).

In another poem "Christ in Alabama" (1931) Hughes writes:

> Christ is a nigger,
> Beaten and black
> Oh, bare your back!
> Mary is His mother:
> Mammy of the South,
> Silence your mouth.
> God is His father:
> White Master above
> Grant Him your love.
> Most holy bastard
> Of the bleeding mouth,
> Nigger Christ
> On the cross,
> Of the South. (Culp, 243-44)

Dhasal in his poem "Ode to Dr Ambedkar: 1978 EQUALITY FOR ALL OR DEATH TO INDIA" writes about Ambedkar's treatment of religion.

You performed God's autopsy

You shoved into sewage;

All those hollow folk-tales that speak of heaven and hell, karmic merit and the burden of sin;

You deprived the 33 *crore* sucker gods of their business making their shops empty;

You set water ablaze. (84)

Both Dhasal and Hughes knew about the negative aspects of religion and its socio-political implications. Through their poems, they want to highlight the idea that realisation of self and consciousness is more important than the mere performance of rituals. On the surface, many people would find their poems to be attacks on religion, but on deeper reflection, one will realise that the segregation of a community(ies) shows the bankruptcy of religion in providing real happiness, the happiness of being human and equal. As Hughes says, "Anything which makes people think of existing evil conditions is worthwhile. Sometimes in order to attract attention somebody must embody these ideas in sensational forms. I meant my poem to be a protest against the domination of all stronger peoples over weaker ones" (Culp, 244). Thus, in order to provide some hypothetical solution, a writer needs to have both the perspectives, of centre as well as of the margins.

The power politics in India also exploits these ruptures that exist in our social movements in order to make these inequalities persist in our society so that they can rule without any resistance. 'Vote bank politics' as we usually call this tendency! Dilip Chitre writes about power politics, "Dalit votes can cause decisive swings in electoral politics and caste leaders are not only aware of this but also base their political stance and manipulation on the Dalit factor" (Chitre 7).

However, poets and artists are not engaged in such dirty mind games. All they do through the medium of their poetry and artistic works is further the vice of the 'subaltern.' Dhasal and Hughes are well aware of their roots and draw the material for their creative instincts from the margins, which is creative as well as productive in terms of output. In his poem, "Ode to Ambedkar:1978", Dhasal writes about people who aspire to become leaders without actually feeling the pain of the people they want to become leaders of as "Monsters of factionalism":

They-who never make the error of going,
One step forward or backward from the pioneer
Don't possess the fuel and the velocity

. . .

He who digs his own grave in the presence of his mentor,
And eagerly embraces decreed concessions,
And rides high horse for the sake of a chair that has no successor,
He who does not change the flavour of the day or the night,
Or the saliva on the tongue, or the water in the saliva,
He who loses touch with life in the soil, and creates the black and white
Monsters of factionalism
For such a one I cannot shed one heart-felt tear. (Chitre 40)

Even Hughes furthers a similar opinion in his essay "The Negro Artist and the Racial Mountain,"

"For racial culture the home of a self-styled "high-class" Negro has nothing better to offer. Instead there will perhaps be more aping of things white than in a less cultured or less wealthy home. . . The family attends a fashionable church where few really coloured faces are to be found. . . Nordic manners, Nordic faces, Nordic hair, Nordic art. . . A very high mountain indeed for the would-be racial artist to climb in order to discover himself and his people." (Gates and McKay 1268)

In the present condition of social decay, by virtue of their birth, a sort of 'forced disability' is imposed upon marginalised people by the forerunners of the society. They are still not given ample opportunities to come to the forefront. We constantly read or hear news of atrocities and dehumanising acts done against the people at the 'fringes' of the society. Why is it so? And being a part of the literary arena, is it not our duty to do something for these people? Why is it that we look towards the West for solutions instead of trying to find them in our ancient Indian traditions?

Even if we look towards the West, why don't we accept the fact that despite being blamed for eating the forbidden fruit, every woman in the West has broken free of the chains of patriarchy? We in India must accept that our society is gender prejudiced and it is high time we must change our mindset because women also have a life beyond *ghar, rasoi* and *aangan*. Kamla Bhasin says, "Every woman in this country is dishonoured, degraded / with your hand on your heart, say, how can such a country be free?" (qtd. in Omvedt 83)

In literature, substantiating the truth is more important than adhering to one ideology or the other. Gopal Guru and V. Geeta in their article *New Phase of Dalit-Bahujan Intellectual Activity* observe, "While ideology is important, it is not enough for developing an emancipator social theory. That has to be achieved through a nuanced understanding of a complex social reality" (130).

From a psychological point of view, it seems that initially, the upper caste people (who followed a biased ideology) got some sort of a sadistic pleasure in inflicting pain on the Dalit, but in due course of time, they started believing it was their birth right to do so. These interpolations in our belief system have aggravated the problems faced by the Dalit all the more. Writing about Dalit identity and also about what shaped Dhasal as a writer, Chitre observes:

"A Dalit identity is the identity of a person uprooted several times in a single lifetime. He or she is the quintessential lumpen, the constantly degraded human being and a weak and struggling member of the community of the deprived and disposed, and with a scarred if not cracked identity. Being treated as less than human through one's growing years and at the most impressionable age, is not a burden easy to carry; and to shed it after years of conditioning requires superhuman strength of spirit." (152)

It is almost as if the urban and the so-called high class people think that the rural folk, people in the countryside, and the marginalised people are backward and uncivilised and it is their duty to civilise them, very much like the colonial project of the Britishers who came to India and thought that it is an uncivilised and a backward country and it is their duty to civilise the Indians. The central question, however is what is meant by the term 'being civilised' in the first place?

It is high time we should realise that paintings of starving children and mothers with dried bosoms, or photographs of farmers struggling in their farms and girls with two small braids carrying earthen pitchers to the nearby well have a lot to say than just fetching *lakhs* and *lakhs* of rupees for a painter/photographer who gives a temporary and distorted aesthetic pleasure to people like us, the self-proclaimed connoisseurs of aesthetics in ethnicity and poverty. We need these depictions and portrayals in our paintings and literature, but we need them to bring some change, to say to this modern world that the poor and the marginalised are also human beings and they also deserve a respectful life, and their culture is as rich and vibrant as ours. A writer who depicts the peripheral world must understand its intricacies and make them manifest in an unbiased manner.

Dhasal talks about the identity of Dalit entrenched in Dalit culture, which is beautiful, and one can feel proud of it rather than being ashamed of it in any sense. One obvious question that could be asked is what is there in this community full of pain and suffering to feel proud of? Folk culture and folk identity are elements that one feels proud of. Equality and freedom, if gained on others' terms, will again lead to another kind of subjugation or mental slavery. This instinct and feeling of being inferior and downtrodden should be eradicated completely from the minds of the marginalised sections of the society. Dhasal writes in his poem 'Kamatipura': "This is hell / This is a swirling vortex / This is an ugly agony / This is pain wearing a dancer's anklets/ Shed your skin, shed your skin from its very roots" (74-75). S.P. Punalekar observes in his essay "Dalit Literature and Dalit Identity" in the collection 'Dalit Identity and Politics', "Dalit literature upholds the view that this vast majority which is vulnerable and poor, untouchable and isolated, must be brought together. And to bring them together, they must be made conscious of their capacity as creative and worthy members of humanity. It is not a matter of shame or indignity to be a *Mahar* or *Mang, Dhor* or *Chamar*" (238).

Marginalised people should refute the idea that they are inferior, through their art, literature and other means of creativity because they not only have a rich cultural heritage but they are also a part and parcel of our national history, a part of our nation's rich and diverse culture, and comprise the strong human resource of our nation. Hughes writes in "The Negro Artist and the Racial Mountain" (1926), "It is the duty of the younger Negro artist . . . to change through the force of his art that old whispering 'I want to be white' hidden in the aspirations of his people, to 'Why should I want to be white? I am a Negro—and beautiful" (Gates and McKay, 1271).

The characterisation and portrayal of the marginalised community in art and literature should be of primal concern of a writer because the stark reality of life and the human predicament is more important than an ideal world of equality. If our means are ideal or utopian, then how are we going to achieve a rational and just destination? Hughes describes the dangers of an immaterialised dream in his poem "Harlem", thereby warning the African-Americans to rise and make their voices heard:

> What happens to a dream deferred?
> Does it dry up?
> like a raisin in the Sun?
> Or fester like a sore
> And then run?
> Does it stink like rotten meat?
> . . .
> May be it is just sags
> Like a heavy load
> Or does it explode? (Gates and McKay 1267)

Vijay Tendulkar has epitomised this idea of portraying reality by describing Dhasal's world using stark imagery and potent metaphors:

"The world of Namdeo Dhasal's poetry—the world known as 'Golpitha' in the city of Mumbai—begins where the frontier of Mumbai's white-collar world ends and a no-man's land opens up. This the world where night is reversed into the day, where stomachs are empty or half empty, of desperation against death, of the next day's anxieties, of bodies of left over after being consumed by shame and sensibility, of insufferably flowing sewages, of diseased young bodies lying by the gutters braving the cold by folding up their knees to their bellies, of the jobless, of beggars, of pickpockets, of holy mendicants, of neighbourhood tough guys and pimps. . ." (qtd. in *Underworld*, 10)

There is a general perception that a man can never be a feminist, a non-Dalit can never write truly about Dalit and a person born with a silver spoon can never understand the plight of downtrodden people. On the basis of this argument, can we say that Sharat Chandra and Premchandra were not feminists, or Rabindranath Tagore was biased in his depiction of downtrodden people, or Vijay Tendulkar did injustice in depicting the condition of Marathi Dalit? There are some aspects of human life that are universal in their appeal and literature does not pose limitations, in fact it provides space for healthy and fruitful debates and arguments. I have juxtaposed Dhasal and Hughes to give a flavour of this universality. Because of preconceived notions, people compartmentalise literature, but the reality is that unbiased and flexible thought processes will provide some viable solutions to problems rather than we thriving only on utopian ideals. The Marginal matrix has always given birth to outstanding writers and caressed them in her lap like a mother. So we must do something for its emancipation and development rather than just exploiting it. We must trash out these preconceived notions and differences and give this world its due respect, an identity of being the centre of creativity.

REFERENCES

Chitre, Dilip (selected, trans. and intro.) (2007), *Namdeo Dhasal: Poet of the Underworld: Poems 1972-2006*, Chennai, Navayana Publishing.

Culp, Mary Beth (1987), "Religion in the Poetry of Langston Hughes", *Phylon*, 48.3, 240-45, http://www.jstor.org/stable/274384, 8 Feb. 2013.

Eyerman, Ron, (1981), "False Consciousness and Ideology in Marxist Theory", *Acta Sociologica*, 24.1, 43-56, http://www.jstor.org/stable/4194332, 19 Feb. 2013.

Gates, Henry Louis, Jr. and Nellie Y. McKay (eds.) (1997), "The Black Arts Movement: 1960-1970," *The Norton Anthology of African American Literature*, New York, W.W. Norton and Company.

Gayle, Addison, Jr. (Fall 1970), "The Harlem Renaissance: Towards a Black Aesthetics", *Midcontinent American Studies Journal*,11.2, 78-87, http://www.jstor.org/stable/40640915, 8 Feb. 2013.

Guru, Gopal and V. Geetha (2000), "New Phase of Dalit-Bahujan Intellectual Activity", *Economic and Political Weekly*, 35.3, 130-34, http://www.jstor.org/stable/4408822, 8 Feb. 2013.

Kumar, Ajay (2006), *Dalit Panther Aandolan* [*Dalit Panther Movement*], Ed. S.S. Gautam, New Delhi, Gautam Book Centre.

Michael, S.M. (ed.) (2007), *Dalit in Modern India: Vision and Values*, 2nd ed., New Delhi, Sage Publications.

Omvedt, Gail (2012), *Dalit Visions: The Anti-Caste Movement and the Construction of an Indian Identity*, rev. ed., Tracts for the Times, New Delhi, Oriental Black Swan.

Puligandla, Ramakrishna (1975), *Fundamentals of Indian Philosophy*, New Delhi, D.K. Printworld.

Punalekar, S.P. (2001), "Dalit Literature and Dalit Identity," *Dalit Identity and Politics: Culture Subordination and the Dalit Challenge*, Ed. Ghanshyam Shah, New Delhi, Sage Publications.

Singh, Maheep and Chandrakant Bandiwadekar (2000), *Sahitya Aur Dalit Chetna* [Literature and Dalit Consciousness], New Delhi, Abhivenjana.

18

'ASTITVA' AND ASTITVA OF A WOMAN : A MOVE BEYOND MARGINS

Anuradha Deepak

Itna na mayoos ban tu kar zara zindadili
Kyon nahi dikhti tumhe vo kabra par khilti kali
Jisko kehte ho andhera din ki vo shuruaat hai
Zindagi kya baat hai, zindagi kya baat hai.......

These endings lines of the beginning song from the movie *Astitva* very aptly present and instil the hope, the positivity as well as the possibility of crossing the boundaries of one's clustro-phobic existence and move towards the brighter side of life.

Whenever there is any talk or discussion on the 'marginalised', the 'have not's, the 'under privileged' ones, one very common and single thing that comes out as the main goal is their desire for a status equal with the 'haves', the 'privileged' ones. And the journey of desire, beginning from the very 'periphery', aims to move in the direction of the 'centre', the 'centre' being its final destination and the sole and the chief goal to achieve.

The present paper is an attempt to speak of the similar situations: the victimization, the oppression, the suppression, the desire to get free and aspire, but very significantly, not for the 'centre' actually. The life and character of Aditi (Tabu), the protagonist of the Hindi movie *Astitva (2000),* directed by Mahesh Manjrekar is a portrayal of the 'defining' boundaries of a women's life who is 'marginalised' within the confines of her 'defined' identity set by the so called patriarchy; her realisation of her own self that desires to exist beyond those strict and suffocating 'definitions' and ultimately her daring decision to cross every bounding boundary in search of the real identity of 'herself', carved out by her own self and more importantly to know and feel her 'natural' and 'real' self. So this 'victimised visitor' standing at the margins, does not wish to move 'inside', towards one more point of stagnation, of being bound, actually a full stop, but rather 'outside', towards the 'open' space that is waiting to embrace the 'victorious visitor' who has chosen to move beyond margins where exist no binaries. What exists there and what is of utmost importance and significance is that a person there is himself or herself to the full, just 'to be' there, with all openness and dignity.

Astitva is a thought provoking film that defying the social structure of this rude society, has attempted an issue that has beleaguered and fraught Indian women since generations. What is a woman born with and what does she die with? Absolutely nothing except her female biological body which does not possess even a name of her own as we all know the history and the story of how a woman acquires her name that remains changing with the changing men dominating her life in different stages. In her journey from birth to death, the same body of hers is used differently and variously at various levels, but nowhere is understood the real importance of her 'body' that is not just a 'physical' and 'biological' entity. Hers is more importantly the 'living' and the 'lived' body, the 'communicating' and the 'communicative' body, and in fact the 'most important body' through which she seeks to define herself, identify herself and express herself in different and various situations and contexts of day to day life.

Aditi is a quintessential middle class wife we see around us every day, educated and intelligent ; devoted to her home and family ; aware of her husband's needs and constantly working at keeping him in comfort. Her husband Srikant Pandit treats her as a chattel, sets do's and don'ts for her. She is relegated to kitchen affairs and upbringing of kids. (there too, ironically, the planning of kids in their life and any decision about that is a male prerogative) Aditi raises a pertinent question in this context: "*tumhare plans tumhare khud ke liye hain, usmein main kahaan fit hoti hoon ?*"

The husband has often one-night stands with other women and if ever he showers any love on the wife, it is when he needs to satiate his own sexual desires, without being the least bothered about her desire as a woman and her rights as a wife. Aditi, too, takes it all very stoically like an ideal Indian wife (*ek aadarsh bhartiya patni).*

Despite repeated complaints of Aditi of feeling lonely without Sri and even a child, Sri is bothered about his own progress giving a deaf ear to Aditi's demands and actually the needs, for both the emotional as well as physical fulfilment. She is not even allowed to take up a job even though the husband is away from home for months at a stretch. The only reason is behind this is the 'male as provider syndrome'. At no cost is Sri ready to allow Aditi to take up any job as he considers himself the 'bread earner' for the family and is dead against the *"bibi ki kamai"*. Meghna (Smita Jaykar) Sri's friend's wife very aptly and bluntly sums up Sri as a "male chauvinist pig".

The movie begins with Aditi in a typical Indian household with the husband going to office. Srikant's old friend Dr. Ravi Bapat and his once divorced wife Meghna arrive from Goa and are promptly invited for lunch. Srikant "important appointments are instantly cancelled; son Aniket, who is engaged to a rather progressive woman Revaty, is ordered to bring fiancée home and it is understood that Aditi will whiz up a *chatpata* lunch".

Ravi and his wife arrive. The two friends down a few drinks and the situation is very symbolic; the women in the kitchen, the men in the garden; the women talking about their identity and self-respect or the lack of it, the men talking about women and beaches and bikinis, that is quite enough to understand the gap between the two sexes as propagated by the society, for centuries. Srikant shares with Ravi his uncomforting at the thought of a working daughter-in-law and his confused reaction to the fact that Meghna is a divorce with two daughters. And this is enough to put before us the real character and mindset of Sri. In the next situation when all are sitting together, we can see Sri very bluntly taking and opening the letter meant for Aditi (clarifying *are biwi to meri hai na! kya farak padta hai ....*), laughing in an exaggerated manner reading that letter and cruelly teasing her about the fact that she has received a large legacy. He makes fun of her that she is now rich and salutes her very ironically pretending to ask her for a loan. Aditi feels embarrassed and Meghna is shown to be expressing a feeling of shock at such behaviour of Sri but then everything stops there and then with lunch as the conclusion.

The seed of suspicion is however, sown in Srikant's mind with that letter and the legacy that Aditi acquires. He flips back through the pages of the diary he regularly writes and comes up with the conclusion that he could not have conceived their son. He calculates all the dates and comes to realise the fact that their son Aniket was born in eight months after he got to know about Aditi's pregnancy, and he was not a premature baby also.

He asks Aditi directly about it and instead of hiding the truth or trying to manipulate the situation at any possible level (that she could have done very easily), she frankly admits the truth and tells him that Aniket is the son of Malhaar Kamat, her music teacher. The startling honesty of Aditi is a brilliant moment in the film. Immediately after her confession, she gets a slap on her face which actually is, a slap on honesty and truthfulness. Sri Kant's veneer as the loving husband melts. Ego shattered, he only looks to balm his hurt manhood by emotionally devastating his already broken wife. The next day, Ravi and Meghna are called and despite Aditi's requests to tackle the issue personally, she is forced to speak out and confess everything even in the presence of Aniket also. Here Sri violates her right to privacy also and exposes his marital relationship to the public view thus humiliating Aditi even more. Even Ravi's reminders of his own marital infidelities are swept aside under the blanket of, "I did not bring the result of my infidelities home." And he goads Aditi mercilessly for her infidelity.

Moreover, even the son Aniket, on knowing the truth, gets too harsh to Aditi and rejecting even her touch says : "Do not touch me you bloody-Don't you dare touch me." Later on, when Aditi goes to his room, he even asks her very bluntly to "get out" saying:

Oh God! Is aurat ke pet se mujhe paida hi kyon kiya!

An unforgiving Srikant, however, wants her to stay back, actually to guard his secret from the prying world. Then Revaty refuses to marry Aniket and all hell is let loose. But what about the shattered dream of Aditi whose big fault is actually her honesty. Neither the husband who she loved despite his ambitious work holism, his dalliances with other women and even his own inability to father a child, nor the son, are ready to accept her. For them, she is just like every other 'thing' in the house which she cares. For those cold callous cruel men, she doesn't exist at all as a human being : a woman, a wife, a mother. They don't wish to forgive her, are not ready to accept her and at the same time expect her to beg forgiveness and stay back, that too, very authoritatively as Sri says to her :

> *tum kahin nahi jaogi. Isis ghar me rahogi apne pati ke saath jo tumse kabhi baat nahi karega........................*

So she is asked to stay back, or rather ordered to stay back, not for the sake of her identity, her honour and dignity but rather for their own sake, and more importantly for the sake of their safe and unblemished social identity.

She is still at the margins, despite giving her whole being for the welfare and case of the family, and the men, including both the father (not actually even the biological one) and the son, remain at the centre, the bosses of the family, the chief decision makers who can pass judgements on Aditi, simply forgetting the significance of her presence and existence in their lives. The marginalised actually get so accustomed to all the oppression that sometimes they just fail to recognize their own 'self', they rather forget the 'real' self that lies with them but takes a back seat because of constant oppression and due to strict moral and social codes and situations that surround them so much that they become all pervading, putting an end to all their mental growth. But as we all know, the 'reality' of 'real' cannot be suppressed for long. All suppression accumulates angst and bitterness and ultimately results in a natural blast, just like the eruption of a long asleep volcano. Aditi's life is a perfect example of this situation.

A woman is a man's shadow. This the film brings to the fore as it is so intricately embedded in the socio-cultural fabric that unless a woman is jolted out of it, she goes on accepting it unquestioningly and reconciles to it as her lot. Aditi is like that. Meghna, from the very beginning, dislikes and disapproves what Sri does to his wife. When tired of her drab existence and repeated insults, the marginalised, the oppressed and the suppressed Aditi decides to leave home, the decision is painful, coming as it does after long years of marriage, loneliness and subordination. But her husband's callousness forces her to realise her own condition of homelessness and worthlessness. It is then that she decides to draw upon her strength.

Aditi's decision portrays her progress from shock to realisation. Sri is the accuser, the jailor and the judge- all on his own. Now it is Aditi's decision to choose between a life of indignity and humiliation or freedom in the real sense. And obviously, she chooses the freedom with dignity. It is in the nuances of the character of Revaty and Meghna also that womanhood emerges. Revaty finds the reflection of her own future in the mother-son relationship and breaks engagement with Aniket. Meghna always has been supporting Aditi asking her to sustain and maintain her self-esteem : "Never mortgage your self-esteem...." She has always tried to make Aditi realise her own worth asking her to start doing something instead of being merely a housewife and on Aditi's reluctance she even motivates her saying : It's never too late." So ultimately realising her reality and her worth, the docile and submissive Aditi emerges a resolute and resilient person. She walks out of Sri's life, her own family, aspiring and moving towards some more open spaces, the vigorous and fluid world full of love, life and spontaneity. She moves beyond all the boundaries and margins set for her, listening to the call of her inner urge, the urge to be herself and the film ends with the lines :

mai thee,
mai hoon,
mai rahoongi.

The film is not merely a portrayal of female desire or sexuality, nor about marital infidelity but actually about the power relationships as they work and govern the society. The woman as the powerless one unable to take any decision even if it is her own life and the man as the powerful one having all hold on a woman's life in all its possibilities. It is not merely about existence, as the name may suggest on the face of it. It is "the assertion of all that which constitutes a personality with its distinct relationships, anxieties, dependencies, dispositions, impulses and aspirations, prejudices and predilections." [Mehta, 258]

According to the German philosopher Martin Heidegger's concept of 'existentiality', each is cast into a world, not of his own making, that he refers as 'fact city'. From this 'fact city', each has to appropriate, assimilate and transcend the given world. [as quoted by Mehta, 258] And Aditi does her bit, thereby breaking her silence and moves on to the final crusade that brings to her the dawn of a new day after a dark and horrifying night. In the end she says,

Aaj mujhe ghar chhodte hue koi afsos nahi ho raha hai. 'Srimati Aditi Srikant Pandit'...is naam me Aditi kahin kho gayi thee. Aaj khula aasmaan mujhe bula raha hai. Mai besabra hoon apna astitva dhoondhane ke liye. Man me bechaini zaroor hai lekin darr bilkul nahin..........mera naya janm hua hai.

And the beginning lines of my paper [as taken from a song in the film] stand justified.

Jisko kehte ho andhera din ki vo shuruaat hai.............

REFERENCES

- Manjrekar, Mahesh. dir. *Astitva* : 2000.
- Mehta, Ranju. *"Battling for Being : Manjrekar's Astitva"* in, Jain, Jasbir and Rai, Sudha eds. *Films and Feminism (Essays in Indian Cinema).* Jaipur, Rawat : 2009.

19

REPRESENTATION OF ANTI-GANDHIAN PRINCIPLES IN ROHINTON MISTRY'S *A FINE BALANCE*

Pragya Bajpai

Mahatma Gandhi believed that there is no better teacher than life itself; but do we learn from life's lessons? He taught us peace, non-violence and brotherhood but does it really exist in the independent India? His dream of ideal nation is brutally shattered by those who don't realise the relevance of his principles. The government was given power to benefit the citizens of India but did anyone know that the power would be misused and the poor citizens would suffer its cruelties. Our nation has a glorious past as well as a painful history and it is quite evident only through the work of art that it was never devoid of domination, oppression, exploitation, violence and criminalisation.

The writers find literature, the best way to expound in detail the darker side of the modern history of India. It not only captures the face of the cruelty in an evocative manner but also makes the readers aware of the lives of the neglected section of the society while drawing their attention to the reactions and responses of the minority to the unfair treatment. The traumatic past is rediscovered through various perspectives by the Indian writers in English. Violence being the extreme stride of expressing anger and hostility against any class or caste in city or in village is dealt skilfully by Rohinton Mistry in his novel *A Fine Balance*. The critical reading of any such work of literature suggests that violence generally results from frustration, insult and hatred of people with a destructive tendency and is used as a means to threaten a group or a community. An attempt has been made in this paper to analyse the illustration of denial of Gandhian principles like existence of untouchability and violence, and its dire consequences on the individual member of a community and the society as a whole.

Rohinton Mistry's *A Fine Balance* is a poignant saga with all the gory details of the Indian past when internal Emergency of 1975 was imposed by Prime Minister Indira Gandhi. Indira rightly defines Emergency as "a defence of an insecure leader" (110) that truly disturbed the peace of mind of the common man who were unaware of the impending havoc, as a result of which the sense of insecurity, sense of loss and above all the sense of perseverance and sustainment among the subaltern prevailed. The novel is a "testimony of torture victims" (FB: 583) engrossed in unveiling the most appalling realities of contemporary India. It is rightly mentioned in a quote of Honore de Balzac, *Le Pere Goriot* at the beginning of the novel that this is a "story of great misfortunes" and that "this tragedy is not a fiction, all is true." The hidden facts of Emergency and post-independence riots are depicted as the anti-Gandhian principles in the novel. It is set in socio-political scenario of "the city by the sea" Bombay (now Mumbai) as well as small villages and towns clutched in the hands of violence where "justice is sold at the highest bidder" causing pity, fear and anger in the mind of the readers. The threatening facts that run through the story grab the reader's attention towards the physical and psychological harm done to the deprived section of the society.

While recalling the horrors of Indian politics, Mistry has made a conscious attempt to portray the increasing criminalisation in the society and its brutal effects that worsened the lives of the unfortunate characters. It is depicted by the marginalised characters like Dukhi mochi, tailors named Ashraf Chacha, Ishvar and Omprakash, the rent-collector Ibrahim that undergo oppression and savagery of the highest degree in the novel and are subjected to persecution and injustice on social grounds. Their low caste is depicted as the social stigma and the dregs of the society. The protagonist of the novel is a middle-class widow, Dina Dalal who runs a tailoring business from her flat. She is not only dominated by her brother but also is repressed by Mrs. Gupta, the lady who owns the Au Revoir Export Company. Dina faced threats, uncertainty, harassment and exploitation as a result of power politics. Almost all the characters of the novel are directly or indirectly affected by Emergency that clearly confirms the vulnerability of the common/marginalised people. As a consequence of which they are reduced to begging or depending on others.

Mistry's *A Fine Balance* is also a record of all the brutal and traumatic sufferings and heart-rending consequences of the caste oppression. The caste violence, oppression of the underprivileged and the misuse of power were the different manners of the working of democracy which was only a thing of joy for the upper-middle class people of the society as represented and advocated by Dina's brother Nusswan, Thakur Dharamsi and Mrs. Gupta. During Emergency, forced sterilization and vasectomies done to achieve daily quota in the family planning camps in the name of eradicating poverty brought misery to innocent people like Ishvar and Omprakash Darji, who were unaware of the power politics and the sinister motive of Thakur. They turned out to be the victims of undeserved retribution of the upper-caste. Emergency as delineated in the novel sheltered the unlawful and immoral actions of upper-caste people giving way to criminalisation in the small towns and villages. Pramod K. Nayar rightly opines, "In Mistry, it is the Government which is castigated as undemocratic and unparental. Throughout *A Fine Balance*, the Government's exploitative power, cruelty, and the evil of juridico-political machinery is emphasised. Herein lies Mistry's savage irony…Mistry seems to suggest that exploitations remain "unadulterated," impersonal, and inhuman" (122).

The tragic reality of the post-colonial India comprised of hatred, violence and revenge. The lower caste is represented as the victim of hate and envy in an ego-centric and chauvinist society of dominating upper caste. Through the characters Ishvar and Omprakash, Mistry has successfully depicted the struggle to survive against the cast violence and power politics in a lawless society; and also how they tried to maintain a fine balance between hope and despair. The writer has spared no effort to bring out the causes of hatred of the upper caste towards the marginalised like resisting the suppression, daring to abandon leather for cloth, assertion of right to vote. As Dukhi's son Narayan expresses his grief and bitter truth, "Government passes new laws, says no more untouchability, yet everything is the same. The upper-caste bastards treat us worse than animals" (FB: 142).

Ishvar and Om belonged to the *"Chamaar"* caste of tanners and leather-workers, the untouchables. Their family in the village was cobblers. Ishvar's father Dukhi mochi was only five when he began to learn the *Chamaar* vocation. When he grew old, he realised that his prime life had been spent in obedient compliance with the traditions of the caste system, yet he was under paid, was thrashed instead of getting a glass of goat's milk that was promised as a reward to his hard work but was treated like an animal. For *Thakur* and *Pandits*, "The crimes were varied and imaginative: a *Bhungi* had dared to let his unclean eyes meet Brahmin eyes; a *Chamaar* had walked on the wrong side of the temple road and defiled it" (FB: 101). Mistry delves deep into the village life to create a painful image which is suggestive of the fact that people denied the laws of the government and continued to harass and exploit the subaltern by unfair means.

Once, Thakur Premji gave Dukhi a job of grinding red chillies into powder to be finished by the sunset. Dukhi agreed to do it all alone to earn some money. When Dukhi was about to finish grinding it in the mortar and the sack was almost empty, an accident occurred. The heavy pestle of the massive stone mortar landed and split in two pieces and collapsed. On side fell on Dukhi's foot and crushed it badly. Thakur refused to listen anything. He called him a "stinking dog" and thrashed him across the back with his stick. He told this to his wife, Roopa after two days, "But this time he had done nothing wrong. He had worked hard all day, yet he had been thrashed and cheated of his payment" (FB: 105). He said, "I spit in their upper-caste faces. I don't need their miserable jobs from now on" (FB: 105). As a result of such unfair treatment to his caste, Dukhi took a bold decision to turn his sons Narayan and Ishvar, tailors. He dared to break the timeless chain of caste. He called the notion of untouchability, a disease "ravaging us for centuries, denying dignity to our fellow human beings" (FB: 107).

The iniquitous treatment of the untouchable caste evoked a feeling of alienation in their own village and sooner or later compelled them to rebel. Another brutal episode happened when Narayan and Ishvar were punished by the school master. The brothers knew exactly where their caste permitted or prohibited. Spending time near the village school and listening to the upper-caste children recite the lessons was much loved by them. One fine morning they found the schoolhouse empty and dared to enter through the window. Fascinated by the chalk and slates, they both sat on the floor and began to draw pictures. They were so engrossed in drawing that did not notice the children and teacher coming. The teacher grabbed them by their ears and dragged them outside and said, "You *Chamaar* rascals! Very brave you are getting, daring to enter the school! He twisted their ears till they yelped with pain and started to cry" (FB: 110). The teacher began to punish them brutally for defiling the tools of learning and knowledge. He slapped them six times in quick succession across the face. When his hand was sore, he asked for a cane. "The cane was presented, and the teacher asked four older students to hold the trespassers to the ground, face down, by their heads and ankles. He commenced the punishment, altering strokes between the two. The watching children flinched each time the cane landed on the bare bottoms. A little boy started to cry" (FB: 110). The teacher stopped after the two received a dozen strokes each and said, "Now get out, and don't let your unclean faces be seen here ever again."

The unfortunate fate bound to *Chamaar* community haunted Dukhi's generations only to ensure its disaster. He suffered everything silently but the unjust beatings of his sons made him shudder and he went to Pandit Lalluram to seek justice. Pandit justified teacher's brutal punishment and said, "Punishing your sons for their misdeed was part of the teacher's duty. He had no choice. Do you understand?" (FB: 113). Thereafter, Dukhi sent away his sons to his tailor friend Ashraf in a nearby village to apprentice tailoring. He told his sons, "Ashraf *chacha* is going to turn you into tailors like himself. From now on, you are not cobblers. If someone asks your name, don't say Ishvar Mochi or Narayan Mochi. From now on you are Ishvar *Darji* and Narayan *Darji*" (FB: 114). When the boys returned to their village, the *Chamaar* community was proud of them. Narayan settled his tailoring business in his village and he prospered. They were "the one who had done the unthinkable: abandoned leather for cloth" (FB: 133). People began to look upon them with high hopes as their unelected head among the *Chamaars.* Every member of the family struggled to wipe off the age old bane associated to their community only to overcome the frustration; nevertheless, the eternal bias paved way to their affliction.

In the novel *A Fine Balance,* the most horrifying scene of violence was displayed during the election in the village against the subaltern for the act of assertion of right to vote. Every voice raised and every initiative taken by the untouchables in favour of their community was ruthlessly silenced to terrorise and humiliate them by the misuse of the power. During the Parliament elections, Narayan decided to mark his own ballot as it was his right. He insisted for his own ballot at the booth inspiring others to practice their rights. After a short while a man from the polling station came with a dozen men. The men seized Narayan and other two and were taken to *Thakur's* farm where "they were flogged throughout the day as they were hung naked by their ankles from the branches of a banyan tree…In the distance, in the far field, his men urinated on the three inverted faces" (FB: 146). In the mean while *Thakur* had instructed his men to prevent the news from spreading that might disrupt the voting. In the evening, after the election got over and the ballot boxes were taken away, "burning coals were held to the three men's genitals, and then stuffed into their mouths. Their screams were heard through the village until their lips and tongues melted away. The still, silent bodies were taken down from the tree. When they began to stir, the ropes were transferred from their ankles to their necks, and the three were hanged. The bodies were displayed in the village square" (FB: 146).

Thakur's horrendous retribution meant to teach a lesson to the *'acchoot jatis'* terrified the villagers. He said, "I want it to be like old days, when there was respect and discipline and order in our society. And keep an eye on that *Chamaar* tailor's house, make sure no one gets away"… "The *goondas* began working their way towards the untouchable quarter. They beat up individuals at random in the streets, stripped some women, raped others, burned a few huts" (FB: 146). That was not enough for *Thakur*; he aimed at something even more atrocious. He was furious at Dukhi's arrogance, turning cobblers to tailors and distorting society's timeless balance. He chose to punish them with utmost severity. In front of the whole village, Dukhi, his wife Roopa, Narayan's wife Radha and the daughters were bound and dragged into the room. Recognising her son's corpse, "A long howl broke from Radha. But the sound of grief mingled with the family's death agony; the house was set alight. The first flames licked at the bound flesh. The dry winds, furiously fanning the fire, showed the only spark of mercy during the night. The blaze swiftly enfolded all six of them" (FB: 147). It happened when Ishvar and Omprakash were away in town, as a result of which they were saved from *Thakur's* retribution for the time being. Later after a few years when they go back to their village to get Om married, they too were not spared. The cobblers turned tailors were punished and put down in the most atrocious manner for being rebellious; they were castrated in the family planning camp for the act of defiance by Om, who spat at *Thakur* Daramsi in the village. The pessimism prevailed at every step in the novel.

In *A Fine Balance*, the events are arranged chronologically starting from the year 1975 when internal Emergency was declared till the assassination of the Prime Minister in 1984. In the novel everything ends badly. Mistry has consciously depicted the communal violence that took place in the country with its brutal effects worsening the lives of the miserable people who were totally unaware. As Ishvar said to Dina, "What is this Emergency we hear about?" "Government problems – games played by people in power. It doesn't affect ordinary people like us" (FB: 75). The Hindu-Muslim riots that started with the independence of India were spread in the country even after the Partition. The sporadic riots had threatened the citizens of small towns. It was during one such riot when Narayan wanted to go back to village to set up his tailoring business when Ashraf *chacha* wanted him to stay back till the town was at peace and advised him that it was not the opportune time to start a new business.

The town scene was very disturbing. Although, an instance of brotherhood between Muslim and the lower-caste can be witnessed amidst the violence that helped relieve some pain during the course of reading the novel. Nilufer Bharucha aptly defines the instance as, "The novel is exposed for the first time to the message of Mahatma Gandhi who was fighting a dual battle against colonialism and casteism – the external and internal enemies of India" (153). Stories of Muslims attacking Hindus in many parts of the country were brought by the soldiers. He warned them to get ready to defend themselves from the impending attacks. "The stories kept multiplying; someone had been knifed in the *bazaar* in town; a *sadhu* hacked to death at the bus station; a settlement raised to the ground… reports about arson and riots in large towns and cities; about mayhem and massacre on all sides; about the vast and terrible exchange of populations that had commenced across the new border" (FB: 123). Next day, the scene got even worse. The only bakery shop in the bazaar, owned by a Muslim, was burned to the ground. The killings and "butchering one another" began to spread. Ashraf was agitated at the thought of being killed in the riots; hence he decided to go to the other side of the border reluctantly. His neighbour, a coal-merchant tried to convince him to stay back and fight. He said, "Everyday trains are crossing that new border, carrying nothing but corpses. My agent arrived yesterday from the north; he has seen it with his own eyes. The trains are stopped at the station and everyone is butchered. On both the sides of the border" (FB: 126). They then planned to change the board of the shop with a Muslim name to a Hindu name in order to survive the sinister attack by the Hindus. When Ishvar went out to get a new board, he saw, "Lots of shops and houses on fire… some people with axes. They were chopping a man" (FB: 127).

The violence did not end with it. In the epilogue, 1984, once again a blaze of anger was displayed by the precise narration of Prime Minister's assassination by her Sikh bodyguard to take revenge of attack on Golden Temple. It took a serious turn when the religious sentiments of Sikh community were disrupted provoking further violence. "And then she made the problem worse and worse, telling the army to attack the Golden Temple and capture the terrorists. With tanks and what-all big guns they charged inside, like hooligans. How much damage to the shrine. It is the most sacred place for Sikhs, and everybody's sentiments were hurts" (FB: 572). It was the time when Maneck returned from Gulf after almost eight years to attend his father's funeral. He hired a taxi to be transported to the railway station. The taxi driver advised Maneck to shave off his beard in order to avoid being mistaken for a Sikh and made him anxious. The driver told him that it was safe for him and on realizing that Maneck was absolutely oblivious, he preferred to brief him. The driver said, "Sikh are the ones being massacred in the riots. For three days they have been burning Sikh shops and homes, chopping up Sikh boys and men. And the police are just running about here and there, pretending to protect the neighbourhoods" (FB: 570). He added the details of the slaughter that took place in the capital:

She created a monster and the monster swallowed her. Now it swallows innocents. Such terrible butchery for three days...They are pouring kerosene on Sikhs and setting them on fire. They catch men, tear the hair from their faces or hack it with swords, then kill them. Whole families burnt to death in their homes. (FB: 572)

The novel suggests that all the Gandhian principles were disregarded either by the government itself or the people doing so were sheltered by the government. Corruption, revenge and violence are inter-related. The common man blamed the police and the politicians for all the violence spread in the capital city. They firmly believed that the Prime Minister was not much liked by the people and gave a sound reason telling. "But let's suppose she was beloved, do you think ordinary people will behave this way? *Aray,* it's the work of criminal gangs, providing official lists of Sikh homes and businesses. Otherwise, it's not possible for the killers to work so efficiently, so accurately, in such a big city" (FB: 572). The insecurity of the politicians is clearly evident by such immoral actions done after the Emergency and the elections got over. This shows the extent of awareness, helplessness, shattered faith and the pain of the ordinary citizens. Such things ruined families, separated them and dislocated them as a result of deeply seated fear in their own nation, by their own government. The driver himself had the scars on his face, the scene of "mutilation and bludgeoning and decapitation" (FB: 573) made Maneck shudder. The stark reality was shocking to him and he was psychologically disturbed by the narration. As always he again realised that everything ends badly.

The author has the power to compel the readers to think about the evils of the society and all the issues that weaken the spirit of an individual or a group that ultimately leads to nowhere and still exist even after Gandhiji's earnest fight for it. It has clearly demonstrated that the government and the system is a total disaster and swallows only the weaker section of the society in the form of a monster. Those who have power and money get the right to abuse, threaten, rape and murder. The "invisible line of caste" not only provokes violence but keeps brotherhood at bay forever. The darkness that prevails in the depressing story is for a cause, to bring about awareness and incite us to raise voice against it. At the end we realise that everything seems to be familiar yet were unknown to us.

WORKS CITED

- Bharucha, Nilufer E. "*A Fine Balance*: Making the Subaltern Speak." Ed. Jasbir Jain. *Rohinton Mistry: Ethnic Enclosures and Transcultural Spaces.* New Delhi: Rawat Publications. 2003. pp. 142-167.

- Indira, B. "Designer Quilt: A Study of *A Fine Balance*." *The Fiction of Rohinton Mistry*. Ed. Jaydipsinh Dodiya. Delhi: Prestige Books, 1998. pp. 110-14.

- Mistry, Rohinton. *A Fine Balance*. New York: Vintage International. 1997.

- Nayar, Pramod K. "The Text(ure) of Cruelty: Power and Violence in *A Fine Balance*." *The Fiction of Rohinton Mistry*. Ed. Jaydipsinh Dodiya. Delhi: Prestige Books, 1998. pp. 119-26.

20

CELEBRATING MARGINS : REJUVENATION OF BLACK ART AND CULTURE IN JAMES BALDWINS 'IF BEALE STREET COULD TALK'

Asha Sharma

Racial injustice and protest has always been predominant theme of Afro-American Fiction. In the years following the Second World War the Afro-American writings especially the novel marked a change of spirit and mood. The spirit to protest which dominated the depression era was brought to an end by America's entry into the World War II. Though the Wright School with its racial protest writing survived into the post war period, The Negro writer of the period found himself in newer situation where he could not confine himself to mere protest because protest as literary genre offered the writer little flexibility, no subtlety and circumscribed possibility. The Negro writer discovered a narrow protest dehumanises every one and turns the fiction into sociological treatise beside being reduced to a "*Little question*" as Ralph Ellison has said of Civil Rights. Negro writer also sensed the danger of falling into anonymity, invisibility and of disappearance into stereotypes those either of prejudice or overliberalism, of protest or mere assimilations. The Negro novelist in the post war period therefore made a conscious effort to break free from the tradition of protest writings.

There is a growing realisation to redefine, to move beyond rebellion to what Klein term as spirit of accommodation. For the Afro American writer, however, this accommodation was far more complex and complicated. For him, "accommodation implies not mere coming to terms with the nightmarish American reality but also the physical or psychic traumas of cruelties and injustices of a racial society." The Negro writer has added burden of discovering his 'Non racial identity', within the circumstances of race. Ralph Ellison and James Baldwin, during the period came to epitomise the new strains in Afro-American

Ralph Ellison was engaged with countering the threat of invisibility for the Negro writer exploring not merely the Negro experience of every man and any man in America. This compulsion to write as an American and not merely as Negro and got stronger and more insistent into Baldwin. Balwin aesthetics represents a new departure. It seeks to extricate Negro fiction from the confining boundaries of an exclusive social arena to take up as its subject the private self void from which the tide of history flows. Instead of mere protest literature Negro literature is sought to be presented as literature of universal application.

In the course of his fiction writing Baldwin confronts himself with the fate of black man made complicated and complex by external as well as existential anxieties. Baldwin is fully conscious that black man is different from other human beings because his life is defined and characterised by being black. He realises that the black man has been left at the margins, denied all rights to live a dignified existence in the white dominated America. The problems forced by the black man certainly have roots in racial discrimination and injustices. Any attempt to deal with black man's predicament cannot afford to ignore the exterior and social causes of his suffering. But at the same time, there is within the black man the inner being comprising complex existential dilemmas leading to the complexity black writer's his urge to maintain distinct racial characteristics and at the same time, achieve universality. Baldwin also tries to achieve this universality, a common bond with humanity but in his fictional writing this attempt is made through Negro consciousness.

The present paper makes an attempt to study Baldwin's novel '*If Beale Street could talk*', to trace the black artist's constant struggle to secure the meaning of his existence and fulfilment of self. While the black protagonist of Baldwin's earlier novels confines himself to finding out the personal solutions to the problems of black man's to the problems of black man's existence, in his later works Baldwin's perspective widens to explore questions of wider and social significance specially in his later fiction written during Civil Rights Movement and the following period. It was during this time that Baldwin tried to confront himself with the problems of the Negro not merely as an individual but also as a social being. By the time he wrote his penultimate novels, "*If Beale Street Could Talk*", he came to question the authenticity of principle of art for art's sake and give some thought to art for social purpose. In this novel Baldwin confronts himself with the problems of black artist trying to define his role and seek his true identity in fulfilment of self his artistic creativity. Here Baldwin concerns himself with searching answers to the issues relating to the role of black artist and depicting his affirmation of faith in black self. The protagonist of the novel, *'If Beale Street Could Talk',* Alonzo Hunt nick named as Fonny is a black sculptor who takes pride in making sculptures for the blacks and his sculpture are symbolic of entire black creativity. In this novel, the influence of the 'Black Aesthetics' and its emphasis on celebration of blacks art and culture can clearly be discerned.

The black aesthetics revolves round dedicated black artists and audience capable of conscious response of striking works of Black art. Addison Gayle, the main propagator of Black Aesthetics and editor of an anthology of critical essays called 'The black Aesthetics' defined the movement as a "Corrective" a means of helping "black people out of the polluted main strain of Americanism" Black aestheticism laid emphasis on affirmation of celebration of black culture and on maintaining Negro identity. The black aesthetics in its various uses and effects has given birth to a newly realised black collectivity and its artist a sense of holism, a sense of an essential reciprocity between black art and black culture. It envisages black artist writing and creating only for black audience and it assures that the black spokesman need never suffer the isolation of the art. The black aesthetics is indicative of rebirth of blacks, a rejuvenation of black art and culture. Larry Neale, who along with Addison Gayle propagated Black Aesthetics, defines New Black Art as an "art that speaks directly to the needs and aspiration of black American" The Black Arts Movement proposes a radical reordering of western cultural aesthetics. It proposes a separate symbolism, mythology, critique and iconology. Baldwin also creates black myth and iconology to celebrate black folk culture standing for its going back to black roots especially in his novel, *If Beale Street Could Talk*. This novel is only illustrative of Baldwin's affirmation of faith in black Art and Culture. Houston A. Baker has very appropriately remarked that "Black artist's quest for selfhood and a concomitant alliance with his culture culminates in a lyrical vision in this novel."

The novel, *If Beale Street Could Talk* is an affirmation of Baldwin's new belief that black artist along with black masses can seek fulfilment in the celebration of black self manifested through strong humanistic bonds in black family and community and through art of sculpting black figures. Fonny, the young black sculptor, protagonist of the novel, tries to explore whether going back to black roots and celebration of black art and cultural could help him sure in this world. Fonny attempts to find some meaning in his life by concentrating on his art of creating figures from wood and stone. He takes pride in his creativity as he makes figure of black men struggling in their live. Fonny not only makes figures of black man in pain struggling to escape an entrapping block of wood but he also shares a tender love affair with Tish, a young black woman. The result of Tish and Fonny's relationship is a baby conceived in the artist's studio. As Fonny is jailed later on, Tish and her family persevere for the safe birth of their child. Like the creative art of Fonny, this unborn child is also symbolic of black people's efforts seek freedom through their unique creativity. The protagonist's struggle to get out of prison is not only his personal struggle but a struggle of entire community for freedom.

In *If Beale Street Could Talk* Baldwim tries to resolve artist's dilemma by relating his problem and questions to black masses. The protagonist Fonny and his fiancée Tish belong to the Harlem to the downtrodden, poverty stricken black masses and the resolutions and answers they arrive at would relate to common black people too. In fact the struggle extends beyond Fonny and his fiancée Tish to Tish's entire family and Fonny's father. Although Fonny's father Frank Hunt provides assistance in the effort to free his beloved son, Fonny's mother and two sisters do not step down from their high yelled superiority to concern themselves with a "nappy headed backward and wayward son and brother". But Tish's family stands for endurance, patience, love and fortitude and serves as a secret strength and hope in otherwise black and hopeless life of Fonny. Here Baldwin while revealing in celebration of black art, culture and folk lore, also indulges in celebration of black family, and its spirit to bind its members together, to sustain them from series and misfortunes and its spirit provide them strength to struggle in oppressive conditions. The artist protagonist Fonny's derive great moral strength from the efforts make by the family not only for his release but indirectly for his search of an acceptable solution for the problems of the blacks in America. The birth of the child and Fonny release suggested at the end of the novel is indicative of birth of black creativity and its freedom from suppression. Baldwin has depicted this struggle through not only the efforts of the protagonist Fonny as he is imprisoned but also through the efforts of Tish his fiancée, her family and Fonny's. It would be appropriate here to quote Houston A. Baker who while discussing Baldwin's novel observes that in this novel Baldwin came to imply that the black writer's embattled struggle for fulfilment in America was a "recapitulation of the quest of all black Americans for expressive wholeness".

NOTES

- Ralph Ellison. "The World and The Jug", New Leader 46 (August 1963) : 22-26.
- Marcus Klein, "James Baldwin", After Alienation: American Novels in Midcentury (New York : World Publishing Co., 1962) 148.
- Addison Gayle Jr. ed. The Black Aesthetics (New York : Double day).
- Larry Neale, "The Black Arts Movement", Gayle, 272.
- Houston A. Baker Jr., "The Embattled Craftsman : An essay on James Baldwin", Critical essays on James Baldwin, Stanley and Burt, 76.
- *Ibid.*, 17.
- James Baldwin, *If Beale Street Could Talk* (New York : Dell,1974). 23.

Index

C

D

E

F

G

V

W

Z